FRIENDLESS OR FORSAKEN?

STATES, PEOPLE, AND THE HISTORY OF SOCIAL CHANGE

Series editors: Rosalind Crone and Heather Shore

The States, People, and the History of Social Change series brings together cutting-edge books written by academic historians on criminal justice, welfare, education, health, and other areas of social change and social policy. The ways in which states, governments, and local communities have responded to "social problems" can be seen across many different temporal and geographical contexts. From the early modern period to contemporary times, states have attempted to shape the lives of their inhabitants in important ways. Books in this series explore how groups and individuals have negotiated the use of state power and policy to regulate, change, control, or improve people's lives and the consequences of these processes. The series welcomes international scholars whose research explores social policy (and its earlier equivalents) as well as other responses to social need, in historical perspective.

1 Writing the Lives of the English Poor, 1750s–1830s
Steven King

2 The People's Health
Health Intervention and Delivery in Mao's China, 1949–1983
Zhou Xun

3 Young Subjects
Children, State-Building, and Social Reform in the Eighteenth-Century French World
Julia M. Gossard

4 Indentured Servitude
Unfree Labour and Citizenship in the British Colonies
Anna Suranyi

5 Penal Servitude
Convicts and Long-Term Imprisonment, 1853–1948
Helen Johnston, Barry Godfrey, and David J. Cox

6 In Their Own Write
Contesting the New Poor Law, 1834–1900
Steven King, Paul Carter, Natalie Carter, Peter Jones, and Carol Beardmore

7 Looking After Miss Alexander
Care, Mental Capacity, and the Court of Protection in Mid-Twentieth-Century England
Janet Weston

8 Friendless or Forsaken?
Child Emigration from Britain to Canada, 1860–1935
Ruth Lamont, Eloise Moss, and Charlotte Wildman

Friendless or Forsaken?

Child Emigration from Britain to Canada, 1860–1935

RUTH LAMONT, ELOISE MOSS,
AND CHARLOTTE WILDMAN

McGill-Queen's University Press
Montreal & Kingston • London • Chicago

ISBN 978-0-2280-2127-8 (cloth)
ISBN 978-0-2280-2128-5 (paper)
ISBN 978-0-2280-2180-3 (EPDF)
ISBN 978-0-2280-2181-0 (EPUB)

Legal deposit third quarter 2024
Bibliothèque nationale du Québec

Printed in Canada on acid-free paper that is 100% ancient forest free (100% post-consumer recycled), processed chlorine free

This book has been published with the help of a grant from the Canadian Federation for the Humanities and Social Sciences, through the Awards to Scholarly Publications Program, using funds provided by the Social Sciences and Humanities Research Council of Canada.

We acknowledge the support of the Canada Council for the Arts.

Nous remercions le Conseil des arts du Canada de son soutien.

Funded by the Government of Canada | Financé par le gouvernement du Canada | Canada | Canada Council for the Arts | Conseil des arts du Canada

McGill-Queen's University Press in Montreal is on land which long served as a site of meeting and exchange amongst Indigenous Peoples, including the Haudenosaunee and Anishinabeg nations. In Kingston it is situated on the territory of the Haudenosaunee and Anishinaabek. We acknowledge and thank the diverse Indigenous Peoples whose footsteps have marked these territories on which peoples of the world now gather.

Library and Archives Canada Cataloguing in Publication

Title: Friendless or forsaken? : child emigration from Britain to Canada, 1860-1935 / Ruth Lamont, Eloise Moss, and Charlotte Wildman.
Names: Lamont, Ruth, author. | Moss, Eloise, 1986– author. | Wildman, Charlotte, author.
Series: States, people, and the history of social change ; 8.
Description: Series statement: States, people, and the history of social change ; 8 | Includes bibliographical references and index.
Identifiers: Canadiana (print) 20240283007 | Canadiana (ebook) 20240283015 | ISBN 9780228021278 (cloth) | ISBN 9780228021285 (paper) | ISBN 9780228021810 (EPUB) | ISBN 9780228021803 (EPDF)
Subjects: LCSH: Immigrant children—Canada—History—19th century. | LCSH: Immigrant children—Canada—History—20th century. | LCSH: Poor children—Canada—History—19th century. | LCSH: Poor children—Canada—History—20th century. | LCSH: Canada—Emigration and immigration—History—19th century. | LCSH: Canada—Emigration and immigration—History—20th century. | LCSH: Great Britain—Emigration and immigration—History—19th century. | LCSH: Great Britain—Emigration and immigration—History—20th century.
Classification: LCC HV887.C3 L36 2024 | DDC 305.23086/9450971—dc23

This book was typeset by True to Type in 10½/13 Sabon

Contents

Figures and Table

FIGURES

TABLE

Acknowledgements

We are indebted to the support and guidance of numerous colleagues, archivists, and the advocates of British Home Children. We would especially like to thank John Sayers and Dennis Kelly, of the British Isles Family History Society of Greater Ottawa, for their incredible support, for sharing their experiences of researching the histories of home children, and for granting access to the archive of Dave Lorente. Lori Oschefski of Home Children Canada (previously British Home Children Advocacy & Research Association) kindly lent us her time and advice, and circulated our research to members of Home Children Canada. Research in Canada would have been impossible without the Shirley Greenberg Visiting Fellowship, awarded with the support of Professor Angela Cameron and Professor Constance Backhouse at University of Ottawa.

Our ability to undertake this research has relied on the expertise and support of numerous archivists and heritage experts, particularly Helena Smart and the archives team at Liverpool Central Library, and Liz Sykes, archivist for the Together Trust, without whom this project would not have been possible. Karen Backhouse, at Liverpool Hope University Archives, has been unfailingly helpful and efficient, even digitising key documents for us to review during the COVID-19 pandemic: thank you! We must further thank the Nugent Care Trust for giving us permission to reproduce images from its archives at Liverpool Hope University. We also owe a significant debt of thanks to the University of Manchester for providing an initial scoping grant, followed by a Humanities H-SIF grant. The funding not only ensured we could access hitherto unexplored archival material but also facilitated the diligent research assistance undertaken by Dr Luke Kelly to whom we are very grateful. We thank the participants of the Arts and

Humanities Council-funded Challenging Domesticity Network who helped to shape the direction of our analysis, especially around the themes of the deviant and curative 'home'.

Thanks also to wider academic audiences who have provided valuable feedback on our research, including the Modern British History Seminar at McGill University, the Social History Conference, the ManReg Research Seminar in the Department of Law, and the Department of History Staff Seminar Series at the University of Manchester. Julie-Marie Strange acted as a wonderful line-manager for several years, and has remained a fantastic supporter of this project, providing insightful and constructive feedback on chapter 4. The team have enjoyed delivering our research to public audiences, and we thank the participants of the Being Human Festival who attended workshops in Liverpool and Manchester in 2019. We also thank the publishing and editorial teams at McGill-Queen's University Press, especially Richard Baggaley and Joanne Pisano, for their work in bringing this book to publication. Our colleagues at the University of Manchester have provided thoughtful suggestions and opportunities to discuss our work, and have fostered a lively environment in which to develop our expertise. We also thank our friends and our families; we fully appreciate their encouragement and patience as we have brought this project to fruition. Finally, we would like to acknowledge the thousands of children who were emigrated from the North West of England to Canada, whose stories and experiences have long been obscured and ignored. We hope this book helps to redress some of the silences around child emigration history, and we aim to treat these often harrowing and difficult stories with the care and respect they deserve.

Some of this research has been published in previous forms, including in articles for *History Compass*, *Liverpool Law Review*, and *Cultural & Social History*. We thank the publishers for granting permission to reuse the material in this book.

NOTE ON THE USE OF ANONYMISATION OF NAMES IN THE TEXT

As a condition of access to certain archives that our research team used in the course of researching this book, some child migrants' real names were required to be anonymised. We have indicated in the text and the footnotes where a process of anonymisation has taken place, whilst retaining the relevant file numbers so future researchers may consult these records if they wish. Elsewhere, when there was no condition of anonymisation, we have retained children's real names. This inconsistency of approach is a product of our conversations with surviving child migrants, their descendants, and researchers working on behalf of child migrant charities, who are often frustrated at what they perceive to be an enduring institutional concealment of the fate of child migrants through these conditions of access. Our decision not to anonymise all names therefore reflects our ethical position in relation to these stakeholders.

Archives and Abbreviations

Archdiocese of Toronto Archives (ATA)
Archive of Dave Lorente (ADL)
Archives of Ontario (AO)
Archives of the Manchester and Salford Refuge, held by the Together Trust
British Home Children Advocacy & Research Association (BHCRAA)
Brunel University, Burnett Archive of Working-Class Autobiographies
House of Commons (United Kingdom; HC)
Library and Archives Canada (LAC)
Liverpool Hope University (LHU)
Liverpool Records Office (LRO)
The National Archives (United Kingdom; TNA)
Together Trust
University of Liverpool Archives (UL)
University of Ottawa Law Library (UOLL)

FRIENDLESS OR FORSAKEN?

Introduction

One day, during the first new and exciting years of the twentieth century, the four girls in the photograph (figure 0.1) stood on the docks in the port city of Liverpool, North West England, waiting to board a ship to Canada. We do not know if they stood together or alone; whether they were sisters or strangers; or what they thought about the life-changing journey on which they were about to embark. We don't even know their names and ages, since the pamphlet in which the photograph was published used their image in a purely illustrative sense, to emphasise to readers the amazing, transformative power of emigrating children (girls and boys) to another country.[1] Described as 'once destitute,' these girls were now dressed respectably with ribbons in their shining hair. One of the older girls, the beautiful young woman in the centre of the photograph at the back, even wore two strings of pearls around her neck; quite a transformation indeed. How did they arrive at this point in their lives, about to be emigrated to the so-called 'land of plenty'? Did they want to go? What did they know of the people to whom they were sent in Canada, or of their 'adoptive' country? Did they ever see England again? What did they think about as they stood there?

This book is about these four girls, and the thousands of other children, who were emigrated to Canada from the North West region of England between the years 1860 and 1935. Figures vary, but a consensus exists among scholars and researchers that between 80,000 and 100,000 children were emigrated from the United Kingdom to Canada during this period.[2] The fact that figures vary is, in itself a troubling aspect of this history. It bears testament both to the scale of child emigration and the patchwork of formal and informal emigrating organisations – religious, charitable, and philanthropic, as well as

Figure 0.1 Photograph of four children resident in the Father Berry's Homes, Liverpool, who were subsequently emigrated to Canada (1903).

those overseen by local government in the form of workhouses, industrial schools, and reformatories – in operation during these decades.[3] The range of charitable and state actors engaged in promoting and organising child emigration, along with the slow, piecemeal regulation of the practice, meant that the experience and arrangement of emigration was highly contextual, with some children's welfare monitored more closely than others. Accordingly, whilst readers of this book will encounter many children's stories characterised by abuse, neglect, and exploitation, there are also others about those who successfully forged independent lives in Canada and were grateful to leave England behind. The history of child emigration is not simple.

The majority of children bound for Canada passed through Liverpool's docks at their departure, though they originated from many different parts of England including Liverpool, Manchester, Birmingham, and other urban centres in the North West and the Midlands. London was also a prominent recruiting-ground, where child emigration first emerged as an experimental antidote to poverty instigated by philanthropist Maria Rye, who sent the first group of children to Canada in the late 1860s (followed, famously, by the Barnardo's charity among others, from 1870).[4] Children were additionally emigrated from Wales, Scotland, and Ireland.

There are no accurate figures to calculate whether one city or country within these Isles sent more children than another, although Gordon Lynch's study of child emigration indicates that whilst approximately just under half of the c. 82,000 children sent between 1868–1924 were from London-based organisations such as Barnardo's and the Salvation Army, the remainder came from agencies around the United Kingdom, with at least 15,000 likely to have been taken from the North West via the Catholic Emigration Association, Manchester and Salford Boys' and Girls' Refuges, and Louisa Birt's Liverpool Sheltering Homes in this period alone.[5] Victorian social commentators tended to concentrate their concerns about child poverty on London, Liverpool, and Manchester, as well as Manchester's satellite towns including Bolton, Salford, and Prestwich. As, respectively, the capital city, the key trading port with the British empire, and the city whose manufactures of cotton and textiles were world-renowned, London, Liverpool, and Manchester comprised a triumvirate of hopes and fears about the success of Britain and its empire in the nineteenth and early twentieth century. These concerns found greatest expression in the attempts of middle- and upper-class officials to regulate the wealth, health, morals, and family life of the cities' workers and their children.

Among these urban centres, Liverpool had high levels of immigration (especially from Ireland), severe problems of poverty and destitution, an extraordinary concentration of emigrating societies, often Catholic (see table 0.1), and direct access to the shipping companies needed to transport children. Consequently, the city became a nexus or 'hub' of emigration activity. After Rye began emigrating groups of children to Canada out of Liverpool's port during the 1860s, the Liverpudlian priest Father James Nugent (1822–1905) initiated a scheme to do the same for what he estimated were 23,000 destitute Irish Catholic children living in the city at that time.[6] Subsequently, other organisations emerged for the same purpose, including Birt's Liverpool Sheltering Homes and a range of schools, orphanages, and institutions operating under the auspices of the Liverpool Catholic Children's Protection Society: the St Vincent de Paul's Homes for Friendless Boys, and the Father Berry's Homes for Friendless Catholic Children (founded by Father John Berry and later run by the barrister and devout Catholic, Arthur Chilton Thomas). This book primarily focusses on these Catholic institutions together with the Protestant Manchester and Salford Boys' and Girls' Refuges and Homes. Father Berry's Homes, whose surviving fundraising pamphlets and correspondence we analyse at length in this book, were the last known residence of the four girls in the photograph before they were sent to Canada.

For these reasons, and due to the already extensive historical scholarship on London emigrating societies such as the Barnardo's charity, this book is focussed on North West emigrating agencies.[7] We explore the understudied local factors that made child emigration not only possible, but a highly popular solution to the perceived poverty problem. At its simplest, *Friendless or Forsaken?* therefore asks the question all historians of child emigration have struggled to answer: How did this happen? We began this project by breaking down this problem into specific lines of enquiry:

1) What were the primary reasons behind emigration schemes, and what were the priorities for child 'rescue' work in the North West? What ensured the schemes' longevity – to what extent were they legitimised by social, cultural, political, economic, and/or legal structures at the time, and transnationally?
2) How was consent to emigration negotiated between parent, institution, child, and state? To what extent did children have agency to embrace, or resist, the experience of emigration and the 'new life' it offered?
3) Has the overwhelming scholarly emphasis on narratives of victimhood and abuse obscured the resilience and entrepreneurialism of children whose biological families were perceived as offering little emotional or practical support?
4) How far did money awarded through local patrons, and the payments of bonuses on numbers of children emigrated to shipping and emigration agents, underpin a commercial rationale for child emigration and create a distinctive economy of welfare in the North West region?
5) What aspects of the original rationale for child emigration schemes can be seen to have endured in modern adoption law and twentieth-century child separation policies enacted towards other vulnerable groups?

Table 0.1
List of known emigrating agents/agencies operating in North-West England, 1860–1935*

Name	*Location*	*Religious denomination/other affiliation*
Birkdale Farm Reformatory	Southport (Merseyside)	Roman Catholic
'Child Home'	London and Lancashire	Unknown
Church of England Waifs and Strays Society	Branches across UK	Church of England
Father James Nugent/Liverpool Catholic Children's Protection Society	Liverpool	Roman Catholic
Father John Berry and Arthur Chilton Thomas/Father Berry's Homes	Liverpool	Roman Catholic
Leonard Shaw/Manchester and Salford Refuges, Strangeways Institute, Salford Boys & Girls Refuge	Manchester and Salford	Evangelical Protestant
Liverpool Children's Friend Society	Liverpool	Unknown
Liverpool Lodge (Girls Friendly Society)	Liverpool	Church of England
Liverpool Self Help Emigration Society	Liverpool	Church of England
Louisa Birt/Liverpool Sheltering Homes (absorbed by Barnardos from 1925)	Liverpool	Quaker (Birt) with a strong Roman Catholic influence within the Sheltering Homes Committee
Newsboys' Home	Liverpool	Unknown
Salford Catholic Protection and Rescue Society	Salford (Greater Manchester)	Roman Catholic
Stanley Boys' Home	Liverpool	Unknown
Working Boys' Home	Liverpool	Unknown

Table 0.1
List of known emigrating agents/agencies operating in North-West England, 1860–1935* (*continued*)

Name	*Location*	*Religious denomination/other affiliation*
Workhouses ('Unions') from which children were sent to societies for emigration:		
Barnes' Home Industrial School	Stockport (Cheshire)	Local govt.
Barrow-in-Furness Union	Historically, in Barrow-in-Furness Lancashire (incorporated into Cumbria 1974)	Local govt.
Barton on Irwell Union	Salford (Greater Manchester)	Local govt.
Beesdale Reformatory (also known as Lancashire Reformatory or Bleasdale)	Bleasdale, Wyre, North Lancashire	Local govt.
Birkenhead Union	Birkenhead, Wirral (across river from Liverpool)	Local govt.
Bolton Union	Bolton, Greater Manchester	Local govt.
'Brownwell' Union Liverpool (likely Brownlow Hill)	Liverpool	Local govt.
Bucklow Union	Macclesfield, Cheshire	Local govt.
Burnley Union	Burnley, North of Manchester	Local govt.
Bury Union	Bury, Greater Manchester	Local govt.
Chester Union	Chester	Local govt.
Chorlton Union	Manchester	Local govt.
Clarence Reformatory Ship	Liverpool	Roman Catholic
Everton Terrace Industrial School (also known as Liverpool Industrial Ragged School)	Liverpool	Local govt.
Haslingden Union	Haslingden (North of Manchester)	Local govt.

Kirkdale Industrial School	Liverpool	Local govt./affiliated with Maria Rye
Liverpool Industrial School (also known as Liverpool Farm School)	Liverpool	Local govt.
Liverpool Union	Liverpool	Local govt.
Manchester Union	Manchester	Local govt.
Newton C. William Reformatory School	Liverpool	Local govt.
Oldham Union	Oldham (Greater Manchester)	Local govt.
Ormskirk Union	Ormskirk (near Liverpool)	Local govt.
Preston Union	Preston	Local govt.
Prestwich Union	Prestwich (Greater Manchester)	Local govt.
Rochdale Union	Rochdale (Greater Manchester)	Local govt.
Salford Union	Salford (Greater Manchester)	Local govt.
Sandbach Reformatory	Sandbach (Cheshire)	Local govt.
South Manchester Union (possibly Withington/Chorlton – integrated into 'South Manchester' 1910	Manchester	Local govt.
St George's Industrial School	Liverpool	Local govt./Roman Catholic (affiliated with Liverpool Catholic Children's Protection Society)
Stockport Industrial School	Stockport (Cheshire)	Local govt.
Stockport Union	Stockport (Cheshire)	Local govt.
St. Vincent Certified Orphanage/Industrial School	Liverpool	Roman Catholic
Toxteth Park Union	Liverpool	Local govt.
Waddington Union	Ribble Valley, Lancashire	Local govt.

Source: Table compiled from: Kohli, *Young Immigrants to Canada*,; LAC, Register, *British Children Emigrated to Canada*; LAC, 'Guide to Sending Organisations and Receiving Homes.'

The chapters that follow chart the impact of child emigration work on working-class families in the region, including the frantic efforts some parents made to prevent their children being sent abroad or to retain contact with them after they left. Our study exposes the difficulties of retaining parental rights in the face of aggressive publicity campaigns to characterise parents as neglectful and dangerous, and their children as likely to descend into the same depths of depravity, theft, and drunkenness if they stayed in situ. This campaign was engineered by the British and Canadian national and local governments in co-operation with the church (both Catholic and Protestant), and all those individual patrons, organisers, and societies who gradually acquired a stake in emigration work, whether financial and/or moral. By highlighting the role of key institutions in Liverpool and Manchester, the book demonstrates the widespread influence of the Catholic and Protestant Church in shaping and facilitating child emigration policies. Their approach was part of their philanthropic work as they dealt with large numbers of poor across the North West, but was also a product of sectarianism and power struggles in the region, and Catholic leaders were particularly concerned that Catholic children would be 'lost' via emigration with Protestant organisations. Liverpool and Manchester were the centres of religious power for the Catholic and Protestant Church, but their influence was wielded over congregations throughout the North West and therefore impacted the experiences of children across the region. Moreover, we look at the influence of agents in the North West on the nascent national and international child protection legislation of the late nineteenth and early twentieth centuries, and on Anglo-Canadian relations in this era. Though we recognise that imperial relationships were often dictated by, or overlapped with, those orchestrated in London, we argue that a regional perspective affords a unique perspective on the everyday administrative and financial concerns that characterised exchanges over child migrants between the Canadian Department of Agriculture and emigration agencies in England.

Friendless or Forsaken? exposes how a system of colonial resettlement was romanticized as rehabilitation, and the chance to make a new home in the 'land of plenty.' We illuminate significant tensions between institutions' publicised ideology of child welfare and religious salvation, and the market-driven, transactional nature of the way the emigration system operated in reality. By exploring how the benefits offered by Canada were presented to both children and the local patrons of child emigration agencies, we offer important new insights into the legal and emotional contours of consent to emigration and the imperial economy of welfare at a local level. By linking North West archives with those held in Canada for the first time, we also reveal a crucial phase in the development of modern child-welfare systems transnationally. The separation of parent and child remains a key feature of certain state-led practices wherein a child is deemed at risk of harm from their parent. The transnational element entailed in child emigration, notionally for the child's welfare, is a challenging feature of the history of child protection law and practice, and our analysis contributes to understandings of the current law on child protection and adoption entailing the severing of ties between parent and child.

Who is the 'we' in this introduction? The authors of this book all currently work at the University of Manchester, UK, as senior lecturers in modern British history and child law. Our specific areas of expertise drew us together as colleagues and friends with intellectual interests that fuelled this research: histories of crime, gender, and urban space (Eloise Moss and Charlotte Wildman), local politics, poverty, and religion in the North West (Wildman), and the law relating to children's rights and welfare in the UK and across national borders (Ruth Lamont). Our professional status, including the academic reputations we have established through our teaching, publications, policy, and media work, carries with it the privileged access to and familiarity with archival research that we needed to accomplish this project. We also had the institutional connections, financial resources, and online database access to conduct research between two countries on the opposite sides of the Atlantic, even when completing this work was made significantly more complex by the COVID-19 pandemic that began in March 2020.

As authors, our roles, resources, and experiences – what is known as our 'positionality' – are worth being unusually transparent about because of the difficult and sometimes controversial history we are telling in these pages. During the 1980s, it took extraordinary courage on the part of researchers to draw attention to the history of child emigration systems to former British colonial territories, including Canada, Australia, Zimbabwe, and Zambia (formerly known as Southern Rhodesia, after the controversial imperial politician and businessman Cecil Rhodes).[8] These researchers' brave demands for truth in recognising both the existence of the system and its abuses not only helped bring about some justice for survivors, including reconnection with extant family members in the UK, but also precipitated an historic apology from Prime Minister Gordon Brown, delivered in a speech to the House of Commons on 24 February 2010:

> Until the late 1960s, successive UK Governments had over a long period of time supported child migration schemes. They involved children as young as three being transported from Britain to Australia, Canada, New Zealand, South Africa and Zimbabwe. The hope was that those children, who were aged between three and 14, would have the chance to forge a better life overseas, but the schemes proved to be misguided. In too many cases, vulnerable children suffered unrelenting hardship and their families left behind were devastated. They were sent mostly without the consent of their mother or father. They were cruelly lied to and told that they were orphans and that their parents were dead, when in fact they were still alive. Some were separated from their brothers and sisters, never to see one another again. Names and birthdays were deliberately changed so that it would be impossible for families to reunite. Many parents did not know that their children had been sent out of this country.
>
> ... To all those former child migrants and their families, to those here with us today and those across the world – to each and every one – I say today that we are truly sorry.
>
> ...I would also like to pay tribute to the work of the Child Migrants Trust and the International Association of Former Child Migrants and their Families, which have campaigned for justice over many years. I know that the House will join me in paying special tribute to Margaret Humphreys, who founded the Child Migrants Trust and has been a constant champion and fighter for child migrants and their families.[9]

Humphreys, a Nottingham social worker, began a decades-long investigation into child emigration to Australia after receiving a letter from a survivor searching for her family in 1986. Her book *Empty Cradles* (1994) sparked documentaries, further books, and advocacy via her foundation, the Child Migrants Trust. In 2010, a film entitled *Oranges and Sunshine* was made of the book. Starring Emily Watson as Humphreys, this work raised global awareness of a system that had been quietly swept under the carpet, even though child emigration continued until 1967.[10] Further, by demanding and encouraging former emigrating societies to place their archives in the public domain for consultation (though some remain resistant), campaigners on both sides of the Atlantic ultimately made the current book possible.

Pioneered by those who had none of our institutional capital to draw upon, and indeed, who did so under hostile conditions (Humphreys received death threats), the history of child emigration remains indelibly bound up in histories of empire, racism, labour, and the sexual exploitation of juveniles.[11] We care deeply about our position within this history, and the politics of empire that shaped, and continues to influence, *who* is equipped to conduct *what* research into the lives of those who were emigrated and their descendants. Often, cruelly, this tends to be people like us: those with no immediate emotional and/or personal connection to the individuals and families affected. How, then, to contribute to knowledge in a way that is ethical, without causing further injury or reinforcing gatekeeping around the subject?

The most appropriate way to record our experiences grappling with these issues is to briefly tell the story of this book project. In doing this, we seek to avoid merely listing characteristics in analysing our positionality, instead providing a reflexive account of how the underlying research developed, and of our perspectives were shaped by the overall research process and experience.[12] In October 2013, the Nugent Care Charity – a modern organisation working with vulnerable children and adults through schools, care homes, community and social work – deposited its archival collections dating back to the time of its founder, Father Nugent, with the Liverpool Records Office (LRO) and Liverpool Hope University (LHU). With admirable transparency, the charity's website highlights that among the nearly 300 items deposited at the LRO were '2,500 files of children who emigrated to Canada under the auspices of the Liverpool Catholic Emigration Association.'[13] In total, 564 items were deposited between the two archives which, in September 2014, when our project team first met with the LRO's archivist Helena Smart, amounted to ninety boxes of archives that needed cataloguing within the Central Library (where the LRO is housed) and a new finding guide to facilitate access by researchers.[14]

At that stage, we had not yet homed in on histories of child emigration as the focus of our research; we had, in fact, only a vague notion of the system, mainly informed by Seth Koven's brilliant analysis of Barnardo's charity in his 2004 book *Slumming: Sexual and Social Politics in Victorian London*. Koven writes of Thomas Barnardo's 'array of child rescue institutions, vocational training, and immigration schemes for boys and later girls that laid the foundations of the Barnardo's philanthropic empire in the century after his death,' that grew from 1870s, coinciding with Nugent's comparable child welfare interventions in Liverpool.[15] Unlike Nugent, however, Barnardo's work was jeopardised when in 1877, he was charged with distributing falsified before-and-after photographs of children he claimed to have rescued from poverty. Visually documenting their 'improvement' from starving children dressed in rags to well fed and respectably clothed, the images were discovered to have in fact been taken on the same day as part of the admission process to Barnardo's homes, with some children dressed to appear poorer than they were, and to make their parents seem more feckless and uncaring by extension.[16]

Already alert, then, to the way in which child welfare organisations concealed a range of questionable practices (even by Victorian standards), our conversation with Helena Smart about the contents of the Nugent archive was enough to make us want to learn more. We began with scoping exercises, sampling different types of files from different periods in the archives that we knew held some connection to child emigration practices. These included diaries and correspondence, financial ledgers, admissions and discharge registers, and publicity pamphlets. Among these were: letters from children asking carefully after relatives and friends, whilst making sure to praise the institution for the opportunities they had been given; case files that detailed damning assessments of their parents' poverty, drunkenness, and sometimes violence; and meticulous financial accounts recording the sums of money spent clothing, feeding, and housing children, shipping them to Canada, and noting monies paid or owed them by the Canadian Department of Agriculture. The more we read, the more we began to apprehend the scale of the local networks of emigrating organisations across the region, and to disentangle Catholic from Protestant emigrating societies, charitable organisations, and local government-run schemes (later, we would learn that an excellent 2003 resource guide by the acclaimed Canadian genealogist Marjorie Kohli had effectively mapped out these agencies using the Canadian National Archives, Federal Sessions Papers, and British Parliamentary Papers).[17] We also slowly identified how relationships were built between officials at local, national, and transnational levels, illustrating the potential for a regional study to offer a fresh perspective on how the system had been sustained beyond London. This took us to the UK National Archives and other archives in the region, including the Together Trust in Manchester whose founders, Protestant Sunday school teachers and philanthropists Leonard Shaw and Richard Taylor, established the Manchester Refuge which sent over 2,100 children to Canada between 1872 and 1925.[18]

With our project gaining momentum, we were awarded two grants by the University of Manchester, one from the School of Law, and the other a seedcorn grant that enabled us to hire a postdoctoral research assistant, Dr Luke Kelly, with whom we would go on to write our first journal article about the project, published in 2017.[19] The most important aspect of this development was, however, the fact that we could now employ Dr Kelly to help catalogue the Nugent Archive at the Liverpool Records Office, and were in a position collectively to author a finding guide, ensuring that visitors to the Liverpool Central Library could also access the majority of these records.[20] As child migrant campaigners, advocates, and researchers (who tend to inhabit all three roles) argue, access to records has an enduring significance for those deprived of the usual documentation required to prove one's existence, connection to family, and indeed origins in the world: "Retrieving files from both migrating agencies and government departments is often a vital step in building a more detailed picture of family backgrounds and early childhood. Since the late 1980's, CMT [Child Migrants Trust] has helped to change both policy and practice on this issue. Consequently, there is now a much better appreciation of the needs of former Child Migrants to access these records.[21] We also held a range of public talks and workshops on how to use the archives, publicising their existence through free events at the Manchester Histories Festival (2016) and Being Human Festival (2019). Yet our North West-based understanding of the emigration system would not be fully realised without tracing the work of local agents and institutions through the archives in Canada as well.

In 2018, the Law Department at the University of Ottawa granted the Shirley Greenberg Visiting Fellowship to Eloise Moss to spend three months connecting with historians, researchers, and child migrant charities in Canada and conducting archival research around the country. We sought to locate records that documented interactions between Canadian and North West officials, philanthropists, and religious figures who organised the emigration system and directed children's labour where it was needed (most frequently, onto agricultural farms for boys, and into domestic service for girls) to better understand their relationships and motivations. We also wished to trace evidence of some of the post-emigration experiences of North West child migrants (or 'Home Children' as they are known) and the receiving institutions, workplaces, and adoptive parents that greeted them on arrival. Home Children were often called 'friendless,' an idea that suggested their families' literal and imaginary abandonment of them to justify emigration, and a term used liberally by English child emigration agents, even during schemes that sent children to South Africa in the 1830s.[22] Yet it was apparent that many children still had family in Britain who did not always realise they had consented to emigration until it was too late. Did their families try to contact them? Did the children still feel a connection to England, or wonder about their relatives there? How far could children successfully integrate, particularly when facing barriers such as the perception they had been brought over because of their criminality, as cheap labour, and to situations where they did not speak the language (in French-speaking regions such as Quebec)? Finally, we also wanted to make sure that our analyses and outputs, including our articles and books, would reflect the perspectives of surviving child migrants and their descendants, serving some useful purpose in the ongoing project of understanding how and why the system functioned and its enduring legacy today.

Friendless or Forsaken? subsequently brings our original research into the Nugent Care and Together Trust archives into conversation with archives of Home Children in Libraries and Archives Canada (Ottawa), the Archives of Ontario (York University), the Archives of the Catholic Archdiocese of Toronto (Toronto), legal papers held at the Law Library of the University of Ottawa, as well as privileged access to memoirs and correspondence from the private archive of Dave Lorente, former child migrant and founder of the organisation Home Children Canada. Access to the Lorente archive was offered when, by extreme good fortune, an introduction was made to John Sayers at Libraries and Archives Canada (henceforth LAC). Sayers is a member of the British Isles Family History Society of Greater Ottawa (BIFHSGO), whose incredible work includes leading the team of volunteers that spent three years transcribing the 'R917' files of Home Children records at the LAC for the years 1869–96 (extracting 14,169 names of children from the Canadian Department of Agriculture papers that comprise this record series and making them available to the public). He also co-built a database of the Home Children who died, mining over 2,200 records from the RG76 General Correspondence files at LAC, newspaper obituaries and death notices, Barnardo's *Ups and Downs* magazine, and information supplied by descendants of Home Children.[23] Sayers, in turn, offered introductions to Dennis Kelly, a fellow volunteer whose father was migrated from Liverpool to Canada in 1925 aged fifteen, and Lori Oschefski, founder of the British Home Children Advocacy and Research Association (BHCARA), whose mother was emigrated to Canada at the age of two.[24] We have gratefully benefitted from their support since; Kelly granted us an oral history interview, the testimony from which informs the pages of this book, and Oschefski has kindly helped circulate our research articles to members of the BHCARA to provoke ongoing dialogue with child migrants and descendants in Canada.

The support received by archivists, genealogists, and other volunteer researchers is usually found within the 'Acknowledgements' section of academic books. Lifting the veil here on these relationships, and the decades of historical digging and advocacy accomplished by Sayers, Kelly, Oschefski, Lorente, and many others, provides a clear illustration of the ongoing scale, politics, and emotional labour involved in researching child emigration histories. As Kelly recalled of the decades of research that preceded our oral history interview in 2018, held at the Ottawa Public Library in Blackburn Hamlet,

> DK: 'And then I used to go to the archives on Wednesdays, and he [Sayers] would get an email from somebody and I'd research it and give it to him, and then he would send it off to whoever was involved, so it was just, it was more for – at the same time, I'd be looking up different things for this [points to his own ancestry research] but mostly just family history in general, it would help them, helping John out, if you know what John is like he'll go out of his way to do anything for you.'
>
> EM: 'Yes he's extremely kind. So what were the nature of the sorts of emails that you were getting from people who thought that their parents [were emigrated], or who had been emigrated themselves?'
>
> DK: 'Well, some of them were just, a lot, not all of them, but some of them come from kids, maybe teenagers, you get a bug in their bonnet, and they send one email and you never hear anything more.'

EM: 'Sure.'

DK: 'And then there's the next sort of people that send the emails, they already know all this, they just want to confirm it, you know they don't tell you that, but – and when you're looking up you find new stuff, and you send it back, "oh yeah, we were aware of that", so its – and then there are some people that haven't got a clue, and they want to find out things, but most of them already have a clue about what's going on, and they just either want to confirm it or get a little more.'

EM: 'Mmm. And do you get a sense of how they view it?'

DK: 'No, because most of the things I give to John, and John would send it to them, and sometimes they get telephone calls or something. A lot of times you send the information back and you don't hear anything. They just take it, forget it.'

EM: 'Which must be quite difficult, after doing that work and finding out about them.'

DK: 'Well you take the hours John spends on this stuff, you wouldn't believe the hours … '[25]

This book is therefore not only the product of our project team's archival research and analysis, but also decades of work by volunteers, many of whom were/are personally connected to histories of child emigration. They have patiently and painstakingly sought to render information accessible, to answer questions from affected families and individuals even when they received no reply, and have offered supportive feedback on our own research. We have allowed some of their views to shape our analysis, particularly when critiquing narratives that exclusively treat child migrants as victims. This approach echoes recent work by Gillian Lamb, whose study of philanthropists' efforts to remove children from harmful family environments during the period 1850–1900 explains that 'children could make decisions in unexpected ways, sometimes actively choosing life in institutional homes over family life and on other occasions demonstrating their agency through their power to leave.'[26] We therefore seek to understand the full range of factors that shaped children's experiences of emigration, looking for how children found a way to survive and in certain situations, flourish.

WHAT DOES THIS BOOK DO?

> Herewith I send you the Emigration Account for the children I have sent to Canada this year ... As regards the children emigrated – they were all most deserving cases and if they had been allowed to remain in England they would have suffered shipwreck both in faith and morals.
>
> Letter sent from Father Berry's Homes for Catholic Boys, Liverpool (1908)[27]

Shipwreck stories fascinated Victorian and Edwardian Britons. Years before the sinking of the Titanic in 1912, the shipwreck functioned as a key metaphor for crystallizing people's bravery, morals, and investment in Britain's imperial project through codes of valour such as saving women and children first, and by sailors demonstrating 'manly discipline' in the face of life-threatening disaster (symbolically affirming their racial superiority over a wild, untamed beast: the sea).[28] In the extract above, the reference to children experiencing a 'shipwreck both in faith and morals' should they remain in England served to communicate to readers, in the strongest possible terms, the ideology underpinning child emigration work: as a means of salvation from 'drowning' in sin, with which children were surrounded among their families and in the slums of British cities. Emigration purposefully severed such children's relationship with family members and required them to integrate into a new community in Canada, where they were placed with families for adoption, as child labour, or both. This book explores how child emigration was conceived of and publicized as a method of securing children's welfare and economic prospects against a background of poverty, crime, and moral degradation, concentrating on the North West region of England and the cities of Liverpool and Manchester.

Friendless or Forsaken? analyses how emigration was conceptualised as a means of channelling imperial power through narratives of children's gradual transformation from 'criminals bred on our streets' (as Catholic emigration agent Father Berry described Liverpool's impoverished children in 1894) to contributing colonial citizens, contrasting these objectives with the financial rewards for emigration.[29] This study builds on excellent recent work by historian Ellen Boucher that illuminates the centrality of imperialism to child emigration schemes, even in the face of growing nationalist sentiments in former British colonial territories. As Boucher writes, 'by the early 1920s and accelerating in the 1930s, government officials across the settler territories were implementing a rush of eugenics-inspired social legislation, much of which focused especially on the young. Whereas prior settler attempts to promote "Whiteness" had remained within a conceptual framework that presented all native-born Britons as indisputably "White," now dominion authorities began to assert distinct standards of race. The trend provoked immigration officers, first in Canada and then in Australia and Southern Rhodesia, to examine the physical and mental "fitness" of child migrants with an unprecedented scrutiny.'[30]

The imperial ideology that underpinned child emigration schemes was reflected in the racialised choices made about those selected for emigration, as well as those children featured in the publicity materials that institutions issued. Pamphlets included pages of photographs of exclusively white children bound for Canada, posed both individually and in large group photographs (figure 0.2). Coupled with the wearing of matching uniforms, these images reinforced the homogeneity and 'quality' of the racial 'stock' being deported. This policy, and the accompanying exclusion of children of colour from the institutional record, has created particular absences within the histories of those written about in this book: the children and survivors whose lives we record here were/are overwhelmingly white and working-class. This is not to suggest that these children did not also encounter different forms of prejudice based on their class and ethnicity, i.e., the knowledge that these children had been born in the slums of England. As Rebecca Swartz observes in her study of children emigrated to South Africa during the 1830s, white working-class children occupied a complex position in the hierarchy of coloniser and colonised. Sent to the colonies to reinforce the white racial stock, children could variously find themselves treated as genuine adoptees deserving of care and education or be subjected to performing unfree labour in the harshest of conditions. Whether working on farms or in service, the latter group of children suffered horrific forms of corporal punishment and were treated with general disdain arising from the perception they had been sent away because of their criminality. In Swartz's words, 'In spite of their race, their class positioned them somewhere between the other servants in the household and the families they worked for.'[31]

Yet, despite the overwhelming focus on the 'rescue' and emigration of white children, it is possible to build up a picture of the hostility faced by children of colour within the emigration system from fleeting mentions of their treatment within institutional correspondence. Arthur Chilton Thomas, who took over as general manager of the Father Berry's Homes in Liverpool in 1897, wrote a diary recording his visits to emigrated children in Canada during the early 1900s. In 1904, he reported on the case of Alice Jeenan, formerly of Everton Crescent, who was emigrated to Canada on 2 June 1904: 'This child does not seem to be getting on too well. I am a little doubtful whether it is wise to send children who are not quite white. They seem more difficult to settle although I do not despair of this case being ultimately well settled. She wrote to Sister Francis once but received no answer. Home not visited.'[32] As Thomas's account intimated, children of colour experienced greater obstacles in finding a secure home in Canada – though his assertion that 'they seem more difficult to settle' placed the blame for this squarely on the children's young shoulders. Tellingly, Alice's attempt to contact Sister Francis, the nun identified as her point of contact with the institution from which she was emigrated and therefore responsible for her welfare, was met with silence. One can only imagine the loneliness and terror of the child upon discovering she was unable to get help in her new country (we will never know what had prompted her to contact Sister Francis, though as chapter 1 demonstrates, emigrated children most frequently tried to reconnect when they were experiencing abuse, ill-treatment, or wished to talk to their relatives back home in England). Thomas himself admitted he had chosen not to visit Alice in her new home, unlike the other children he personally met and whose living conditions he reported on when in Canada. This lack of sustained communication between Alice and the institutions responsible for her emigration stands out in comparison to the persistence with which others maintained connections with their charges, as we shall see in later chapters. Despite Thomas's breezy assessment that he did 'not despair of this case being ultimately well-settled,' he offered scant support to ensure this outcome. Prejudice here took the form of social ostracism towards a vulnerable girl; without visit or communication, Alice was left entirely alone.

Such examples of hostility and neglect towards people of colour, and of unkindness and abuse of non-white children, were repeated in the wider chronicles of Canadian 'welfare' work in this era. The *Third Report of Work Under the Children's Protection Act of Ontario*, 'presented by the Superintendent of Neglected and Dependent Children of

A Group of Girls, Inmates of Father Berry's Homes.

A Group of Boys, Inmates of one of Father Berry's Homes.

Figure 0.2 LHU: Groups of children photographed at the Father Berry's Homes, Liverpool, 1902.

Ontario' for the year 1895, mentioned two incidents. The first took the form of an update on the work of the Guelph Humane Society, which included a single line: 'A colored family is still before us to deal with, it being very difficult to find homes for colored children.'[33] The lack of detail in this brief report was itself an active silence, indicating the Society's derision; other children discussed on the same page, presumably white, were described with details about their abandonment by parents, their criminality, or descent into poverty. The fact that this family of colour were 'still' being dealt with by the Society gestured at the broader barriers to finding citizens willing to offer homes for children of colour within the community, leaving these children to the Society's 'care' – suffering the combined stigma of institutionalisation and racism – for a disproportionately longer period of time than their white peers.

The second incident was more explicit. The Children's Aid Society of St Vincent de Paul's, a Catholic organisation in Toronto, described its work with the police on 'the case of a colored lad 13 years of age, an inveterate thief who lives with his married sister, father and mother being dead.' The child, who told the Society's agent of his unhappy family life, reportedly volunteered to go into an institution at which point the agent, Mr Hynes, removed him into the St Nicholas's Institute for forty-eight hours. Cruelly, however, he instructed the Reverend Mother to place the boy in solitary confinement for the duration, 'in order to disabuse his mind as to the happiness of living in such places.' Upon visiting the boy at the end of the forty-eight hours, Hynes 'found that he had completely broken down, that he had lost all fancy for such living, and was most anxious to pledge himself to everlasting probity [honesty].'[34] Once again, segregation and isolation functioned as correctives to the expectations of children of colour that they might receive care, or even loving homes, through institutions nominally created to promote their welfare in Canada – even had they been born there. Consequently, migrant children of colour from England could expect little better, and, given they did not fit late Victorian and Edwardian notions of racial supremacy shared across the Atlantic, it is small wonder that mentions of them in the records of emigration agencies are few.

This does not, of course, mean that children of colour were not emigrated *en masse* through similar schemes within the British empire, albeit those that did not herald their work as 'child rescue' or as part of the imperial project. Sumita Mukherjee's study of South Asian child migrants offers an important corrective to the overwhelming concentration on white child migrants in existing studies. As Mukherjee observes, indentured servitude, child marriage, and the widespread demand for child labour meant that Indian children were also separated from their families and emigrated in astonishing numbers throughout the British empire during the nineteenth and twentieth centuries.[35] For this reason, the absence of children of colour within the North West child emigration schemes was all the more profound, though the rationales for separation of children from family differed. In fact, the racist character of child emigration systems did not pass without notice among child migrants themselves. Born in Liverpool in 1910, Joe Ayre was sent to Louisa Birt's Liverpool Sheltering Home in 1920 after running away with his brother from their abusive stepmother. Emigrated to Canada in May 1923, some fifty-five years later he recalled, 'One thing of interest was when I look back on it was that all the kids were Anglo-Saxon and Protestant, amazing for a cosmopolitan city such as Liverpool.'[36]

Ayre's comment revealed not just one but two sites of cultural conflict within competing emigration schemes. The first was the pressure placed upon agents to only send white children from highly diverse urban centres, where the lack of infrastructure had contributed significantly to the poverty that led children to institutional care in the first place. The second was religious competition. Ayre himself was born to a Spanish Catholic mother and a Protestant father, who insisted that the children were raised as Protestants. However, as we will see in chapter 3, Birt was at times alleged to have passed off Catholic children as Protestants, which reflected wider concerns amongst leaders of both the Catholic and Protestant churches in the North West that children's refuges were proselytising their residents. Among these leaders was Bishop Vaughan of Salford, who in 1889 declared that 'hundreds and thousands of Catholic children had been sent from this country by those proselytising institutions to Canada or America.'[37] Two years previously, Bishop Vaughan had been involved in an unsuccessful attempt to bring a case of child stealing against the Manchester Boys' and Girls' Refuge, who had taken in a four-year-old Catholic boy when his mother was in gaol.[38] Although we cannot substantiate these concerns about proselytising children, the widespread tensions between Catholic and Protestant leaders were brought to the fore around the 'rescue' and emigration of children, which they both saw as having significant implications for the survival of the church. Emigration of children through the North West therefore served the institutions' religious priorities in ways that often put them in conflict with each other and the local state.

The methodology of this project channels an interdisciplinary approach to history, social policy, and law (disciplines reflected in the co-authors' areas of expertise, and within the tone and focus of each chapter). Accordingly, we read and analyse our sources through a range of methods. Publicity materials for child emigration agencies, such as the fundraising pamphlets and images of children discussed in chapter 1, as well as some of the published letters from children discussed in chapter 3, are considered through the lens of cultural history: i.e., to understand how they communicated an idea of the cities and towns of the North West as dangerous criminal hotspots, of working-class parents as negligent and dissolute, and children as both sympathetic victims and potential future thieves, murderers, and sex workers. This focus on representation and its power to solicit middle- and upper-class charitable patronage builds on analyses of how Victorian juvenile criminals were portrayed by scholars such as Heather Shore and Gillian Lamb.[39] Starkly similar depictions of parents' failure to adequately nourish, dress, and care for their children has also been noted as an important feature of child welfare rhetoric in Claudia Soares's exploration of the Waifs and Strays Society, another London-based child welfare association that also emigrated children to Canada as part of its operations between 1881 and 1920.[40] Whilst the language and imagery of children's impoverishment – materially and morally – were shared across institutions, we look at the specific tactics used by North West agencies to generate local support for emigration in their advertising.

We also take a legal history approach to understanding how child emigration sat within the framework of late-nineteenth and early-twentieth-century responses to what we would now call 'child protection.' Chapter 2 is concerned to understand the evolving legislation that governed emigration in its historical context, charting a shift away from the assertion of parental rights and authority over children and how a child's environment could be deemed sufficiently harmful to separate them from their families, and indeed, their country of origin. By contrast, chapter 4 concentrates on very different sources – financial ledgers and correspondence over accounts – to better understand the economic structure of the system at a local, national, and transnational level. Here, we treat payments both as a commercial apparatus necessary for child emigration and as symbolic, acting as a register of the strength of relationships between the Canadian Department of Agriculture and North West emigration agencies, between agencies and children, and in relation to how children perceived themselves as being bartered, with either traumatising or empowering effects. Gordon Lynch notes that 'The relationship between child migration agent, child and receiving household remained, for the duration of the Canadian migration schemes, predominantly one between that of employment agent, employee and employer,' yet this directly contradicted the moralising language of "salvation" deployed by emigration agencies and was often a source of tension or confusion for children themselves.[41]

We examine how the Christian doctrine of salvation was used to justify removing children from parents, ostensibly before children fell into sin (i.e., crime). This became the ideological basis for child separation policies, underpinning the legislation crafted to regulate the schemes transnationally. Criteria for separating children from parents and launching them on the path to emigration were based on institutional assessments of health, education, and criminal activity of children and parents. These criteria and practices have had a profound legacy within the modern child protection system, to which debate this book contributes by considering how historic systems of abuse and neglect were both challenged and sustained by 'philanthropic' local actors. Indeed, chapter 5, which builds on the sub-disciplines of public history and studies of memory and autobiography to explore the aftermath of child emigration schemes today, notes that 'in comparison to First Nations children who were subjected to the Indian residential school system, the popular memory of British Home Children has come to successfully emphasise their contribution to Canadian public life as worthy, assimilated citizens,' or in essence, 'good migrants'.

Friendless or Forsaken? therefore analyses the causes of the system's longevity and its legacy from local, national, and transnational perspectives, to make several important interventions. First, it analyses how the system was popularised and routinized throughout the

North West of England. Second, it unravels the economy of emigration schemes and its impact on sustaining religious and charitable work of this nature transnationally. Bringing the Nugent records into conversation with those held at LAC has revealed scandals surrounding an attempt to defraud the system through double payments of bonuses on migrated children, including at Father Berry's Homes for Boys in 1906–7 (see chapter 4). Financial frauds such as these suggest the market-based nature of welfare intervention, exposing an economy of emigration that scholars are yet to examine.[42] Research into the local economy of child emigration also adds a fresh layer of understanding why children were removed from families, and the parameters of consent to their removal. By auditing the financial payments and economic relationships between emigrating institutions, patrons, parents, and the provincial and state governments of Britain and Canada, this book reveals how material transactions created the scaffolding for these relationships, alongside shared religious and political ideologies.

Third, *Friendless or Forsaken?* constitutes an important shift in focus towards the mass emigration of children prior to the Second World War. Pre-1945 emigration schemes to Canada have been surveyed in older works by Kenneth Bagnell and Joy Parr, Roger Kershaw and Janet Sacks's 2008 book, and garnered recent discussion in studies of national emigration schemes and specific organisations (the Waifs and Strays Society) by, respectively, Gordon Lynch and Claudia Soares.[43] Our work reinforces the significance of understanding this older context as a key period in which child emigration not only achieved a new scale of operation but also a distinctive ethos in its simultaneous drive to make use of children's labour whilst asserting that children were *children*; vulnerable individuals in need of moral guidance, care, and education, a view that coincided with the debates around the introduction of compulsory schooling for children aged between five and ten in the 1880 Education Act. In this regard, our study modifies Lynch's assertion that 'The principle of using children's labour both as a means of making migration schemes economically viable, and as a source of practical and moral training for the child themselves, was also common to many of these initiatives.'[44] Correspondence among North West emigration agencies about where children would be situated rarely made reference to the *moral* value of their labour, although the virtues of their productivity and the employment opportunities Canada offered were often espoused in purely financial terms. Our study therefore demonstrates the importance of mining older schemes for fresh insights, broadly in terms of region but also specifically, in terms of revealing localised power plays between working-class families and institutions, agencies, and national governments, and the distinctive experiences of those emigrated. It is troubling that the earlier phase of mass emigration was not a prominent focus of the Independent Inquiry into Child Sexual Abuse, whose report on the 'Home Children' phenomenon (2017) dwelt predominantly on emigration post-1945 (in part, justifiably, so that recommendations for compensation could be made).[45] However, this means that the historical antecedents of this practice are often effaced, obscuring how entrenched the emigration of children was already by the mid-1860s and how it worked at local, national, and transnational levels.

Analyses of child emigration highlight the abuse and exploitation emigrant children experienced, depicting conditions in some institutions and adoptive homes as similar to prisons.[46] Though this abuse was often communicated using a different language historically, it is vital to recognise that it was still identified as abuse. As early as 1875, Poor Law Inspector Andrew Doyle issued a widely publicised report on emigration schemes as a thinly-disguised vehicle for exploitative child labour on Canadian farms, denouncing the cruelty and squalor children faced.[47] By exploring how knowledge of the criminal mistreatment of children circulated among emigration agents in this book, we demonstrate the culpability of those involved in sustaining the system, and illustrate the longstanding systematisation of mistreatment. These are vital features to recognise for those children who received no acknowledgement of their trauma, nor justice in their lifetimes. At the same time, we also identify a more complicated picture of how some children did receive emotional and material support from institutions and agents, and prospered in their new lives in Canada. As Kelly recalled, 'I mean if most of those kids would have stayed in England, I don't think they'd be any better off, they might even be worse off than the ones that came to Canada. Now, some of them had troubles also, of course. But some did rather well too.'[48]

Fourth and finally, our book recentres histories of child separation and emigration away from the existing scholarly focus on

London-based institutions such as Barnardo's. Recent work has begun to expand the geographical scope through examining national agencies although, again, many of these originated in the capital.[49] By understanding the North West's commitment to the policy of child emigration even as public opposition grew, *Friendless or Forsaken?* unearths how child separation became a normalized local welfare practice, offering insights into the conditions that sustain child separation policies globally today. It demonstrates the far-reaching impact of small-scale, local, and religious institutions in shaping child protection policies and forms of welfare. From modest roots, institutes established by local philanthropists such as Louisa Birt's Sheltering Homes, Father Berry's Homes, and the Manchester and Salford Refuge, largely without any contribution or scrutiny from the local or national state, responded proactively to the problems of poverty and deprivation that they witnessed around them, growing into large and comprehensive systems that became responsible for the emigration of tens of thousands of children. The practices and policies innovated by these institutions became the foundations for state-endorsed postwar child emigration schemes and wider child protection legislation, by reiterating the principles of separating children from pernicious influences and recreating them as ideal imperial citizens.

Friendless or Forsaken? is organised into five chapters. Chapter 1, entitled 'Criminals Bred on Our Streets', charts how, following the cessation of transportation of criminals to colonial territories in 1857, child emigration schemes emerged that were concentrated particularly in the North West. The region's high levels of Irish immigration and poverty, combined with well-established shipping routes to the empire, afforded a unique landscape for child emigration schemes to flourish. The cultivation of patronage for the scheme among local dignitaries, in collusion with transnational state sponsorship, is analysed with reference to publicity materials and correspondence, which emphasized the likely descent of children into criminality should they remain in the North West.

Chapter 2, 'Legal Legitimisation for Emigrating the "Friendless" Child' examines the legal rights of parents of children identified for emigration, and how charities and state institutions obtained the authority to emigrate children. The lack of a clear basis for the legal emigration of children meant that the activities of the charitable organisations engaged in this practice were initially unmonitored and controlled. This chapter will examine how the state legitimated legal intervention in the family to protect children from risks of harm and incipient criminality. The eventual controversy generated by the failure to effectively monitor placements and the problems of reporting of abuse of children will be considered, and the partnership between the state and charitable provision to secure the emigration of children, separating them from allegedly negative influences in England, identified.

Chapter 3, 'Letters from the Land of Plenty,' explores the emotional survival of children within emigrating institutions and as they adjusted to new lives in Canada. Analysing letters from children in Canada to the institution responsible for their emigration, it complicates the assumption that such institutions were wholly uncaring and uninterested in the emotional welfare of their charges by demonstrating the importance of affective bonds between the emigrant children, the institution, and the kinship relationships with fellow migrants they formed during their time at various 'homes.' However, the chapter also explores coded disclosures of abuse within the letters, looking at how far children were able to expose working and family conditions that were physically and psychologically damaging within the constraints of the aftercare systems.

Chapter 4, 'Rescue or Reward?' reviews child emigration schemes' fees and frauds, through analysing shipping and financial ledgers and correspondence relating to the payment of bonuses on emigrated children by the Canadian Department of Agriculture. It interrogates the previously unexplored economy of child emigration as a point of comparison with the moral and regulatory framework for emigration used to sustain it publicly. The chapter builds on case studies of fraudulent bonus payments, including at Father Berry's Homes during 1906–7, when W.T.R. Preston, Commissioner of Emigration for Canada, became aware of a double-payment of bonuses to the Homes – in the sum of £112 for fifty-six children. Further inquiries revealed double payments on hundreds of children sent from the Homes since 1903; worse, at least twenty of the children in whose names the bonuses were claimed appeared never to have arrived in Canada.

Chapter 5, 'Aftermath,' analyses the popular memory of child emigration through its representation in media such as autobiographies, novels, and film, and through charting the emergence of the British

Home Children's Association Canada and its campaigning activities. It suggests that at a time of important discussions confronting the difficult histories and continuing problems caused by the residential schools system in Canada, public heritage has represented emigrant children from Britain as assimilable through narratives of the 'good immigrant.' The chapter also analyses how far the North West's role in child emigration has been marginalised from the region's history, and how the vast popular culture emerging around British Home Children in Canada both brings important public attention to hitherto unknown experiences and the abuse many suffered, whilst also risking overshadowing the varied stories and narratives of those emigrated to Canada as children.

Our book aims to support the work of Canadian organisation the BHCARA and the Child Migrants Trust. We also endeavour contribute to the efforts made to render child emigration histories transparent by extant local charities Nugent Care and the Together Trust, organisations that want to reconcile the troubling historically specific schemes of their founders with their current child welfare work. negotiating contentious histories for public appraisal in a transparent manner. Indeed, we can only echo the words of Oschefski, whose BHCARA states its main goal is: 'to catalogue Home Child information and Home Children stories, to reconnect families unjustly torn apart by these migrant programs and to promote the story of the Home Children across the world.'[50]

1

Criminals

The emigrant boy, as a rule, is originally taken from the gutter of our great cities, London, Liverpool, Birmingham, Manchester, Leeds, Sheffield, &c. Drunkenness, foul language, immorality, want, and cruelty have been familiar to him from infancy. As if by magic, he is transported to a land where such wretchedness is unknown. He finds himself a member of a fervent Catholic family. In Canada, to miss Mass is a crime practically unknown.

The Very Reverend Canon Keating,
'Emigration Work in Canada', c. 1902[1]

Children are left here I don't know how, and it is with great difficulty we are able to dispose of them when they grow up. We sent them out to the farmers to the country, and there they were too often made slaves of.

Letter to Father Cazeau from Bishop Lynch
of Toronto dated February 1873[2]

'Taken from the gutter.' This pithy expression, along with the similarly catchy 'criminals bred in our streets', 'friendless', and 'nobody's child', became cornerstone phrases of the origin stories of children destined for migration to Canada under the auspices of child rescue and emigration organisations that flourished in late Victorian Britain.[3] The word 'stories' is used deliberately here. As historians of child emigration have long since observed, children placed under the guardianship of, and emigrated by, industrial schools, workhouses, philanthropists, and charitable and religious organisations, often had extant family members (including parents). They also came from homes that, although shaped by poverty and sometimes neglect, did not constitute 'gutters' in the literal sense of being outdoors, exposed, on the streets; nor in every case did these homes reflect a metaphorical gutter, filled with dirt and other polluting influences, although this was how working-class lives were overwhelmingly portrayed by emigration officials.[4]

Such inconvenient truths were beside the point for authors invested in the project of child salvation through relocation to Canada, which as historian Gordon Lynch asserts, 'reflected a growing interest internationally in the idea that relocating poor children to more healthy moral and physical environments could greatly improve their future prospects, both as citizens and workers in this world and their eternal souls in the next'.[5] The Very Reverend Canon William Frederick Keating was destined for a glittering career in the Catholic Church, going on to hold appointments as Bishop of Northampton (in 1908) and Archbishop of Liverpool (in 1921).[6] Keating wrote the first statement above after accompanying a group of fifty children on the nine day voyage from Liverpool to Quebec via rescue homes attached to the Catholic Emigration Association, circa 1902.[7] Notably, he chose to couch the emigration process in a language of 'transportation' rather than transformation, an oblique reference to the defunct (since 1868) practice of transporting convicts to serve prison sentences in British colonial territories.[8] Children were 'taken from the gutter' and 'transported to a new land' because, as he recounted in some detail, they had spent their early lives engulfed by various sins ranging from alcoholism to 'immorality' (a metaphor for sexual abuse).[9] As this chapter will discuss in more detail, children's exposure to these experiences was regarded as tainting them with an irreparable loss of innocence and virtue, despite their powerlessness to prevent it. Hence a journey and forced separation from past connections and environment were required, though whether this fate constituted a form of punishment or simple rescue was decidedly, and perhaps deliberately, left ambiguous. Keating assured readers that at the termination of the process, however, children would be bathed in the purity of Canadian familial and religious life where even the 'crime' of missing mass was supposedly unheard-of (a slightly humorous jibe that enabled him to reemphasise emigration as the alternative to a life in prison).

Yet Keating offered no guarantees the experiment would have the desired result: a fundamental reformation of the child's behaviour. In that sense, there was little to differentiate child migrants from the convicts who had crossed the oceans decades prior. As an ostensibly more sanitised form of transportation, Keating's words anticipated the linkage between the two practices that has since been drawn repeatedly by scholars.[10] The implied association with criminality was also reinforced by the urban geography of child migrants' former lives, which he sketched at a comparable length. Besides London, four of the six cities from which migrants originated listed by Keating were in the North of England, including Liverpool and Manchester in the North West. This concentration of candidates for emigration in the region indicated the perception that poverty and crime were inextricably linked with these urban centres, famed for their industrial manufacture, shipping, dense populations, and high levels of immigration. Even Birmingham, the fifth city mentioned by Keating, had a particular connection to the North West as the main conduit between London and the region on the West Coast Main Line railway. Who was to say, Keating appeared to suggest, that the interconnectedness of these sites wasn't channelling the problems of poverty and crime (via the mobility of transient workers and their families) between these locations? Emigration was thereby presented as the necessary means to disrupt the cycle.

Decades before Keating penned his thoughts on child emigration, however, correspondence between Bishop John Joseph Lynch of Toronto (1816–1888) and his colleague Father Cazeau demonstrated their awareness of abuses within the child emigration system (seen in the second quote above). Problems in removing children to new families/employers, where their status was viewed primarily in economic terms, rather than as family adoptees, were recognised by the 1870s.[11] Indeed, Lynch's purpose in writing was to refuse to receive any more emigrant children from England for precisely this reason. Lynch observed evils not only present in the treatment of English migrants but also of impoverished Canadian children sent from the cities to the countryside as part of domestic 'rescue' projects. In such situations children were 'too often made slaves of' Lynch commented, noting further: 'Boys were returned to us completely broken down, at the age of 16. Others left their hard masters and went off to the States. The girls were more exposed; they were poor orphans, "Nobody's Children"; were made the drudges of the barnyard; and often fell victims to the farmers' boys.'[12]

These experiences of exploitation were similarly documented in the notorious Doyle Report of 1875 that sparked initial condemnation of child emigration in England (see chapter 2).[13] Less familiar in the scholarship, however, are examples of officials themselves discussing and acknowledging these abuses as crimes, which this chapter will examine in detail. The juxtaposition between these conversations and reports, alongside characterisations of migrant children as inherently criminal, affords an important lens through which to explore the elasticity of definitions of criminal responsibility within the peculiar logic of the child emigration system (perhaps especially because it had a quasi-judicial similarity to transportation, as discussed). Just a few lines after Lynch referred to the dire treatment of boys and alluded to the rape of girls, facilitated by their placement in new homes, his letter began to wrestle with the contradictory impulses of whether to cast them as victims or sinners: 'We have received occasionally, those called "gutter-children" from London, but they turned out very unsatisfactorily. Lying and stealing seemed to be the sins impregnated in their existence. As for immorality, they appeared to have but little conscience: the sad effect of their position in childhood. With this experience before us, we could not undertake the responsibility of inviting, and adopting, those children. Will their condition be worse with us, than if they were left to the fate of the poorhouses of England?'[14]

Lynch suggested that children's environment had conditioned them to lie, steal, and become familiar with 'immorality' (again, holding a sexual connotation), making them the source of danger. By contrast, removal and adoption of those children would see them descend to a fate equivalent to, or worse than, life in the workhouse – a logical conundrum. Neither circumstance could support the notion of emigration as a viable means of salvation; hence it is striking that the system flourished despite of such internal doubts and criticisms. Reflecting on this, one can surmise that the narrative value of asserting children's criminality, or likely future imprisonment, became even more crucial to the survival of emigration schemes. The criminal potentiality of the child migrant was an idea that both sustained public support and funding for emigration and provided a psychological or faith-based justification for officials working within emigrating organisations. As this chapter will show, internal correspondence documenting abuses of child migrants and acknowledging the inconsistency of publicised claims of rescue were often accompanied, in the same breath, by accounts of the crime-ridden environments from which children had been removed, and suggestions of children's complicity in their own mistreatment. Further, emigration officials both in the North West of England and in Canada, habitually sought to minimise maltreatment of children through casting such cases as rare, or casting doubt on the veracity of children's claims of neglect, even as they recorded successive examples of cruelty in their files.

In a chapter analysing the nature of criminality in child emigration schemes, both as a trope applied to children and through evidence of their maltreatment, it can be difficult to ensure that the actors involved are understood in appropriately complex ways. Child migrants were victims of treatment that, even in the Victorian and Edwardian periods, was recognised as criminal. As the 2018 Independent Inquiry into Child Sexual Abuse's report on child emigration asserts, 'We are ... satisfied that if a child migrant was being sexually abused, there was indeed the language available to describe it, although it was different from the language which would be used today.'[15] The report goes on to highlight the legal mechanisms in place in the UK to prosecute this abuse, dating back to the 1885 Criminal Law Amendment Act raising the age of consent for girls from thirteen to sixteen. It does not explore the limited extent to which this legislation was duplicated elsewhere; in Canada, the age of consent was raised from twelve to fourteen in 1890, and only raised to sixteen as recently as 2008.[16] As a result, some care is required to identify the different definitions of assault among English-versus Canadian-based officials although, ironically, the archival evidence demonstrates considerably greater consternation by Canadian officials than those orchestrating emigration from England.

Child migrants themselves showed tremendous courage in reporting cases of maltreatment to visiting priests and emigration officials, which is largely the reason the evidence exists. Though often disbelieved, child migrants refused to stay silent and would sometimes alert neighbours to their condition, assert themselves through other forms of disobedience, or run away. These actions speak loudly, despite being characterised as further evidence of children's criminality by the officials reporting them. At the same time, we need to understand the paradoxical situation in which emigration agents, religious or otherwise, tried to sustain a system about which many patently had misgivings. Emigration schemes formed a sanitised version of transportation, *as well as* a genuine attempt at welfare and rescue work, however misguided in many instances.[17] While wrestling with the inherent contradictions of punishment and rescue, emigration agents witnessed a similarly complex set of domestic conversations about childhood from the 1880s, with conflicting views about the age when childhood ended, the proper treatment of children, whether they should be made to work, and sexuality and children's (in)ability to consent to sex, often determined within the context of social class.[18] Views of childhood ranged from the 'romantic' view of it as a discrete life stage oriented around innocence, play, and learning, to an older Evangelical view of children requiring their 'wills to be broken to achieve salvation,' as Ginger Frost notes.[19] In Liverpool, the Society for the Prevention of Cruelty to Children was founded in 1883, the age of consent was raised in 1885, and in 1889, as Frost observes, the Prevention of Cruelty and Protection of Children Act 'formally made violence and neglect of girls younger than sixteen and boys younger than fourteen a crime.' Admittedly, this latter Act played into the hands of emigration officials by permitting authorities to remove parents' custodial rights if convicted, and prior to that, to remove children to a safe place before trial.[20]

Accompanying these developments, bespoke and more humane ways to deal with juvenile criminality as a problem were evolving in the penal system. As Pamela Horn writes, a preference for avoiding placing children in gaol in favour of placement in institutions designed to effect rehabilitation, including reformatories and industrial schools, became a 'new philosophy' of the Home Office from the Late Victorian period. Even this shift met with doubts about the wisdom of long-term confinement of young people in institutions, and magistrates increasingly 'made use of refuges, shelters, and orphanages set up by philanthropic organisations' (though Horn notably highlights that the stipendiary magistrate for Liverpool in 1901 was quite 'satisfied' to send children straight to the workhouse). In 1907, the Probation of Offenders Act created a practice of placing 'reclaimable' offenders under supervision of a probation officer to avoid the stigma of imprisonment, a system that saw officers (akin to social workers) 'befriend' young criminals and visit them in their homes with their parents.[21] The advent of the probation system and other 'softer' options illustrate a growing uncertainty about whether children could truly be held responsible for criminal behaviours, and a sense that their trajectory as good citizens could be reinstituted locally, and without removal from their birth families.

Child emigration schemes appeared to occupy a sort of hinterland between the logics of the criminal justice system and the more humane impulses of social welfare and charitable work among the poor. Oddly, child emigration schemes are either absent or appear only intermittently in key texts on the history of juvenile criminality (perhaps because of this complexity). Horn's otherwise excellent work on young offenders in Britain 1700–2000 asserts that 'In the second half of the nineteenth century the emigration movement concentrated on pauper children rather than juvenile delinquents, on the abandoned and destitute rather than the criminal. As such it falls outside the scope of this study.'[22] Although child migrants were rarely convicted criminals, since they would not have been admitted to Canada with a formal criminal record, the stigma attached to them still arguably renders their experiences an important dimension of the history of crime and punishment. The enduring uncertainty over how to define child emigration within the broader state apparatus does go some way to explain how officials failed to confront their own complicity in a system that created the conditions for other criminal behaviours, including abuse. It also underlines why child migrants struggled to shake off the stigma attached to them when their status was so ill-defined and open to contradictory labels.

The first section of this chapter examines how the notion of child migrants as criminals evolved, and specifically how this idea was rooted within the correspondence and imagery used in pamphlets disseminated by Liverpool-based emigration societies, taking on a specific flavour of the fears associated with the North West region and the city itself. The imagery is of particular importance to understand the visual tropes deployed to indicate poverty and criminality by emigration agencies – specifically ragged clothing, disability, and visual cues such as the presence of bars looming in the background. The same images were often used again and again in publicity materials, indicating their cultural currency. Similarly, the practice of inspecting children to assess whether they had inherited their parents' criminal tendencies, was still in evidence during the early 1910s. We do not have surviving evidence of how North West emigration agencies defined a child's likely criminality after 1911, but it is notable that the assumption of criminal heredity survived into the Edwardian period, even though studies by social surveyors Benjamin Seebohm Rowntree and Charles Booth were encouraging a stronger link between environment, poverty, and criminality by this time.

The marketing materials of child emigration agencies reflected both environmental and hereditary (or criminal anthropological) concerns about the dangers posed by working-class children. Though they urged readers to fear the detrimental effects of urban environments on children's health and morals, they also treated working-class children as part of what Neil Davie describes as a larger schema of groups that could turn into 'born criminals,' situating them within the imperial discourses of 'savagery' associated both with citizens of colour and members of the poorer classes.[23] As the second section analyses, it was extremely difficult for children to shake off this taint when they arrived in Canada, where many were exploited and abused despite ostensibly forming another generational pillar of white colonization of the territory. This section analyses how reports of maltreatment of child migrants were dealt with in correspondence between North West-based emigrating agencies and officials in Canada. It considers the way these reports confronted institutional actors with the broader forms of criminality sustained by emigration schemes, and how this in turn prompted officials to double down on the language of children's propensity to criminality.

'OUR CRIMINALS ARE BRED IN OUR STREETS'

Father James Nugent was not only a conscientious record-keeper, but also had an ear for a good story. The man who would go on to innovate child emigration schemes in Liverpool left two volumes of personal notes on his work as both a prison chaplain and his later schemes for assisting the impoverished children of the city, though the tone of these notes suggests they were designed to be read by a wider audience. Beginning his reflections on what had inspired him to take up the mantle of child welfare, Nugent related the following tale:

> I was on my daily rounds through the wards of the prison and turned into the cell of a prisoner not more than twenty years of age. He was a bright intelligent Irish lad, with a sparkling humorous eye and a face which did not bespeak a bad heart. He came to Liverpool when nine years of age and having no friend in that town, he was cast upon the streets + soon afterwards became a frequent visitor to the gaol. Before he was fifteen, he was transported for five years + now again, he is condemned to seven years penal servitude. Turning to me he said 'Well, yer Reverence, I know all you say is true, but believe me, its little or no use you wasting your money + time upon us old guvs, just try your hand upon the lads. If you can keep them from being thieves up to sixteen, you will find very few of them take to it after that.'[24]

This story wove together the distinctive features of Liverpool that associated the city with criminality in the Victorian mind: Irish immigration, the culture of poverty and homelessness on the streets, and its role as the main port from which criminals had been transported to British colonial territories for centuries. Cleverly, Nugent's description of his prison encounter rendered the young criminal a sympathetic character, isolated from stable family life, but with a 'sparkling humorous eye' and a kind face, a 'lad' who was both self-aware and intelligent, directing Nugent's efforts towards rescuing the under-sixteens. Irrespective of whether the encounter was real, the retelling of it placed the clergyman in the position of being asked for help by a now-fallen representative of the vulnerable young boys of Liverpool, a mission for which, he suggested, he had personally been selected.

The origin story of the child emigration schemes associated with Nugent (and later, the Catholic Emigration Society) was inextricably linked with the prevention of crime and the reduction of inmates within the (Liverpool) prison system, as were those origin stories later attached to many child migrants themselves. Canadian fears of the likely criminality of child migrants from England tended to refer to the Dickensian stereotype of them as 'artful dodgers' (pickpockets).[25] By 1927, a more generalised concern about the likely criminality of children underpinned a legal caveat permitting juvenile immigration into Ontario only on condition that 'if any such child becomes, within five years of his immigration, an inmate of a prison, hospital or other charitable institution where such child is likely to become a permanent charge, the Inspector of Prisons and Public Charities shall notify the society or agent … in order that such child may be deported.'[26] Yet the spatial context of Liverpool as both conduit for these migrants and nexus for the Catholic child emigration schemes would only have augmented such ideas about such children's moral failings.

Distinctively within the cities of North West England, Liverpool had a reputation for crime that led to it being labelled by Victorian journalists and social commentators as 'the black spot on the Mersey.'[27] In 1850, the Cambridge lawyer Joseph Kay was commissioned by the university to conduct a survey of the poor in Western Europe, later edited and republished internationally in 1868 as *The Social Condition and Education of the People in England*. Kay's work described 'the extraordinary criminality of Liverpool,' with a particular emphasis on Irish immigration. It also quoted a statistical report of 1849 that deplored 'how much the combined criminality of Manchester, Salford, Bolton, and Preston – the great "manufacturing centres" – falls below that of Liverpool alone.'[28] Similarly, in 1864 Mary Carpenter, founder of the ragged schools and reformatory movement in England, wrote of how such institutions were being trialled in the city to 'check' the 'supply of daring, reckless young persons' given the 'extraordinary incentives to crime in Liverpool.'[29] Consistent fears about crime in the famous seaport endured throughout the next decades and, perhaps most damningly, Liverpool was reported to have its own 'Ripper' murders in 1909, imaginatively reincarnating the serial killer 'Jack the Ripper,' and the conditions of poverty, prostitution, and degeneration associated with London's Whitechapel in 1888, as Liverpudlian evils some twenty years later.[30]

In this context, and bearing in mind Canadian concerns, emigration agents in Liverpool took particular care in navigating the theme of criminal responsibility when describing the situations and moral character of the children they wished to emigrate. Father John Berry was a Catholic priest appointed to take charge of the financially struggling St Vincent de Paul's Homes for destitute boys in Liverpool in February 1893.[31] Pamphlets issued by the rebranded Father Berry's Homes during the period 1894–1904 chose to face the subject of crime in Liverpool head-on – perhaps the best option, so as not to appear disingenuous whilst diplomatically implicating parents (rather than children) as the cause. This delicately negotiated the issue of children's criminal behaviour by admitting that it happened, whilst focussing greater attention on the causes and their remedy. A statement that typified this strategy appeared in the 1894 pamphlet, asserting that: 'Our criminals are bred in our streets … an over-scrupulous regard for parental rights makes English lawgivers hesitate to act … In some cases boys who have come to us have been claimed by their parents, and have been forced by them, to our great regret, and, in spite of themselves, to return to the miserable life of a street arab. These miscalled parents have led their children away from comfort, in order that they might obtain a few pence from their miserable earnings, regardless of the desire of their children to better themselves, and caring not that their offspring, by such a career, must assuredly develop into the corner-men [thieves] of our City – a disgrace to our civilization and themselves.'[32]

This dual focus on the urban environment and the malign influence of parents coincided with a developing sociological and criminological consensus about the relationship between crime, poverty, and the city, marking a shift away from ideas of personal responsibility and inherent biological predisposition to crime This shift was argued for most famously by social surveyors Benjamin Seebohm Rowntree and Charles Booth, whose respective studies of poverty in York and London during the early 1900s described a cycle of poverty stemming from unemployment, a lack of universal insurance and pension provision, and malnutrition and disease in the slums.[33] Canada was the idealised rural alternative to the harrowing urban playground in which children were indoctrinated into crime by malicious parents; by implication, Canada was also a responsible imperial satellite that would share English concerns for the safeguarding of civilization by helping to reform such children. As historian Ellen Boucher explains, this rationale for emigration was a familiar aspect of British imperial psychology and a key justification for emigration to Canada propounded by other Liverpool-based emigrating agents such as Maria Rye. Believed to be a 'distinct master race' in this era, British children needed to have their inherent superiority cultivated in the 'underpopulated yet bountiful dominions,' simultaneously 'extending the reach of the British settlement.'[34] Thus the irony of proclaiming to the world that the streets of British cities were so overridden by poverty, crime, and other forms of pollution that children needed to move countries to escape them could be reconciled with the broader goals of empire-building.

The reports issued by emigrating charities and Homes such as Father Berry's were a key marketing tool integral to the spread of this ideology and the survival of institutions, issued as pamphlets circulated around existing patrons and potential sponsors within the city.[35] Accordingly, they developed a sophisticated visual and literary language to communicate to readers the complex reasons for, and benefits of, child emigration. The third of Berry's reports, published for the year 1894–95, featured a single photograph entitled 'On admission' (figure 1.1), showing a young boy asleep outside, only saved from being literally prone on the street by perching on a box and leaning his shoulders against a dilapidated and broken door. This prospective site of shelter, itself exposed to the outside conditions by the gaping slats in the door, was nonetheless a space from which he was barred by a padlock. With his conspicuously bare feet resting in the street, and wearing dark, crumpled clothing, the boy's vulnerability was acute, emphasised by the absence of parents, siblings, or friends. The image therefore appeared broadly in keeping with the conventions of 'before' images used by other organisations such as 'Dr' Barnardo's in London (Barnardo never finished his studies at the London Hospital, but appropriated the title of 'doctor' from 1872).[36] Later on, such pamphlets would juxtapose these 'before' images against 'after' images of the clean, well-dressed child following rescue (both sets of photographs were usually staged, and taken on the same day during admission, as was scandalously revealed in 1877, to Barnardo's cost).[37] 'Before' images simultaneously construed the child as an 'object of innate pathos' in need of rescue (with little agency to effect that change for themselves), and evoked the unsettling independence of a child forced to source their own bed for the night in the dangerous environment of the slum, without the support of stable and respectable family life.[38] Acting as a commentary on the criminal neglect of working-class parents as well as tapping into middle-class fears about the 'unruly' urban poor, the images posed a problem that, historians have argued, contemporaries saw as having a clear resolution: institutionalization, care from 'responsible' citizens, and discipline.[39]

However, the text on the adjacent page struck an individualistic note where the child was concerned, with the institution operating as facilitator for change instead of solving all a child's problems. The aim of the Homes and others then conducting 'social work among homeless children' was, Berry stated, to 'ameliorate their material and moral condition … to lift them above their sordid or dangerous surroundings, and to place them in positions where they may be able to maintain themselves by their own efforts.' Indeed, Berry continued, the best way to incentivise the Homes' children to work was to teach them that 'if a lad will not work, neither shall he eat.'[40] Rather than constituting a 'before' image leading inevitably to transformation, 'On admission' was a photograph in temporal stasis. Demonstrating the conditions under which children were then surviving – just – in the urban slum, it served to indicate that these resources for survival might be put to better use under changed circumstances, provided that the child was willing. Unusually, and illustrating a distinctive culture of marketing by the Liverpool-based Homes, this photograph was never completed by a subsequent image of the child post-rescue. 'On admission' was simply reprinted, unchanged, in subsequent reports for the years 1897–98 and 1901, by which time (in the latter publication) the featured child would, in reality, have been well into his teens.[41] Assuming that regular readers of the reports knew this and recognised the image (a likely scenario since the composition of the committee remained largely unchanged), the purpose of the image was to crystallize a moment in childhood at which intervention might *potentially* interrupt the spiral into decline; again, indicating that the city's reputation for crime may have encouraged its emigrating agents to be more cautious about claiming that rescue would be an unmitigated success.

The ages of the children featured in these leaflets – between approximately five and thirteen years of age, with the exception of one baby photographed in a christening gown in the 1903 *Report* – maintained Catholic subscribers' investment in the pre-pubescent innocence on which rested Christian fantasies of childhood rescue.[42] Simultaneously, it placed them within an age group where they were, according to the Elementary Education Act of 1880, supposed to be ensconced in full-time education and undertaking some form of work to supplement the family budget.[43] These factors implied that the children taken in by the Homes were already becoming independent actors fulfilling social, financial, and familial responsibilities. Commensurately, they were now of an age to be regarded as criminally responsible, even as social surveyors such as Booth and Rowntree drew attention to the links between poor environment and a high incidence of theft and prostitution.[44]

Before the 1908 Children Act introduced specialist courts for juvenile offenders, those under the age of sixteen who committed crimes were tried alongside adults in front of the same judges, and were often subject to corporal punishments in addition to incarceration in a reformatory or industrial school or, from 1902 for those over the age of fifteen, borstal institution.[45] Thus in the 1895–97 reports of the Homes, illustrations depicting, respectively, a young boy selling Christmas carol sheets and walking barefoot in the snow and an adolescent boy on a crutch knocking at a front door (figures 1.2 and 1.3) were designed to register a sense of a child on the precipice of falling into crime. Despite the sentimentality of the angelic-looking child condemned to work the freezing streets at Christmas with only a small dog for company, the text accompanying the first image once again described how 'Criminals are made upon our streets' and the Homes' rescue of the 'street-trading boy' was ultimately an exercise 'in saving the expenses which are likely to be incurred by his more probable transmission to the workhouse or gaol.'[46] This destiny was evoked in the tall spiked gate in front of which the boy stood, visually framing him against a set of prison-like bars that, as readers had been reminded, represented the further expenditure of hard-earned taxes as well as the child's exclusion from the rights and duties of citizenship.

Similarly, the possibility of assisting the handsome adolescent of the second image was somewhat punctured by Berry's warning on the next page that 'The helpless street boy makes the hopeless cornerman [a type of petty thief and scrounger particularly identified with Liverpool in this era], and his whole life is likely to be a burden to the community upon which he preys.'[47] The crutch, signalling the presence of an injury, was a marker of the young man having to beg for help instead of acquiring work. This physical impediment, whether real or faked, would have to undergo a swift recovery, for as the 1903 *Report* made clear the Homes were not prepared to offer financial support or shelter to cripples who could acquire money from specialist charities and/or local authorities.[48] Disabled children were ineligible for emigration, a condition that Canada introduced in the early decades of the twentieth century that was swiftly adopted by Australia and the area of South Africa then known as Southern Rhodesia (after the British colonist Cecil Rhodes).[49] Including images in the reports could, in this instance, act as a salve to such eugenicist impulses by visually demonstrating that only children in peak physical condition would be supported by the institution.

The use of such illustrations (both reprinted in subsequent editions of the 1898, 1899, and 1901 *Reports*) again connoted a kind of stasis, wherein the viewer was presented with a set of unresolved possibilities and asked to donate towards providing the opportunity for reformation.[50] As Shirlee Swain argues, Victorian social reformers could still attract sponsorship when the children featured in publicity photos were known to have criminal pasts, due to what she describes as a prevailing belief in 'the plasticity of childhood' that would render such children 'capable and desiring' of reform.[51] The ambiguity of children's futures may also, however, account for the increasing use of images of the façades and interiors of buildings in the *Reports*, used as a visual metaphor to suggest the kinds of citizenship to which inmates of the Father Berry Homes might aspire even if they fell short in reality.

Both the 1899 and 1900 *Reports* were replete with photographs of the Homes, identifying them as three-storey, imposing townhouses located on clean and uniform streets in residential areas of Liverpool such as Shaw Street, close to the newly-built (1887) St Francis Xavier's

Catholic Church.[52] Inside, bedrooms were organised into large dormitories comprised of neat rows of beds made up with crisp white sheets and overseen by a matron, whose ability to supervise children's behaviour was enhanced by the large mirror overlooking the beds on one wall.[53] A comparable level of regimentation was apparent in another photograph of the 'working boys' dining room,' a large room encompassing a dining area with two long rows of tables bedecked with bowls and plates above hard wooden benches.[54] It is a mistake, though, to read these spaces as either exclusively punitive in ethos or of a design confined to the realm of working-class reformatory schools. Writing of the same period, Leonore Davidoff suggests comparisons between boarding schools for upper-class boys and certain orphanages for the poor, noting of both that the communal spaces and constant surveillance 'offered a crash course in manliness' for inmates through the profound contrast to the atmosphere of home.[55] This is a point more recently echoed by Kelly Boyd, whose own analysis of the education of upper-class boys in this era suggests that the isolation of children from local and familial networks in these schools – an agenda consistent with institutions for poor children – was crucial to transfer boys' allegiances 'to a national elite which would dominate parliament, public life, business, and the empire.'[56] Inculcating values of self-reliance, perseverance, and 'building character,' these were spaces that were meant to cultivate attributes consistent with late-Victorian and Edwardian ideals of 'imperial citizenry,' long identified with prospective emigrants to the colonies and colonial administrators.[57] As Boyd notes, boys' story magazines targeted at middle- and upper-class youths even ran competitions with the prize of assisted emigration to Australia or Canada for the winners, such was this considered the apex of masculine British citizenship.[58]

The slightly jarring presence among the photographs of the Working Boys' Home of a 'Recreation Room' (figure 1.4), resembling the games room of an Oxford college and featuring a plush billiard table, appears to have been a clever attempt to ameliorate the disciplinarian aspect of the Homes and imply further connections between these institutions and upper-class schools. This was reinforced by later photographs of current and former inmates posed in unfeasibly aristocratic settings and clothes. In figure 1.5, the elaborate fretwork on the ornamental chairs and chaise longue against which the two well-dressed children lean are mere set dressings to offset the Grecian columns in the background. Notably, this stately-home style setting –

presumably a photographer's studio – appeared consistently in photographs of children in the *Reports* from 1902, when the Homes began accelerating their emigration scheme to Canada. Generating these comparisons, even in a purely public-facing sense (since we do not know whether features such as the recreation room were merely for show), was particularly important for organisations whose focus was emigration to the colonies. In 1902, the *Report* included an account of their emigration scheme by honorary manager and fierce local supporter Arthur Chilton Thomas, who wrote, 'Canada is willing to take our children, but will not be the dumping-ground for unsatisfactory children. Everyone in Canada must work … the children chosen, therefore, must not only be willing to work, but strong and healthy. A new country is no place for those who will not work: for stubborn children, for sulky children, for weakly children, for diseased children, for children who suffer from any infirmity of mind or body, even if that infirmity is only eczema, weak eyes, or nocturnal incontinency of urine; and finally, Canada is no place for viciously-inclined children.'[59]

Thomas's comments arose in the context of the first backlash against emigration schemes in Canada – where many emigrant children were regarded as cheap labour and second-class citizens – and consequent tightening of the policy of the Catholic Emigration Society to ensure the welfare of children identified as candidates for emigration.[60] Dressing children up to evoke the potential for their social mobility in Canada, and situating them among other 'imperial citizens', served to blur the lines between classes and suggest that such children's destinies were not fixed.

Yet these reassurances held only marginal sway with those Canadian officials who suspected their country was being used as a modern penal colony. Prior to the inclusion of more flattering images of the Homes in the Father Berry's annual reports, in 1898 a new examiner was appointed under the auspices of the Children's Protection Act Ontario 1893 to perform inspections of the emigrating institutions in England. This official was also required to conduct a physical examination and brief mental assessment of children being emigrated to that province before they left Liverpool so that, as the Department of Neglected and Dependent Children of Ontario explained in its own annual report, children would no longer be 'merely inspected in bulk as they passed on ship-board at Liverpool'. Mr Byrne, the Ontario agent based in Liverpool, was given the role, and sent long reports on Homes across London, Manchester, Birmingham, and Liverpool, the tenor of which was overwhelmingly positive. Crucially, however, Byrne instituted a new practice of assessing the children, described in his first report as follows: 'The children were first inspected while drawn up in a line as in a military parade and afterwards brought before me, one by one, for closer and more minute examination. After ascertaining, as far as possible, that they were physically and mentally sound and free from any serious bodily defects, I made careful enquiry into their character and antecedents.'[61]

It is hard not to wince at the excruciating scene depicted in this account. No amount of historical distance can ameliorate the disturbing portrait of vulnerable children being 'paraded' before a senior Canadian official, a stranger to them, before being subjected to 'close and minute' physical examination (the specific details of which were not disclosed) then grilled about their morals and family history – some not having seen their families for several months by this point. Indeed, it is arguably not the role of History as a discipline to sanitise or foster a more comfortable form of encounter for present-day readers when evidence such as this emerges; rather, the opposite reaction is important. Byrne's practice reinforced, rather than mitigated, the criminalisation of children. First dehumanising them by checking they were of prime racial stock, then subjecting them to physical intimacies we can only guess at, the subsequent interrogation of their 'antecedents' was familiar Victorian code for asking about any criminal activities and/or connections. Children would therefore have been made aware, if they were not already, that whatever period of time they had already spent in the institution would be insufficient to divorce them from the stigma of poverty and crime – in fact, it was likely to reinforce it. This would have been children's first encounter with a representative of Canada.

Byrne's practice became entrenched in the system until, in 1911, the Dominion Government of Canada established a formal 'Inspectorate over the work carried on by benevolent societies in colonizing British children in Ontario,' rendering the certification of children's physical and mental suitability for emigration formal and routine.[62] From at least 1902, long, four-page forms were used by the Liverpool Catholic Children's Aid Committee to fulfil the bureaucratic requirements of emigration for each child (it is unclear whether this was an invention of the Liverpool Catholic Children's Aid Committee or whether they adapted it from criteria requested by the Dominion Government; the latter seems more likely). These forms asked questions about the child's age, height, weight, and religious history (whether they had been christened, confirmed, etc.), as well as recording their parents' names, residence, and the details of any nearest living relatives. The next pages then devoted longer sections to 'Character' and 'Medical History,' including questions such as:

> Is the child honest?
> Is it free from sulky temper?
> Is it moral?
> Is it religious?
> Does it try to keep itself clean and tidy?
> Is it obedient?
> Is it willing and anxious to oblige?
> Is its disposition good, fair, or doubtful?
> Is it bright and intelligent?[63]

These questions, using the curt pronoun 'it' to refer to the child, inherently gestured towards the notion of assessors' ability to identify criminal tendencies such as dishonesty, anger, 'sulkiness,' and disobedience. Despite the emphasis of publicity materials on parental neglect and the urban environment as the causes of crime, therefore, internal forms and practices of examination were more consonant with the ideas of criminal anthropology and a Lombrosian ideology of spotting criminal tendencies via physical appearance and temperament.[64] These directives were apparent even in the section notionally entitled 'medical questions,' where the form once again asked: 'Does it show any sign of moral defects or bad characteristics? NOTE Children of bad character are returned to England.'[65] Given the location of this question on the form, doctors may well have understood this as a question about whether a child had been sexually abused, in which case they were thought likely to have impure sexual knowledge and impulses they might transmit to others.[66] Similarly, a question about bed-wetting was accompanied by the note that 'It is impossible to keep children in Canada who suffer from incontinence of urine and the like.' Bedwetting, rather than being understood as denoting anxiety or evidence of the emotional trauma of emigration, was also thought to denote experience of sex and therefore, the hallmark of a potentially dangerous child. As the chaplain of the Salford branch of the Catholic Protection and Rescue Society commented in an 1890 report on his visit to Canada, 'I was surprised to find that some of the children were afflicted with nocturnal incontinence … In Canada, such a case is regarded as evidence of bad moral lives on the part of the child's parents, and people are unwilling to become responsible for physical and religious moral conduct of such children.'[67]

More bluntly, one of the final questions under 'character' asked: 'Does it understand that in Canada it will have to work hard or starve?' The nature of this question illustrates the way that the system itself created the conditions for children to be abused, offering a stark dichotomy between work and starvation that undermined the bolder claims of spiritual salvation, replacement family life, and adventure and opportunity presented in publicity materials. The first section of this chapter analysed the processes through which children's potential criminality was negotiated publicly and privately by emigrating organisations. The second section will now explore the way emigration agencies behaved when confronted with evidence that the system made children victims of crime.

'I DON'T LIKE MY PLACE, THEY BEAT ME YESTERDAY.'

In 1871, at the age of nine, a little girl called Louisa boarded the ship Nestorian at Liverpool and set sail for Canada.[68] Little is known about what had led her into the care of Liverpool emigrating agent Maria Rye; if it were not for later events, a note in the shipping records would be one of the few traces of her existence. Yet Louisa's encounter with Maria would fundamentally change the course of her life and, unbeknownst to Rye, go on to raise profound questions about the levels of aftercare and responsibility for children held by emigrating agents. On arrival in Ontario, Louisa was sent to work as a domestic servant in the tiny township of Perrytown in Durham, at the home of Reverend Hodnett. Six years later, fifteen-year-old Louisa was three months pregnant, 'seduced' by the wealthy seventy-year-old neighbour of Hodnett, a Mr Frooms. Bravely, Louisa presented herself to the local J.P., Samuel Corbett, and though initially reluctant to explain what the matter was, refused to go back to her situation. Corbett forced her to return to Hodnett but again Louisa fled, until Hodnett and his wife drove to find her at the train station in Port Hope and 'insisted then and there on knowing who the author of the mischief was.' Forced into a corner, and later that day, into a doctor's examination followed by a confrontation with Hodnett, Corbett, and

Frooms, Louisa poignantly accused him: "You did it Mr Frooms and you can't deny it and you brought me in a melon the same morning." Indeed, 'interviews' between Frooms and the girl, followed by giving her fruit, had occurred for 'months,' Frooms's wife admitted. Panicked, Hodnett wrote a lengthy account of the situation to Mr J.A. Donaldson, chief emigration agent for Ontario.[69]

To Hodnett's credit, the tone of his letter directed the blame firmly at Frooms. He described Louisa as a 'poor creature' and reported that he had instigated legal proceedings against Frooms, making an affidavit about his neighbour (and his wife, who was complicit in the procurement of the child) to the local magistrate. He also continued to have Louisa stay in his home, though noting that 'the neighbours are surprised that I have not turned the girl away.' Hodnett's sense of injustice at the situation was perhaps unusually modern. His proposed course of action demonstrated that he was attuned to the legal and social quagmire in which child migrants found themselves should they be raped. Imploring Donaldson for assistance, Hodnett argued, 'What I would like would be that Miss Rye being her legal guardian should come down and prosecute this man and make people feel that they cannot tamper with those poor friendless unfortunate girls with impunity.' Further excoriating the system, Hodnett commented on the evils that would occur 'if poor creatures are brought to this country and allowed to go to live without anyone to look after them,' intimating the inconsistencies of aftercare that had rendered Rye a largely absent figure in the life of the child. Rye was, in fact, actively avoiding any involvement; Hodnett explained that he had written to her but 'I did not like it too well that Miss Rye seemed inclined to decline any responsibility in the matter and disposed to trust the burden of the affair on me and while in that word and fact to rely upon the simple relation of matters of servant and try to free myself from the affair like that.'[70]

Hodnett appeared to have no notion that he might himself have intervened to protect the child he had raised as his servant from abuse. His identification of Rye as Louisa's 'legal guardian' firmly characterised his own relationship to the girl in purely economic terms, although it is clear from Rye's apparent response that she shared this view. As Canadian officials sought to respond to the case, Rye became increasingly evasive. By January 1878, the correspondence suggests that she had been forced to acknowledge by letter that she remained Louisa's legal guardian until the age of eighteen, but even after soliciting that information, it was left to Hodnett and Mr David Spence Esq. of the immigration office to pay for the train to reunite Louisa and Rye at Hamilton. It is unclear whether Frooms was ever prosecuted for rape; certainly, Rye does not appear to have acted on this suggestion. As Hodnett concluded in his penultimate letter to Spence, 'It seems to me that Miss Rye has acted as an obstruction in this whole business. Perhaps she thought I would be likely to submit to keeping her [Louisa] here however … this morning I wash my hands of the whole business after having done all that could reasonably be expected of anyone to try to save this poor unfortunate creature.'[71] Sadly, Louisa was unlikely to have met with any sympathy from Rye. As the historian Marion Diamond notes, during the early 1870s Rye set aside a smaller, separate Home in Ontario for girls who returned from 'unsatisfactory placements' (likely unwanted pregnancies) where they could stay without 'contaminating' other children, freshly arrived from England.[72]

Rye's response was not unique: in 1905 Barnardo's opened a similar 'Rest Home for Girls' in Toronto, where, as June Rose describes, pregnant migrant girls were encouraged to have their babies then return to work, so that Barnardo's could bank their accumulated wages until they were twenty-one (it is unclear what happened to their children in the meantime).[73] In the context of emigrant agents' pragmatic approach to dealing with migrant girls' illegitimate pregnancies (and by extension, their sexual activity, unwanted or otherwise), therefore, Louisa's case has a number of compelling features. First, the case reveals the mundane frequency of abuse suggested by Rye choosing to haggle over train tickets and attempting to keep Louisa as Hodnett's responsibility rather than supporting his plan to prosecute Frooms as an example to other employers of child migrants. Second, it underlines the contrasting behaviour of Hodnett, whose identification of what had taken place as a criminal act worthy of prosecution (even though Louisa was above the age of consent at that time), shows that not all those involved in the Victorian child emigration network, or in positions of religious authority, took such a blasé attitude towards the rape of children. As early as the 1870s there were clear examples (that emigration officials registered) of the way child emigration created a perfect system in which criminal behaviour could flourish.

This is a key argument of this section. Abuse of children within the emigration system is well-documented, especially for the post-Second

World War decades.[74] Scholars have, however, tended to reserve judgement on the extent to which Victorian and Edwardian emigration agents and officials understood abuse and maltreatment as criminal practices, rather than as unfortunate adjuncts of disciplining a child, or as responses to a child's own 'fallen' nature.[75] Ellen Boucher's analysis of child emigration schemes highlights a parallel case of a young boy emigrated by Barnardo's to Canada who reported in 1909 that he had been overworked, beaten, and left outside to endure frostbite (later leading to the amputation of both legs). Again, no prosecution of the child's employers appears to have occurred, and Boucher suggests that 'Instances of extreme abuse like this one are rare in the archive, and, given the inadequate nature of inspections and record keeping in the period, it is impossible to know how common they were in reality.'[76] However, by dissecting the reports on individual children sent to the Canadian Department of Agriculture, and those recorded in the emigration diary of Chilton Thomas (manager of the Father Berry's Homes from 1897) this section will demonstrate that officials routinely registered abuse *as* abuse, and sometimes sought legal channels to punish it.

In 1888, a file of inspectors' reports sent to the Canadian Department of Agriculture traced the disturbing experiences of five children from Liverpool (whose surnames have been anonymised here for ethical reasons, although their cases can be traced through the footnotes). John, aged eleven, was sent to work on a Canadian farm. W.J. Wills, the immigration agent for Ottawa, had been sent to inspect the child and reported that John was 'placed with a farmer who is fairly comfortable, but has the name of being rather hard and severe to his own children.'[77] A second child, also named John (aged nine), had gone missing in Quebec: 'Visited the above place, no such person as James Barrett [the man to whom the child had been entrusted] there, no child from workhouse there.'[78] Another nine-year-old boy called James, now resident on a farm in Kingston, 'Ran away after having been chastised for breaking through or into a cupboard where apples were kept Egan [the farmer] does not know where he is. Advised Egan to search for the lad and return him to Rev. Fr... of Westport.'[79] Nicholas, aged fourteen and resident on a different farm in Kingston, had 'become lame,' and although Inspector MacPherson of the Kingston immigration branch could 'not account for it,' the child's 'disobedient and impertinent' refusal to attend school persuaded him to remove Nicholas from the farm and return him to Hotel Dieu, the Catholic receiving home.[80] Finally, Alice, aged seven, was also missing; MacPherson noted that he could not find a Patrick McDermott (the man with whom she was placed) in Marysville nor in the next township over, fearing 'there must be an error in the list as to address.'[81]

Although these notes were provided without additional commentary, they betray a clear concern (whether humane or administrative) on the part of inspectors for the fate of the children they were required to check upon. Wills's caution that eleven-year-old John was housed with a farmer known to be 'hard and severe' even to his own children, can be contrasted with his other assessments of children on the same page as 'remarkably well-placed,' 'comfortable,' 'happy,' and 'warmly-clothed.' These observations showed a general care for issues of emotional and physical welfare and provided testimony to inform other inspectors' decisions should John need to be removed in future. Nicholas, whose sudden 'lameness' had been accompanied by a striking behavioural change, was sent back into institutional surroundings by Inspector MacPherson. In practical terms, this solution may well have been to appease his employer, who was no longer benefitting from the child's labour, rather than a response to indicators of abuse, but as the authors of this book have argued elsewhere, those living and working within institutional homes often had complex relationships with children that did encompass love and a sense of kinship.[82] Therefore, we cannot rule out the possibility that Nicholas was returned to Hotel Dieu as a measure of safeguarding, with the inspector judging that he had a better chance of recovery, or the opportunity of finding another placement there.

Similarly, the missing boy James, once discovered, was ordered to be returned to a priest. The chastisement James had suffered, the implications of a child going to such lengths to steal an apple, and his subsequent disappearance, were of sufficient significance that Egan was no longer to be his employer and was now required to make an eight-mile (fourteen kilometre) journey from North Crosby to Westport to return him. It is possible that mere bureaucratic accuracy, or anticipation of struggling to trace the antecedents of future criminals, may have underpinned inspectors' reports of the disappearance of James and Alice. Yet by recording these absences and seeking explanations, such reports created a structure for flagging problem placements, noting incidents of a severity to terminate such placements, and recording patterns of behaviour and proposed interventions.

The cases above were of a less severe character than many others in the inspectors' reports (however much we may regard these five cases with unease today). As noted in the previous section, in 1890 the chaplain from the Salford branch of the Catholic Protection and Rescue Society returned a report on 141 children he had been instructed to visit in Canada between August and September that year. The chaplain did not visit all of them, however; 'Not visited for want of time' appeared beneath the names of children intermittently throughout the report.[83] In a further sixteen cases, the chaplain recorded a level of mistreatment that had caused the child to be removed from their original placement. One such case was Mary, aged thirteen. Mary's first placement, with a Madame Waters in Montreal, had been terminated due to the 'unkind' treatment Mary had received – which included beatings and the sadistic refusal of Waters to supply the child with gloves during the freezing Canadian winter. The Society had consequently moved Mary to the residence of a postmaster in St Hubert where she liked her work better, but told them 'you know [Friar] I am still English and I like England.' Subsequently, it was noted that 'Mary wants her sisters of 15 and 17 years of age to come next May.' Mary's final comment on her abusive first home – 'Mary said she did deserve some correction, but not as much as she received' – poignantly suggests that she had already been institutionalised into expecting that her behaviour would be regarded as deserving of punishment or 'correction,' perhaps a legacy of her experiences at Chorlton workhouse, from whence she was emigrated.[84] By continuing to isolate Mary from her origins, the Society were administering the supposed moral rescue from her deleterious environment and family connections that their name implied, yet the contentious question of her own agency in this process, or that of her family, remained tangible in the chaplain's notes. Mary's refusal to characterise her life in Canada in wholly praiseworthy terms, her stated identification with England, her desire to be reunited with her family, and the fact that these feelings survived within the report suggests that children's consent and wellbeing were factored into consideration, and occasionally were empowered to offer a disruptive voice to institutional narratives of rescue.

Children's bravery in reporting abuse to the visiting chaplain is as powerfully apparent in the report as the surprising fact of his having recorded these details. 'I don't like my place, they beat me yesterday,' 'I don't like being here. I get up at five and work till seven in the evening. I am lonely,' were just two of the statements, apparently copied verbatim (as indicated by the chaplain's use of quotation marks) that resounded with the defiant voice of the child.[85] A common note in response was 'will be removed.' Though we cannot verify that this took place, the annotation itself suggests that the Board of the Catholic Protection and Rescue Society, for whom the reports were written, expected action – as did their patrons – recognising that it was unacceptable for a child to be treated thus, or kept in place against their will. One case proceeded even further than relocation. Margaret, aged eleven, was 'Currently in a good home,' yet 'Was badly beaten by M. David, of St Hubert, but at once removed by our Agent. M. David and his wife were each fined ten dollars and costs for illtreating the child.'[86] A later explanation of the case described that this had taken the form of a legal prosecution: 'The mistress and her husband were summoned before the local magistrates, and each fined 10 dollars and costs, which brought upon them a great deal of local disgrace.'[87] Clearly, visiting emigration agents were aware (and occasionally availed themselves) of the legal apparatus available for casting hosts in the role of criminals, rather than the children in their 'care'.

In other circumstances, however, the chaplain chose to discredit or ridicule complaints (whilst still maintaining a record of them). Cecilia, whose age was unspecified, told the chaplain she 'likes her place very much' and he noted that 'She was well clad, and looked fat and healthy.' Yet the neighbours had 'told the Curé that the girl was occasionally whipped.' Rather than asking the child about this, the chaplain questioned the girl's master, who promptly denied it; no further action was taken.[88] Silences, rather than arousing suspicion, were accepted at face value by the chaplain, suggesting again that children themselves had to take the extraordinary step of personally declaring their mistreatment to him in order to bring their abusers to justice. Accusations of lying were the risk these children took by communicating what had happened. Another boy who reported being beaten was removed, but it was noted that 'I doubted his tale and the Curé will be asked to make enquiries.'[89] The chaplain then concluded his report in generally positive terms, summing up that 'The Homes were all that could be desired,' though his reports on individual children and acknowledgement of the need to remove several children who had been beaten in the sentences that immediately followed rather undermined this statement. Indeed, although sixteen cases constitute a comparatively small number out of 141 (although not all children were visited), it is worth considering that these were recorded in a two-month period of visitation by one society, and no comments on the report suggested that the incidence of children reporting mistreatment was extraordinary or unusual. As such, if the archives had survived, other visitation reports might well bear out a sustained pattern of mistreatment.

Unfortunately, just as declaring abuse could lead to children being labelled liars, removing them from bad placements could reinforce, rather than mitigate, notions of their criminality, rather than spotlighting their employers' behaviour. Another John, emigrated aged twelve in 1889, 'had several places but left them. Sent back for stupidity; thought to be going 'soft', wrote the chaplain.[90] Similar assessments were made of Patrick, aged sixteen – 'placed in several homes. These he left' – and Frederick, also sixteen, who 'refused many places' until found a job as a porter in Montreal, then returned to the receiving home again after being accused of insubordination and disobedience.[91] Frederick 'wanted to go back to England' and refused to work, after which he was promptly thrown out of the Home and never returned. Transience and mobility were pathologized in the Victorian period, associated with vagrants on both sides of the Atlantic.[92] As Tim Cresswell writes in his study of the stigmatisation of tramps in America from the late-nineteenth century, 'mobility has often played the role of a suspect "other" threatening to undo the cosy familiarity of place-based communities and neighbourhoods'.[93] A pattern of repeated placements would have only augmented suspicions of migrant children's alienation from the rhythms and constancy of normal family life, in conjunction with their inherent otherness as foreign citizens (especially those in French-speaking Quebec).

Removing children from exploitative or otherwise dangerous placements carried unknown perils. Some children's initial responses to the chaplain indicated their awareness of the stigma attached to excessive mobility, as well as the destabilising emotional effects of being introduced to a new family only to experience rejection and institutionalisation all over again. Rosetta, aged nine, was 'Adopted and greatly loved by all. She loves them too, and at first she would not come near me lest I should take her back', noted the report. Likewise Martha, aged ten, 'would not come to see me at first fearing I intended to take her away.'[94] It is impossible to know for certain the thoughts and emotions directing children's behaviour. Logically, though, one can safely venture those earlier experiences of loss of family and removal to a Home in England, as well as the impact of repeated messages about the opportunities for redemption afforded by Canada, would have left children wary of what the chaplain's visit might signify in terms of their perceived success or failure as migrants.

Canadian officials also understood that repeatedly moving children could pose a problem (and continued to publish evidence of their awareness of the potential for abuse in both domestic and agricultural placements). Yet rather than dismantling the system, they instead urged those involved in child welfare schemes to be more rigorous in their selection of families/employers. The superintendent for the Neglected and Dependent Children of Ontario produced annual reports on both the removal of Canadian children from city to countryside (Canadian cities also having poverty and crime, though this was never mentioned in English publicity materials) as well as juvenile immigration schemes into Canada. In 1911, the Superintendent invited C.R. Miller, the Children's Aid Society inspector for Berlin, Ontario (renamed "Kitchener" in 1916 during the First World War) to write a short tract on the proper placement of children as part of the nineteenth annual report. Miller warned that 'There are many people who go to church and prayer meeting, and are possibly considered to be faith workers, but to live with them as a "domestic" or as "orphan child," is to know they are greater slave drivers than church workers. It is to be regretted that many people who apparently are religious, seem to be lacking the real thing, and … consequently only live out their natural inclination, which very often is faulty; sometimes even sensual, and occasionally devilish. In the face of the above mentioned facts we wish to repeat that it is of vital importance to know the disposition of the guardian before placing the child.'[95]

Warnings about children being subjected to 'devilish' behaviour might seem to be sufficient grounds for the cessation of placements and, by extension, emigration schemes, particularly among Catholic agencies. It is a testament to the intensity of belief in this system of child salvation, and perhaps also a reflection of the demonisation of Liverpool and other English cities, that the schemes endured despite these reports. Miller's advocacy of a more careful process of research, monitoring, and surveillance underlined the way that, collectively, officials refused to confront the possibility that child rescue work institutionalised criminal behaviour among a significant proportion of those with whom child migrants were placed. Since child migrants were assumed to have been already conditioned by the criminal impulses of their parents and origin cities, cases of abuse continued to be treated on a case-by-case basis rather than identified as a systemic problem.

CONCLUSION

Emphasising the criminal potential of impoverished children was fundamental to emigration agencies' publicity materials, and broader justification for emigration schemes during the late nineteenth and early twentieth century. Liverpool, with its reputation as 'the black spot on the Mersey' and role as the central shipping port to the empire, provided a spatial context in which narratives of rescue and salvation from malign environmental influences made perfect sense. Small wonder, then, that the city became the nexus of Catholic welfare activities, or that these interventions so closely resembled the earlier punitive system of transportation. Tragically, the success of these organisations in crafting a persuasive narrative of rescue and redemption via emigration to Canada also seems to have overridden any evidence of maltreatment, abuse, and exploitation of children with which both emigration agents and Canadian officials were periodically presented from the 1870s onwards. Whilst sometimes removing children from their surroundings and returning them to the guardianship of institutions may have provided immediate relief from dangerous homes (in instances where children had taken the courageous step of reporting abuse), it did not address the way that child emigration systematised and institutionalised the conditions that led to it. Strikingly, however, abuse was clearly recognised as criminal behaviour worthy of punishment and occasionally, prosecution, even taking account of the elevated age of consent in 1885 in Britain, and much lower age of consent in Canada. Child emigration agencies thus continued operating their schemes in the full knowledge that the 'criminal classes' they claimed to deal with were not the only criminals children would likely be exposed to after emigration.

Figure 1.1 Illustration entitled 'On Admission,' in a marketing pamphlet for the Homes for Catholic Friendless Youths, Liverpool, 1894–95.

Figure 1.2 Illustration of a destitute child worker in Liverpool in winter, in a marketing pamphlet for the Homes for Catholic Friendless Youths, Liverpool, 1894–95.

Figure 1.3 Illustration of a destitute child on crutches, in a marketing pamphlet for the Homes for Catholic Friendless Youths, Liverpool, 1896–97.

Figure 1.4 Photograph of the recreation room at a Catholic working boys' home in Liverpool, 1900.

Figure 1.5 Two children posed for 'after' rescue photographs, in a marketing pamphlet for the Father Berry's Home, Liverpool, 1902.

2

Legal Legitimisation for Emigrating the 'Friendless Child'

In 1879, Maria Rye, one of the earliest proponents and facilitators of emigration for young women and girls to Ontario, suggested to her supporters that: 'our children in Canada are supporting themselves, instead of being supported by charity here in England; we may have pleasure in the knowledge that our money is spent every year in helping fresh cases, starting fresh little ones on the right road.'[1] The informal origins of these arrangements, in both the selection of children for emigration and the arrangement for their eventual placement in Canada, meant that, at least initially, there was no clear legal framework for their regulation and management. As the state started to make use of charitable societies' arrangements for the emigration of children through the Poor Law and from industrial schools, this lack of certainty was unsustainable. The legal framework developed significantly from the late 1880s onwards, with the state increasingly prepared to intervene and support the activities of charities, normally religious Protestant and Roman Catholic organisations, designed ostensibly to secure the welfare of children in their care.[2] Removal of the child from the family, and the potentially permanent severing of ties to relations in the England, were regarded as desirable outcomes of this process. The state increasingly sought to use pre-existing charitable networks to place children from English state-funded organisations associated with the Poor Law and industrial schools for emigration to Canada.[3]

By the early twentieth century, there existed a more regulated environment governing legal processes. The promotion of emigration for children was a policy of Empire, supporting the settlement of Canada especially in rural areas,[4] but also responding to anxieties about child poverty and perceived juvenile delinquency at home.[5] However by 1924, the risk of exploitation of children's labour once emigrated was becoming recognized: 'Taking the system at its best, boarded out children transferred from homes in the United Kingdom to homes in Canada do not seem to us to have gained any appreciable advantage.'[6] Despite these expressed anxieties, the legal emigration of children from England to other countries, notably Australia, continued as a form of welfare provision for children with both charitable organisation and state support into the 1960s.[7]

This chapter will examine the process through which the law was used to legitimise new forms of intervention in the family, ostensibly to protect the child. The inalienability of parental rights over a child was steadily eroded from the 1860s on, as charitable organisations campaigned and asserted authority to monitor parents and intervene in families on behalf of children. This erosion legitimated intervention in families, but there remained significant lacuna in the legal regulation of this process. Charities sought to exploit these legal gaps in ensuring the effective severance of the rights of and the relationship between the child and the parent, a parent deemed deficient by their child's emigration. This provided the initial context in which the permanent removal of children from the family unit was sought to secure the welfare of the child.

As chapter 1 explored, the children who were emigrated were rarely entirely without family in England and were part of a complex, increasingly cross-national community. This chapter will consider the incoherence in approach that developed in removing a child from a problematic family environment, to eventually send them to a placement in Canada without monitoring the performance of the placement. The challenges of placing children in a vast foreign country were significant, both in defining responsibility for the child and in monitoring the child's welfare. The processes of inspection were initially limited and the legal status of the child uncertain, and dependent on the nature of the placement secured. It will be demonstrated that the law failed to provide a coherent framework or status for children aimed at protecting and promoting their welfare. The law was responsive, regulating pre-existing arrangements and problems as they arose, and endorsing the separation of children from parents as the resolution of perceived problems of care. This left the determination of harm to a moralistic assessment, and highlighted the ongoing difficulties of providing effectively for the future of children who are separated from their parents because of the perceived risk posed by parental care.

CHILD EMIGRATION AND THE EROSION OF PARENTAL RIGHTS

The child as an object of abuse, vulnerable and in need of protection, became a key figure of the late nineteenth century. Children and, for the first time, children of poor families, were distinguished as having a specific identity with interests and needs by reason of their age.[8] Children became an object of concern in a range of new regulatory contexts including child participation in economic work, compulsory education, and juvenile delinquency, all within the broader environment of management of poverty. The child within the family, particularly working-class families, became a focus of anxiety regarding their exposure to immorality, vice, physical abuse, sexual exploitation, and their own potential delinquency (see chapter 1).[9]

Within this environment, intervention ostensibly designed to protect children and provide them with services was primarily provided by charitable organisations rather than the state directly. A number of philanthropic individuals undertook personal action, and developed extensive charitable networks to identify abused or vulnerable children and intervene on the child's behalf. The National Society for the Prevention of Cruelty to Children (NSPCC) sought to highlight the risks posed to children by the family environment, the potential for abuse of children, and their need for specific protection.[10] The NSPCC created a national campaign for combatting child cruelty and raised awareness of the impact of familial abuse on children's lives. Cockburn argues that, in seeking to intervene specifically in the lives of poor families, 'The campaigns around child protection can be seen as the appropriation of the working-class child to conformity to middle class ideals.'[11] The activities of these charitable organisations were characterised by prurient language, designed to pique the interest of the middle class to secure funding and support for their methods of intervention in families, and for legislative campaigns.[12] In doing so, they created demand for alternative provision for children's protection *outside* the family for the first time.

Whilst the national campaigns created by the NSPCC attracted attention, the evolution of localised child protection interventions associated with the Church, of all denominations, was significant. This was particularly evident in the industrialised cities of northern England where charities sought to respond to the needs of children in poverty. Religious institutions developed and campaigned for a range of support for poor children and their families, and it is within this context that the practice of child emigration evolved. The activities of child emigration charities were explicitly promoted as providing for children's welfare in two ways; first by providing new opportunities for a productive life in Canada, and secondly by effectively severing the relationship between a child and a potentially abusive, neglectful family and the concomitant risk of poverty. The characterisation of the parent or family environment could be highly subjective, but the child was regarded as being at risk of either moral or personal harm without intervention. Emigration was presented as designed both to protect the welfare of the child and promote their future success: 'remember that if these children do remain here they would never get into your service, they would not grow up into even working, to say nothing of Christian women, but would grow up into our habitual drunkards, our tramps, and the mothers of more tramps, and into those nameless miserable outcasts who fill the black wards of our hospitals and of our workhouses – children whose heritage here from birth to death is sin, shame, misery and destruction.'[13]

Lynch points out that the migration of children to Canada was an evolution in nineteenth-century emigration practices.[14] The criminal sentence of transportation only ceased in 1868, and had included the emigration and training of children before placement in Australia.[15] The practice of emigrating children to Canada as a method of providing for their future employment originated partly with Maria Rye.[16] She had promoted the value of emigration of women to Canada for work in the early 1860s and created a network of institutions providing children for emigration and for their placement in private homes once moved to Canada. Later in the decade, she sought to expand her original scheme to include girls. Rye's activities included the controversial recruitment of girls from Liverpool workhouses. She instigated the practice of providing for the passage of the child to Canada, followed by their brief residence in a home in Ontario run by her organisation prior to their placement with a Canadian family. A range of different origins were identified in annual reports; for example, in 1880, the following children and their placements were listed:

> F.C., aged 10; deserted by both parents – Mr. W.T.H., Farmer, Thornton, O., Ontario. Child adopted.
>
> H.S., aged 11; father dead; mother married again and husband illused [*sic*] the child – Miss T., Bowmanville, Ontario. As little maid.
>
> K.B., aged 11; mother dead; father has very bad health and was left a widower with 5 young children – Mr. T.H., Harness Maker, Clarke, Ontario. Child bound. [17]

The mode of emigration developed by Maria Rye was subsequently used by a range of charities and religious organisations in Liverpool and Manchester. In Liverpool, Father Nugent became concerned that Catholic children were receiving a Protestant education in Poor Law schools and workhouses.[18] Rye had emigrated some children from Liverpool's workhouse, and Nugent sought to emulate this example with the aim of ensuring a Catholic placement and education for the child. From 1870, he began to migrate parties of Catholic children with the aim of securing homes and work for children in settled Catholic communities, particularly Québec, in Canada. The religious foundation of charitable emigration schemes like his provided an additional motivation for separating children from their wider families if there was a risk that they would be cared for and brought up in a different religious denomination.[19] Father Berry also ran 'Homes for Catholic Friendless Youths', maintaining three homes for working children and a 'one night' shelter in Liverpool from the 1890s onwards 'to assist the numerous Catholic lads who were roaming about the streets of Liverpool, and learning amid the city's temptations the nearest road to gaol or workhouse. I think no one who understands the friendless condition of these vagrant lads can have any doubt that the streets are to them, in their weakness and misery, the forcing ground of vice and crime.'[20]

The characterisation of the child as 'friendless' is central to the perception of emigration. Whilst the child might have had relatives, they were without evident means of financial and personal support from family, and this justified intervention that separated them. There was little legal justification for this position, however, and it is notable that the terms 'orphan,' 'abandoned,' or 'deserted,' were avoided, since they bore legal significance under the Poor Law.[21] The connection between Father Berry's Homes and Father Nugent eventually became a network of organisations for the emigration of Catholic children, the Catholic Emigration Society, and by the early twentieth century, this institutional structure was actively utilised and co-opted by the state in its developing provision for the protection of children.

There was a range of local emigration activity across the North West of England, including emigration from the Liverpool and the Liverpool workhouse, and from the wider Lancashire area, including Manchester and Salford. These had more localised support and publicity than the bigger London-based schemes that eventually developed, often associated with the work of 'Dr' Barnardo.[22] The Manchester and Salford Boys' and Girls' Refuges and Homes[23] charity was founded in 1870 by two schoolteachers in a ragged school and engaged in emigration of children to Ontario from the 1890s as a means of providing for children housed in their residential homes. The geographical reach of the emigration charities extended across the North West of England; for example, EF was emigrated at the age of eleven by the Manchester and Salford Boys' and Girls' Refuges in 1897. His settlement parish was Nantwich, a market town in rural South Cheshire, though he was emigrated from Manchester to Morganstown, Canada. He obtained a placement on a farm where he was described as good at farm work, but not keen on attending school, and eventually left to work for another local farmer. He was described as a 'very independent lad.'[24]

Emigration practices were developed by a range of local organisations in the late 1860s without a clear legal framework to govern the process. In particular, the factors determining whether children were eligible to be emigrated and regulating their legal status in relation to their parents were unclear. Under the common law, the paternal rights of the father over the custody and control of the children were clearly established by the mid-nineteenth century.[25] Paternal authority was absolute to determine a child's religious upbringing and education,[26] but carried with it the obverse responsibility to maintain and provide for the child's welfare.[27] These rights and responsibilities could not be relinquished or transferred from the father to another. The mother of a legitimate child had no right to control decisions as to their welfare, although they would have practical control on a day-to-day basis, which was a highly unsatisfactory legal arrangement. By contrast, if the child was illegitimate, the mother would acquire rights of custody and control over the child.[28] On death, the father of a legitimate child could appoint a guardian by will and the mother had no rights to interfere with decisions made by the guardian.[29]

By the 1880s, the exclusivity of the legal rights of parents – primarily the rights of fathers – over their children's physical and moral welfare were open to public discussion, led by the campaigning activities of the NSPCC.[30] The legal framework providing for the care of children, formulated around the importance of progeniture and the passage of property through the male line,[31] by the late nineteenth century frequently did not effectively reflect the practice of family life. In many households, but through economic necessity in working-class ones, the practical reality was that the care, and primary decision-making over children, was the responsibility of the mother, particularly after the death or abandonment of the family by the father.[32] There was legal debate over the authority for external intervention in the family, but the rights of the father were reaffirmed in the courts.[33] However, the increasing intervention by charitable institutions in the working-class home, and the role of middle-class women in managing the poor 'as an extension of the duties of motherhood'[34] undermined the inalienability of parental, or purely paternal, rights. On both a practical level and a formal legal level, parental rights over their children were eroded by state intervention through statute, and by the actions of charitable organisations.

Cretney identifies the fact that the law denied to mothers of legitimate children the legal status of being parents as highly problematic.[35] Though married women were not *legally* parenting the child and were not *legally* responsible for the obligation to provide for them, the role of the mother was nonetheless increasingly policed by the law, so she could be made criminally responsible for failure to provide for them, for example, in ensuring their attendance at school.[36] State intervention in decision-making over children through legal obligations placed on parents was already evident in seeking to ensure their vaccination,[37] despite significant resistance by anti-vaccination campaigns from both men and women.[38] Though only the child's father was legally obliged to provide for the legitimate child, mothers provided the majority of care, and indeed were expected to do so. The intervention to ensure certain expectations of parenting through the law was steadily encroaching on the common-law position of exclusivity of parental rights to determine the treatment of a child.

Section 37 of the Poor Law Act 1868 was the first criminal offence for the neglect of a child, providing for a sentence of up to six months imprisonment, with or without hard labour, for failure by a parent to provide food, lodging, clothing, or medical treatment for their child. Section 37 explicitly envisaged the separation of the child from the parent, potentially through imprisonment, but its scope was uncertain, and it was not enforced.[39] It was replaced and broadened by section 1, Prevention of Cruelty to, and Protection of, Children Act 1889, which enabled the prosecution of anyone having care of a child to be prosecuted if the child died as a consequence of wilful ill-treatment, neglect, or abandonment. Pimm-Smith argues that this section was directed at enforcing middle-class standards of parenting and was highly gendered in its enforcement, with mothers, particularly biological mothers, facing harsh punishment if a child died of neglect in their care.[40] The exception was employed biological fathers who did not provide for their children: 'The deaths of their children were perceived as inevitable due to transgressions of class and gender norms.'[41]

In seeking to protect and support children outside the family environment, charities and the state were engaging directly with families and their attempts to negotiate poverty and circumstances of acute economic distress. Utilising the charitable provision available, some families would place their child(ren) with a charity home on a contingent basis while they were temporarily unable to provide for them. Murdoch has demonstrated that few children were admitted to charitable children's homes due to parental abuse, or as orphans, but were instead admitted by parents as a temporary measure for their care during a period of economic difficulty.[42] Knowledge of such support enabled 'a poor mother to be a "forager" within the mixed economy of welfare'[43], strategically accessing charitable provision to support the family. Lamb notes that children themselves could exercise considerable autonomy in seeking institutionalisation for a range of reasons, including escaping the family environment or alleviating economic pressure: 'Children existed both within and separate to the family and they understood the power they wielded as children with a right to protection in an increasingly interventionist society'[44]

Whilst parents and children were capable of making use of charitable provision for their own purposes, the placement of the child created physical distance from the family and the potential for the charity to undermine the relationship between parent and child by limiting contact between them.[45] Charitable intervention in the family increasingly affected the effective exercise of parental rights but was justified by reference to the child's welfare. The admission of the child, however, opened the parent to judgment, which could be derogatory, 'focused on parents' perceived immorality, their capacity to be industrious, their respectability and their "deservingness" of assistance'.[46] The moral judgments underpinning the assessment of parenting did not clearly engage with the difference between that affected by economic oppression and purposeful negligence or abuse.[47]

Despite the development of emigration as a way of separating children from the parents, ostensibly to secure their welfare, it was not clear whether parental rights over their child could be terminated in such a manner, or whether charities had the right to terminate their rights. Charities were seeking to migrate children to Canada despite the existence of family remaining in England, and the fact that the child's parent(s) retained rights over them. Soares has identified that, whilst the Church of England Society for Waifs and Strays included a statement of permission to emigrate children in the admission form, consent to emigration was 'vigorously disputed' by parents.[48] Pooley argues that 'When fathers and especially mothers expressed suspicion about institutional interventions, they were confident in articulating the parental prerogatives, time-consuming labour and individual expertise that meant that they knew how to care for their offspring.'[49]

Even if they had signed an agreement including potential emigration to place the child with the charity, the legal rights of the father were inviolable over their own child.[50] The statement of permission to emigrate was a common feature on admissions forms for children's homes, but it had no legal effect. The legal right of the charity to remove the child abroad without formally granted permission by a holder of parental rights over the child was therefore highly doubtful. 'Dr' Barnardo was subject to legal action seeking the return of a child unlawfully emigrated to Canada without parental permission by the charity.[51] Barnardo was overt in his determination to remove children to Canada where he regarded the influence of the parent(s) as malign.[52] This led him to entirely ignore the right of the parent to consent to their removal abroad. Removal without formal permission from the child's parent was a recurring theme in charitable emigration schemes.

The legal situation was amended by the Custody of Children Act 1891, which provided that for a parent to remove their child from an institution where they had been placed for their care, having been abandoned by their parent, permission from the organisation must be obtained. The parent would have to demonstrate that they were a fit person to have custody to retrieve them from the institution.[53] Once the child was placed in a charitable institution, parents' rights over their child were significantly abrogated by the 1891 Act. From the perspective of the charity, where the parent or family was regarded as an undesirable influence, emigration provided the potential to fully sever the relationship between parent and child.

Alongside their own activities, charities also supported emigration from state-funded institutions. The Poor Law provided for the emigration of abandoned or orphaned children with the consent of the child and of the magistrates.[54] From 1889 on, when the child was deserted by their parent(s), the guardians of the parish could assume all parental rights through agreed resolution, and this power included providing for their subsequent emigration.[55] The provisions clearly stated that the parental interest in the child was extinguished through abandonment or death of the parents. However, the existence of extended family for most children led to their characterisation as 'friendless', a legally insignificant term which still implicated the disinterested, neglectful parent in failing to provide for their child's welfare. From 1894, a child could also be emigrated if their parent was convicted of cruelty towards them.[56] This was accompanied by the provisions of the Prevention of Cruelty to, and Protection of, Children Act 1889, permitting charitable intervention in the family to prevent cruelty to the child, even where parental rights over the child were being exercised.

In addition to the Poor Law provision for children, legislation provided for the establishment of industrial schools from 1857. Godfrey et al. have identified that 'Child saving charities altered the legislative landscape by driving a new national child protection agenda'.[57] Industrial schools sought to provide a trade and a basic education to children identified as begging, wandering without visible means of subsistence, or in the company of reputed thieves. The magistrates could also commit a child to an industrial school if the parent stated they were beyond parental control.[58] Industrial schools were normally managed by charitable organisations supported by a grant directly from the Treasury, rather than being run by the state directly, and these penal-welfare institutions were rooted in local patronage.[59] The development of industrial schools is evidence of government 'social reform for national economic and imperial reasons and showed a willingness to incorporate the institutions of civil society directly into its social policies.'[60] This is evident in the co-operation between the state and local charities in the running of industrial schools and the arrangements for child emigration from these institutions. From 1891, 'well conducted' children could be emigrated from an industrial school with the permission of the Secretary of State and the consent of the child.[61] These innovations further eroded parental rights by focusing on the child and their perceived need for institutional support, rather than care from within the family.

Child emigration using the resources and networks of the emigration societies became an important aspect of the practice of industrial schools. It was identified as 'one of the best means of disposal open to schools, especially for children coming from bad homes.'[62] Between 1908 and 1910, 410 boys and 197 girls were emigrated from industrial schools, a large proportion of whom were sent out by the Liverpool Education Authority through the agency of the Liverpool Sheltering Homes Committee or the Catholic Emigration Society.[63] Emigration to Canada for children in industrial schools was welcomed as a method of severing the influence of the parent(s) over the child: 'When a child is not physically inaccessible to his parent – when he leaves school, for instance, – no Act of Parliament can prevent the influence of a parent over the child, or the desire of the child to submit to that influence. Under the statute and the Home Office Regulations the parent has to be consulted and the consent of the Home Secretary obtained before a child can be emigrated from a school, and this rule appears to us right, it being understood that objections from the parent are acceded to only when found reasonable.'[64]

The choice made by charities to deliberately sever relationships between the child and potentially both their parent(s) and wider family through the impact of geographical distance provides an insight into the origins of child law in England. The aim of separation was to salvage or rescue children from environments or people regarded as problematic or harmful often, in this context, because of the impact of poverty. The unregulated space created by new forms of charitable intervention to protect a child who had otherwise existed within the private family structure allowed the practice of child emigration to develop. The role of charitable intervention was only later legitimated by the legal authority accorded to charities, both acting alone and in conjunction with state-led provision.

Following the Children Act 1908, the three routes through which a child could be emigrated to Canada were now clarified, but the legal requirements for the authorisation of their travel varied depending on the route adopted. Parental consent was *not* required for emigration from any of the institutions, because the parental rights over the child either did not exist (in the case of orphaned children) or was abrogated by the parents' neglect or deemed abandonment of the child. The child was required to consent to emigration in front of the magistrates for emigration with the support of the Poor Law.[65] For emigration from an industrial school, the child was required to consent, and the consent of the Secretary of State for the Home Office was also necessary.[66]

This legal framework provided for, and legitimated, existing local cultural practices that supported emigration as an outcome where parents had abandoned children, had placed them in an institution, or had been convicted of cruelty. However, the nature of the legal regulation meant there was considerable uncertainty surrounding the circumstances when intervention within the family was legitimised. As noted by the director of the NSPCC, Robert Parr, in 1910, 'the great reason for emigration is to remove a child from the bad influences of undesirable parents.'[67] The assessment of the circumstances of the child and the family justifying emigration could be very limited. Mary E. Fleming was emigrated from a Catholic industrial school on the basis that: 'If the girl is with her parents in Liverpool, we are afraid she is in danger. As to her willingness to go to Canada we are quite sure about that.'[68] The characterisation and understanding of 'care' was influenced by a range of concerns regarding the desirability of removal of the child from their environment, with limited consideration of the understanding of the child, or their relationship with their family.[69] Ferguson has argued that 'A highly restricted notion of "child protection" existed to the extent that children were seen as in need of protection by the state from their own incipient criminality, and society was in need of protection from these children in so far as they might pose a future threat to social order. Child protection ... would require putting into practice new conceptions of abuse that would demand an intimate knowledge of and access to hitherto largely private domestic relations between parents and children.'[70]

The influence of the parents or family on decision-making was highly circumscribed, although the consent of the child themselves to emigration was sought. Whilst the implications of emigration were probably not fully understood by the child concerned, there was a perception that some children actively pursued emigration as an option from their existing circumstances.[71] A report on Father Berry's Homes in Liverpool in 1901 stated that: 'For a number of boys Canada has many attractions, and from the reports we have had of boys sent out there we felt that we wisely undertook emigration as far as our funds would allow.'[72] Lamb argues that children were not necessarily merely 'victims of philanthropic enthusiasm' but were exercising choice within a circumscribed range of options.[73] It is notable that the requirement for the child's consent was maintained, despite the steady erosion of the parental right to determine the welfare of their child. Once the child was identified as suitable for an emigration scheme, they became 'friendless' for the purpose of the process, and the legal frameworks authorised the treatment of the child as separate from their family.

To resist emigration, therefore, a substantial burden was placed on the family, and though some families did manage to prevent the emigration of their child, their scope for agency was limited.[74] When Grace Potts was emigrated in 1910 without the permission of her father, it was recognised that the acceptance of parental rights by the father might indicate potential for parental change in the treatment of Grace.[75] It made no practical difference to Grace and her father, since the emigration had already been legally achieved without such consultation. However, it did lead to a change in approach, requiring parental consultation (but not permission) prior to emigration from industrial schools.[76]

By the turn of the twentieth century, the legal and organisational framework for the emigration of children was established and administered by a range of charitable institutions with the support of the state. Emigration was a means of achieving separation between child and parent and/or family influences to secure the future welfare of the child. This 'child-saving' narrative has underpinned legal frameworks for the protection of children from harm within the family since this period, maintaining the emphasis on separation between parent and child as the policy response to significant harm.[77]

RESPONSIBILITIES FOR PLACEMENT OF CHILDREN AND CARE ONCE EMIGRATED

Once emigrated, the legal responsibilities of the organisation in control of their emigration, and the oversight of their welfare in Canada was also uncertain. The children were now in a foreign jurisdiction and technically subject only to Canadian law. The focus of English regulation was only the process, legality, and authorisation of emigration. The child's arrival, accommodation, and eventual placement in Canada, and the support for after-care of the child once in the community, initially attracted little regulatory attention. It was the concern of the emigration charity to provide effectively for the child, but it was unclear who was legally responsible for the child and the type, or labelling, of placements available seemed to differ in character. This lacuna demonstrates the extent to which the legal framework for this practice was initially lacking in structure and focus on the needs of the children. The extent of the responsibilities of the emigration charity to provide after care and support on reception in Canada was not clearly defined.

According to Rye's reports on children placed in Canada, whilst some children were labelled as 'adopted', others were 'placed in service' or 'bound to a master' in an apprenticeship.[78] The distinctions seem to be drawn between the understanding of the nature of the relationship and the work potentially undertaken. There seems to be little distinction drawn according to the age of the child, since children of a similar ages were apparently in different types of placements. The age of the child came to be more significant over time, with children below the age of ten more likely to be labelled as 'adopted'.

These descriptions may have had an impact on the relationship between the child and the Canadian family, particularly for the small number of girls labelled as adopted.[79] It is possible that these children were intended to be treated as members of the family, rather than put to work. Adoption was not legally regulated in England until the Adoption Act 1926 (despite previous attempts in 1889 and 1890). The 1926 Act severed the legal relationship between child and birth parent, investing parental rights solely in the adoptive parent. Before then, any arrangement would be a 'simple' *de facto* adoption, leaving the legal rights of the birth parents, but assigning day-to day parenting to the adopting parent.[80] The adoption of the child in Canada could be motivated by the need for an extra pair of hands, particularly in rural environments, and perhaps also by the desire to conform to social expectations of the nuclear family.[81] The use of the term 'adopted' clearly implied some element of responsibility for the child on the part of the person accepting the placement. This is also the case for children 'bound to a master' and expected to learn a trade as an apprentice. However, the open nature of the concept of a placement as a potential form of employment left the expectations of the employer undefined, and the child open to exploitation and abuse.

The conditions children faced after placement were highly variable. Children placed on remote farms could be extremely isolated and there were limited, and monitored, forms of communication from their placement (see chapter 4). If the child was exposed to abuse or was unhappy in their placement, there was initially no formal system for following up on complaints. Children could be returned to the charity in Canada by an unhappy employer, but such children tended to face punishment, recrimination, and a subsequent placement. The lacunae in monitoring eventually attracted government attention in the Doyle Report of 1875,[82] which highlighted that this was a largely unregulated space putting emigrated children at risk of further abuse and harm.[83]

Doyle described the children's legal status following emigration as follows:

> In accordance with the municipal laws of Quebec and Ontario, the children upon arrival in these Provinces come under the absolute parental control of Miss Rye or Miss Macpherson, or of others to whose care they may have been committed by persons who have or are assumed to have authority over them in England. Whether children who are brought to Canada have been legally placed under the care of the persons who bring them is a point left wholly unnoticed by the authorities of the Dominion, or of the Provinces. Indeed, there appears to be nothing in the law of either England or of Canada to prevent any person of a philanthropic or speculative turn, who can collect money for the purpose, from gathering any number of 'waifs and strays and street arabs,' and with their easily obtained consent shipping them to Canada.[84]

Doyle saw the placement of children in a range of circumstances, mainly in farm labour and service.[85] He made it clear that 'Some of the places are worse than a Board of Guardians would consent to place a child in England.'[86] Lynch notes that Doyle reflected moral judgments in his discussion on the children emigrated, and the benefits of the Poor Law provision that he helped to administer in England.[87] Doyle suggested that emigration was suitable only for 'the very young destitute children who are not paupers, but may be said to be the raw material of our criminal classes, and who swarm in our cities and large towns.'[88] He echoes the arguments presented by the proponents of child emigration as a means of separating children from undesirable influences in England.

However, the Doyle Report highlights the risks associated with separation of children from the family unit and placement for their welfare. In relation to the placements themselves, Doyle acknowledged that there was little knowledge or monitoring of the homes and work environments to which children were sent, the authorities trusting to local agents. This exposed children to 'great abuses' and placement in homes that Doyle regarded as unsuitable.[89] He identified specific children who had been lost sight of once placed so that their current address was unknown,[90] and he concluded that 'It is to be regretted that some of the Union authorities do not manage to keep up regular communication with their own emigrant children.'[91]

The impact of Doyle's Report was to suspend the emigration of children from Poor Law Unions until 1883, when the Canadian government offered to inspect the situation of emigrated children annually and the guardians subsequently received greater guidance on the requirements for securing emigration of a child.[92] The report highlighted the gap in the legal authority of the charitable organisations in relation to the children placed, and the regulation of this activity once the child had left England. Without the legal framework of parental rights and family interest posing a potential challenge to the activities of charitable bodies, there was far less concern expressed regarding the welfare of the children in their care. Taking the child out of the jurisdiction and into the care of someone other than the parent further blurred legal authority over the child. The child was now subject to Canadian law rather than English law. While the charity might have retained formal legal authority in Canada, the reality of placement at a distance and controlled by the employer meant that the employer was *de facto* parent of the child – if they chose to assume this position. The central legal authority of the state over children and their welfare had yet to be fully asserted, and Doyle highlighted in emotional but precise terms the potential impact of this situation. 'There is a total absence of efficient supervision, and consequently children are exposed to suffering and wrong for which they get neither relief nor redress.'[93]

In *Gossage's Case*,[94] a writ of *habeas corpus*, requiring that an identified person produced from custody and be made available before the court, was issued in the English Queen's Bench Division for the return of Henry Gossage, aged twelve, from Canada to England. Henry had been emigrated to Canada by 'Dr' Barnardo without parental permission and his mother sought his return. The requirement to produce Henry before the court was defeated in a practical manner by the inability of Barnardo's organisation to locate the child in Canada. The legal remedies available in the English court to the parent were practically inoperable because of the failures to monitor and record the placement of children in Canada. The severance of the relationship between parent and child was regarded as important and effectively provided also for the severance of parental rights. The Canadian placement was pre-eminent in the day-to-day experience and relationships of the child and was now central to their welfare.

Whilst Annie Macpherson responded to the criticisms and recommendations made by Doyle and changed her practice on the ground,[95] Maria Rye responded with a press and public relations offensive. She argued to the president of the local government board that her Canadian placements were with a 'substantial, orderly, comfortable, and well established class of people who are the custodians of these children in Canada you would then better understand the enormous boon you are placing within their reach, and why I think inspection of the children of comparatively so small moment, and the reasons I have so largely used correspondence as a means of oversight of the young people once placed out.'[96] She did not seek to change her practice in the light of the report. Having examined Maria Rye and received evidence in relation to her scheme, the Canadian Dominion government Select Committee on Immigration and Colonization accepted that the work of emigration was of a satisfactory character, giving advantage to both the children and to Canada. Despite this positive endorsement in evidence to the Select Committee, there was broad acceptance of the value of more direct supervision that Maria Rye had engaged in. Yet there were also concerns expressed by Mr Young MP (Canada) about the validity of Doyle's suggestions for supervision arrangements in the Canadian environment: 'Mr Doyle had evidently looked at the work entirely in the light of an Inspector of the Poor Law Board of Great Britain, and had not taken into account the different state of society, and different circumstances which exist in this country. He seemed to think that the boys must go entirely astray if they were not constantly watched by a Government Inspector.'[97]

Doyle, in responding to Maria Rye's criticisms of his report, was quite clear that he regarded her practices and monitoring of the children once placed as unacceptable. His reflection and compassion for the children's experience provides some insight into how abuse of children was experienced within the community. He refers to the secondary reporting by people who wished to remain anonymous of 'difficult' placements or, more directly, of harm to children. This was evident in his initial report but in his response to Maria Rye, he explores individual cases, arguing that this was the only evidence available of the harm to which children were potentially exposed and the impact of non-supervision of placements. He highlights one case where 'I asked a coloured man whom I met if he could direct me, and to assist him in doing so, told him I was looking after a little English child who was there in service. "Oh!" he replied, "I am glad that anybody has come to look after her; I have seen that child flogged worse than a slave; but don't mention me as telling you, for I do all the white washing of the house."'[98]

The secondary reporting identifies the difficulties of responding to abuse within small communities. The child themselves had no voice in this situation, but the reporting individual was also limited by their circumstances. It is notable that this 'coloured' person perceived the abuse of the child in question as 'worse' than that of slavery. It is not clear from the report if comment was made by a person of Indigenous Canadian descent, or a person of a different race. Likening the situation of the child to one of slavery may reflect the child being flogged for perceived infractions. However, it may also be directed at slavery as property of the person[99] and the consequential exploitation of their labour. The vulnerability of the child to exploitation in a situation where the child is entirely subject to the conditions of the placement is evident, and conceptually similar to ownership of the child.

The complicity of the community in the maintenance of silence and limited accountability for the treatment of children is evident throughout both Doyle's original report and his later response. Reporting of abuse of a child has two potential impacts; first, it may affect the personal position of the reporting individual, more likely in a small community, as alluded to in the quote above. Secondly, the allegation of abuse could potentially impact on the perception of the community *as a whole* in a colonial society seeking to establish its status. It also speaks to the lack of voice experienced by children in this environment; their background and the perception of their needs meant that their narrative was rarely preferred if they were labelled as unco-operative, or as having a temper, something with which Doyle identified and had some sympathy.

The movement of children abroad left children in an unregulated environment, potentially open to abuse and mismanagement. There was opportunity for some children, but there was also the potential for victimisation in the system as constituted. Whilst the state was prepared to utilise charities' emigration societies, it eventually recognized the problems of sending children abroad in terms of monitoring their welfare and managing their placements in a mainly rural society with less developed infrastructure. Doyle made a significant effort to pay regard to children's feelings, their experience of their environment, and their remaining links to England.[100] However, the practice of emigration did not cease, though there was subsequently much greater management by the state, both English and Canadian, of both the process of emigration and the control of placements once in Canada.

STATE-LED MANAGEMENT AND PROMOTION OF EMIGRATION FOR CHILDREN

By 1910, concerns over the emigration of children through the Poor Law in conjunction with various charitable organisations had been resolved. The charity was in *loco parentis* of the child once they left England. There was 'high appreciation shown by the Canadian authorities of the work of Guardians of the Poor in the emigration of children, and of the value to Canada of the children so emigrated.'[101] The Local Government Board received 1,999 reports from 1909 created by local immigration officers inquiring into the situation of children previously emigrated. Each child had to be visited at least once a year. Only forty-one children were identified as requiring intervention or a change in placement.[102] The government favoured the increase of emigration of children through the Poor Law, from industrial schools and through the operation of the emigration societies, as long as there was training beforehand and monitoring once placed in Canada.

In 1924, the Bondfield Delegation, led by Margaret Bondfield MP, sought to investigate the conditions of immigration to Canada and made a report to the Secretary of State for the Colonies on the system of child migration.[103] First-hand information regarding the system of child migration and settlement, including the arrangements in receiving homes, the selection of placements in Canadian household, the inspection of placements before and during placement, was examined. It focused specifically on the costs of emigration to the state now it was a recognised form of legalised intervention in relation to children. The Empire Settlement Act 1922 had provided explicit financial support for specific forms of emigration to help the rural settlement and economic development of Canada, providing further impetus in policy for emigration.[104] Post-Empire Settlement Act 1922, the Imperial Government and Dominion Government made a joint grant for transportation and placement of each child, clearly seeking to promote the emigration of children.[105]

The Bondfield Delegation identified that the number of applications by Canadians seeking to receive children from the emigration societies exceeded the number of children emigrated. A number of placement characterisations were identified by this point: legal adoption (comparatively rare); boarding out with a foster parent for cash payments (only used by Dr Barnardo's Homes); boarding out without cash payment of children up to fourteen (child expected to do light duties, but not paid wages, and attend school); payment of wages to children over fourteen for full-time work (wages paid to a bank until the child is eighteen; some societies recovered costs from this deposit).[106] There were formalised distinctions drawn between the responsibilities associated with each type of placement, by contrast to the earlier period. Inspection of the placement was recommended to occur within one month of the child entering the Canadian home, though it normally took place within three months. The process had become more highly structured, with co-operation between the Dominion authorities and the emigration societies.[107] The Dominion government was not prepared to accept the dumping of children, and therefore requested the selection of children deemed suitable for placement from the emigration societies. The major recommendation of the delegation was regarding the age at which children were emigrated: 'we feel that, however excellent the placings, the migration of young children is open to objection in principle. In the first place, the comparative helplessness of the child makes this form of migration the most liable to abuse. There is the loss of certain educational advantages. There is the danger of overworking … the children are sent to Canada for working purposes, the general principle to be adopted is that the children should not leave this country until they have arrived at working age (i.e. over 14).'[108] They suggested that children younger than fourteen should be allowed to travel only if the Canadian applicant was prepared to legally adopt the child, or defer the costs of emigration.

There was recognition that emigration might be of great value to young people, but also posed risks associated with their vulnerability.[109] It was clear that children were marked out and referred to as 'Home Children'[110] both at school and in their home environment, identifying them as different and separate within the community. This labelling of children was given as a reason to reduce the number of inspections, since the process of inspection identified them a Home Child, particularly if they had to be contacted at school to complete the visit. Children were not consistently visited on an annual basis, and it was considered that the inspection was not 'a great safeguard.'[111]

By 1934, child emigration was again considered as highly desirable by the state for both working age and younger children. As one aspect of the Bondfield Delegation's assessment of assisted emigration within the Empire, it was suggested that child emigration should resume on the basis of boarding out with Canadian families and 'very careful safeguards.'[112] The Delegation concluded that 'There can, in our view, be no question as to the desirability of encouraging by all available means the migration of young children. Apart from the wide opportunities available in the Dominions for the healthy upbringing of children, the fact that child migrants are brought up from a tender age in the country of settlement generally renders their absorption as adults into the community far easier than is the case with other migrants.'[113] The benefit to the child is in 'absorption' into their community, despite the challenges of this process, to take advantage of the employment opportunities in Canada. This had always formed an aspect of the wider narrative of child emigration, but was now regarded as a positive aspect of emigration for children themselves.

The government was also keen to maintain the balance of co-operation between voluntary emigration societies and its own activities and responsibility. The emphasis remained on the importance of voluntary organisations in encouraging and promoting emigration,[114] but also in organising the process of emigration, including reception, aftercare, and advice.[115] The philanthropic and charitable aspects of child emigration were still central to the effective administration of the schemes, despite the fact that this potentially limited accountability and support for the children placed in Canada. It acknowledged the authority of the Canadian jurisdiction over children within the territory, but there was little reflection on the use and limits of emigration as a means of providing for the safety and welfare of children, particularly given the long experience of the practice at this point.

The concern instead was about the legal eligibility of children for emigration. The 1930 Poor Law Act had included the provision for orphaned and deserted children to be emigrated with the child's consent before the magistrates.[116] Under section 52 of the Poor Law Act 1930, the Poor Law Authority could also provide for the adoption of a child who was neither orphaned or deserted, and whose parent(s) were still living. There was uncertainty over the difference in treatment between orphan and deserted children, depending on whether they had been 'adopted' by the poor law authority or not.[117] The previous disregard for the formalities and legal categorisation of the status of children emigrated had been abandoned, and the complexities of the legal framework within the Poor Law became evident. Whilst these distinctions had largely been ignored to this point, there was discussion over the process through which the child could be lawfully emigrated. The Ministry of Health determined that, depending on the status of the child as being either orphaned or deserted, the child's consent before the magistrates would be required, the parent(s)' consent could be required, or should be obtained where available.[118] It was argued that, from the point of view of the child, there was little difference between being orphaned or deserted by their parents. This underlines much of the approach taken to child emigration: that the child's point of view was heavily influenced and predetermined by the authorities in the Homes or industrial schools where they were placed and, even when sought, was within an environment that favoured the outcome of emigration. The law was acting on children as chattels of the family to be provided for when the family structure was identified as failing.

CONCLUSION

The regulation of child emigration demonstrates the increasing role of the state and the law over the lives of children from the late nineteenth century. As intervention in poor families occurred in a variety of guises, the question of how to respond to the needs of children who were separated from families identified as neglectful or abusive, or otherwise unsuitable, became a pressing question. Emigration allowed for the separation of the child from perceived undesirable influences, and had the additional benefit of forwarding the colonial settlement of Canada. The support of emigration for children provided by philanthropic and charitable organisations was motivated by these designs. This nascent provision for child welfare regarded children as in need of intervention to shape and guide them, yet did not provide consistent monitoring or support for the subsequent management of their placements and the child's welfare in the longer term. Though for some children emigration had positive outcomes, this remained a largely unregulated environment, with limited acknowledgement of their wider connections and family in England or the value of those relationships to the child. This problem will be explored further in chapter 3.

The organisational framework created by the emigration societies was utilised by the state through the Poor Law and industrial school system to provide work and accommodation for children outside the framework of their family. State agencies sought to manage provision for children at arm's length, without clear engagement with how emigration affected children and their future welfare, and a legal framework that only responded to issues as they arose. The movement of children triggered cross-national co-operation regarding the movement of children. However, there was acceptance of the narrative surrounding the opportunities of emigration without clear and consistent examination or questioning of the outcomes for children by government.[119]

The movement of children abroad created an unmonitored space where there was opportunity for the exploitation and abuse of children without likely penalty or further intervention. This was exactly the situation that the charitable intervention originally sought to correct by removing and separating the child from the family, a hitherto unmonitored space. This inevitably led to considerable difficulties in tracing children, managing their placements, and responding to allegations of abuse, as highlighted by the Doyle Report and the associated furore in the 1870s. Whilst Doyle challenged these practices, the regulation that subsequently developed still supported the practice of emigration rather than fundamentally challenging its purposes.

Whilst both the legalities of emigrating the child and the arrangement of placements saw greater regulation from the 1880s on, there remained considerable uncertainty about the circumstances legitimising intervention in the family to protect a child. The process of emigration was more closely regulated by both the English legal framework and Canadian immigration rules to ensure legality in the selection of children and that the appropriate permissions were sought. There were attempts to engage with children after their original placement as well as to retain records of where they were placed and on what basis. Despite this, there was no critical questioning of the role the law should play in engaging with family life when problems were identified, or when a child was at risk of harm. The origins of child law, and modern child protection, lie in this desire to separate the child from the family and their wider environment, realised through the process of child emigration. The statutory framework developed to manage the legalities of emigration began the characterisation of English child law as responsive from the mid-nineteenth century; a process of salvaging children from persons or environments identified as problematic or harmful.

3

Letters from the Land of Plenty

In May 1899, a teenage girl named Lizzie wrote from Montreal to Mrs Birt, head of the Liverpool Sheltering Home. Birt had facilitated the emigration of thousands of children from the North West of England to Canada, including Lizzie. Enclosing two photographs of the young children she cared for, Lizzie wrote movingly of her experiences in Montreal and her gratitude to Birt for changing her life so dramatically: 'I am sending you my two babies photos, the youngest is a sturdy little boy of six months, feeling sure you would like to have them. We have a lovely fall here no cold weather to speak of yet, my sister Annie has been very sick but is getting better again. Dear Mrs Birt this time of the year is apt to bring sad memories back still after eight years. I cannot thank you enough for what you have done for my two sisters and myself at that time when we were all-alone without father or mother … hoping you will have a very merry Christmas and a happy new year when they come as you have been the means of giving me so much happiness.'[1] Signing off, 'I remain one of your girls' Lizzie's letter is perhaps surprising in its intimate and affectionate tone to 'dear Mrs Birt' and its emphatic, 'I cannot thank you enough for what you have done'.

Certainly, Lizzie's message of contentment jars with the narratives of abuse and exploitation that we usually associate with the experience of child emigration.[2] Yet Lizzie's letter was by no means exceptional, and many letters from emigrant children to their 'dear old refuge' have survived.[3] Not all letters were as positive as Lizzie's, of course, and other emigrant children sent complaints about their circumstances or requests for help. For example, a year after Lizzie's affectionate letter, Mrs Birt received an angry missive from another of her émigré girls, protesting that Birt had returned her invalided sister to England. Leonora complained 'you have given me the heaviest blow I have ever had, in taking away the only tie we had left to us in this world away from us, and it can never be lifted from my heart and *I will never forgive you* as long as I live.'[4]

These letters offer an important perspective from the children who made the long journey from the North West of England to Canada, and undermine the presumed voice of the emigrant as an adult one, writing home to maintain connections of kinship.[5] Placing the children's letters at the heart of its analysis, this chapter contributes to an emerging body of scholarship that explores the experiences of children following institutional care, as emigrants in colonies, and their correspondence home.[6] Letter-writing was widespread and provided important communication between children in institutions and their families, and with the staff members once they had moved beyond residential care, and was certainly encouraged by some emigrating institutions. Of the 2,129 children sent to Canada by the Manchester Refuge and Homes, 175 emigration files remain with the charity, now known as the Together Trust. Of these, around eighty, or 45 per cent, include letters written by emigrant children both to Marchmont, the home in Canada where they stayed until a foster or work placement was found, or, more commonly, to the institution back in Manchester. About twenty-five written to Mrs Birt have survived and are housed in the Library and Archives Canada Birt letters collection. It is unlikely to be a coincidence that only Protestant institutions have kept this correspondence. It is possible that Catholic children's literacy skills were poorer or that they wrote fewer letters. Certainly, Protestant institutions used the letters strategically to ensure the viability of child emigration schemes, and especially to challenge criticisms of their emigration policy and to attract donations. By comparison, Catholic institutions had relative autonomy, as they relied less on the state or local philanthropists for support and could utilise the power and influence of the Church to operate with less scrutiny.

Letters were not only used by emigrating institutions to justify their policies and rebuff criticisms of their practice, but also provided valuable opportunities for children to engage with those who controlled their lives. Claudia Soares's analysis of the Waifs and Strays society argues that 'correspondence offers valuable insight into how the poor negotiated with those in power to meet their own ends, their attempts to parent from a distance, and their struggles to preserve relationships with children.' Soares's readings of the letters from family members to children in care suggests that 'these letters are sites where working-class parents routinely articulated their family values, and laid bare their attitudes about parenting and the affective dimensions of family relationships.'[7] Yet, as we shall see, letters from emigrant children to their institutions also helped children to shape and direct their own experiences of emigration, particularly when to isolating and difficult posts in remote areas or when they were faced with unwanted separation from siblings or friends.

This chapter's focus on the letters written by emigrant children therefore contributes to a broader shift away from thinking of children as 'principally as objects of welfare provision' and instead highlights children's agency even within institutions and residential forms of care.[8] Gillian Lamb's research on nineteenth-century welfare has challenged the presumption that institutional care was necessarily harmful for children and instead demonstrates that children could 'use the welfare system to direct their futures', including choosing to stay in residential care rather than living with their own families.[9] Similarly, Laura Mair's analysis of correspondence between those emigrated as children by the London Ragged School Union and their former teachers suggests that their letters were 'emblematic of the agency former ragged scholars exercised in their relationships with teachers after their time at school' and could 'set the tone for the epistolary relationship.'[10] As we shall see, children did not necessarily resist their emigration and frequently reinforced the rhetoric of the emigrating institutions, perhaps out of a belief in the missionary zeal they were subjected to, because they felt powerless to challenge their fate, trusted those who cared for them, or because they welcomed the chance to depart difficult circumstances and embrace new opportunities. Reading children's experiences in these ways helps to understand their complex and contradictory status and identities. Drawing on the insights of recent scholarship that stresses the 'in betweenness' of emigrant children as both marginalized and privileged, and that highlights their liminal position within settler society, we see that although emigrating institutions employed their correspondence as propaganda, child correspondents wrote these letters – to try shape their own experiences within a system that offered them little formal power.[11]

HISTORICISING EMIGRANT CHILDREN'S LETTERS

Institutions interpreted letters in ways that served their own agendas and used them to present positive stories of life in Canada whilst casting suspicion on those who questioned or complained about their treatment. Here, we find similarities with emigrant children's writings and those by refugees, which, as Peter Gatrell, Anindita Ghoshal, Katarzyna Nowak, and Alex Dowdall argue, were 'created and preserved (or not) within particular bureaucratic and administrative systems. Letters and petitions composed and sent to government authorities, NGOs or humanitarian bodies were written with the perceived requirements and expectations of those same organizations in mind, while they were preserved in the archive according to particular institutional cultures and internal organizational histories.'[12] Using this framework, we argue that letters from emigrant children undertook important emotional work both on behalf of the children themselves and for the emigrating institutions in Canada and the North West of England. This kind of correspondence is typically one-sided – we only have letters written by children to their own institutions and do not have copies of the letters sent by the institutions; nor do we have letters from the same children to other correspondents. Read in conjunction with press coverage in local newspapers in the North West, however, we can see how this writing afforded children a powerful way to influence, respond to, or resist their emigration experience.

The use of children's letters by charitable and welfare organisations to legitimise and fundraise for their policies became commonplace into the twentieth century. As Joy Damousi has demonstrated, the plight of children took centre stage in post-First World War humanitarianism as a way to depoliticise the processes that created the need for such aid campaigns. Using the example of the Foster Parents Plan (PLAN), which emerged following the Spanish Civil War and expanded through Europe during the Second World War and through Asia during the 1970s, Damousi stresses the importance of letter-writing schemes as a way to attract donors and elicit an emotive response that was removed from politics or nationalism. Damousi argues that 'in promoting exchange through letter writing, efforts were made to capture the voices of children, but these were severely compromised and appropriated to serve the fundraising endeavours of PLAN itself.'[13] Home institutions encouraged their emigrants to write letters and may have influenced what was written in order to present a wholly positive image of their experience abroad. As we shall see, 'letters of gratitude' often mirrored the propagandist language produced by emigrating institutions and were read aloud at fundraising events and annual subscribers' meetings, and used to publicly condemn claims about emigrant children's ill-treatment.[14] The use of these letters, therefore, was a precursor to what became a relatively widespread exploitation of children by humanitarian agencies to mobilise support for international aid and justify relief policies.[15]

At the same time, however, this chapter suggests that the manipulation and appropriation of émigré letters by the institutions did not silence the voices of children entirely. Their letters are also used to expose their affective bonds both with each other and with the institutions they had emigrated from. Lucinda Matthews-Jones notes how strong emotional ties between the staff of philanthropic 'Settlement Homes' (created for university graduates to administer social work to the poor) in Cardiff were maintained with their former inmates, working-class youths, who subsequently fought as soldiers during the First World War.[16] Such ties might flourish even in more explicitly disciplinarian surroundings. Abigail Wills's work on the High Beech Probation Home during the 1950s, a centre for male juvenile offenders whose staff were largely trained pre-1930s, characterizes the ethos of the Home as a 'substitute family'.[17] Children could also use this language of affect to position their requests for help from the institution, suggesting they knew what their Home institution wanted to hear and how to exploit that for their own advantage.

Finally, the chapter demonstrates how these letters were used by children to make complaints – often coded or veiled – and to object to their placement or their treatment as well as to make requests. Letters were especially influential as the one of the few methods of recourse for children not just against ill-treatment, but particularly to address the enforced separations from their siblings. The letters therefore highlight the significant trauma of child emigrants when they were separated from their brothers and sisters. These insights are important because they show how children developed strategies for survival amid great upheaval and turned to other types of bonds in the absence of parental connections. They also indicate that children had some sense of the power or influence of writing letters and used them to shape and challenge their experiences of emigration. This approach uncovers how the letters and their authors can be understood as contributing to an 'emotional community' through their shared forms of emotional expression and their common use of coded language, even when the correspondent was writing to complain or to obtain information.[18] Building on recent research by Hester Barron and Claire Langhamer, we suggest that these letters represented an important way to understand how 'emotional formation' was developed through relationships rather than being spatially defined, and how children understood their relationships with others.[19]

Our reading of these letters provides a rare opportunity to trace an emotional history of child emigration from the children's perspectives. Penny Summerfield's *Histories of the Self* notes that historians usually use letters as either a method of accessing data or to address the making of the self, whereas these two goals are not mutually exclusive. Summerfield writes, 'letters, seen by some historians as a stage on which their authors performed, recorded both resistance to the operation of colonial ideologies in everyday life, and the reproduction of such dynamics as part of the author's accommodation of them. The fashioning of an epistolary self from culture and experience thus provides clues, in the hands of some historians, to wider social, psychological, and material processes.'[20] Yet children have, until recently, been excluded from these important discussions around epistolary culture and the shaping of the self. Barron and Langhamer's analysis of children's writing for the social research movement Mass Observation highlights 'children's familiarity with adult-defined emotional codes and styles facilitated transitions across physical and imaginary spaces.'[21] Of course, as others have noted, children's narratives, like those of adults, are always shaped by wider social and cultural processes.[22] We show here that emigrant children, subconsciously or consciously, mobilised the propagandist language and imagery created and disseminated by the emigrating institutions in order to help obtain what they wanted. From professing affection to their home institution and fondness for the children left behind to May's insistence that 'you have been the means of giving me so much happiness,'[23] the letters reveal powerful language expedient both for the children and the institution.

LETTERS OF GRATITUDE

Children's letters were used by Protestant institutions in the North West of England to support and justify the policy of child emigration, particularly from the 1880s onwards as it came under increased scrutiny and criticism. Public support mattered, because these institutions relied on donations and the patronage of local inhabitants (employing the children as manual or domestic labour, for instance) to fund their activities. Children in the institutions required food, shelter, an education, and also received industrial training (including farming instruction for boys) in the several years between admittance and emigration. The institutions did more than just emigrate children; for instance, the Manchester Refuge ran training schools and the ship *Indefatigable*, provided night-shelters for children escaping abusive parents, and ran a seaside rest home. They would take any boy or girl up to sixteen years of age and operated on an income of around £14,000 a year.[24] The need to garner public support was less pressing for Catholic institutions because the Church wielded such notable power and authority and benefitted from sectarian divisions, especially in Liverpool.[25] The Catholic Church subsequently required less accountability to the local populations of Liverpool and Manchester, allowing their significant fundraising power to go relatively unchecked, and they facilitated financial contributions from their overwhelmingly working-class congregations with relatively little need to justify their projects or the nature of their welfare work.[26] For example, Father Berry's Homes only began holding annual meetings for supporters in 1893, in honour of Berry's silver jubilee, with the focus on fundraising over accountability or reporting.[27]

The power and autonomy of the Catholic Church ensured it was also relatively more robust in the face of concerns about child emigration policy, which was generally very popular amongst Catholic leaders in Britain. For instance, the 1902 Conference of the Catholic Truth Society included a report on child emigration, to which the Bishop of Southwark remarked, 'it was important that this work should be extended' and the Bishop of Shrewsbury 'said it was distressing to see the number of children in the gutters and slums of great towns, and it was gratifying that some of them could be rescued by emigration.'[28] In contrast, criticism of the emigration system threatened to undermine the wider philanthropic projects undertaken by Protestant institutions and risked the withdrawal of support from local patrons and donors. The policy remained contentious, particularly in light of the 1875 Doyle Report, which as we saw in chapter 2, expressed serious concerns about the care of emigrant children, whilst shifting ideas about child protection and welfare encouraged some local Poor Law Guardians to become outspoken critics of the practice in the 1890s and 1900s. The Manchester Refuge also faced scandal in 1895 when one of its central figures, Gilbert Kirlew, faced accusations of being a paedophile and abusing the boys in his care. Libel cases in 1895 and 1898 attracted significant press attention and required former refuge boys to testify against Kirlew.[29] There was a real need to maintain local support therefore and not just for financial reasons. As we also saw in chapter 2, although the system only nominally required 'consent' from children and their families, familial opposition could disrupt or even halt a child's emigration. Local patronage mattered to the long-term success and viability of child emigration, and it was in this context that children's letters became crucial forms of testimony about its success and to challenge persistent accusations around children's ill-treatment and abuse. This context helps to explain why the Manchester Refuge and Birt's Sheltering Home used letters strategically to facilitate a positive image of the experience of child emigrants in Canada.

The letters to Manchester Refuge were featured relatively frequently in the *Manchester Guardian*, which reported its annual meetings alongside more general discussions, reports, and debates around child emigration, in its role as a leading Liberal paper focussed on local and international issues and communicating with a middle-class audience.[30] In Liverpool, letters to Birt were most commonly reported in the *Liverpool Mercury* prior to its merger with the *Liverpool Post* in 1904, which also reported on local, national, and international issues and circulated in the North West of England as well as London. There was also some discussion of the policy in other newspapers published in the North West of England, particularly in the *Liverpool Echo*, which catered to a more working-class readership, but coverage tended to focus on reports of 'little emigrants' setting sail for Canada,[31] or 'consenting' to their own emigration.[32] The Liverpool press perhaps reported on Catholic emigration institutes more frequently than the Manchester press did, but we have not yet found any examples of letters to Catholic Homes being published or discussed in any of the newspapers.[33] These features of the reportage around child emigration demonstrate that it was commonly accepted in Liverpool and Manchester, where it had become a well-known form of child welfare and where sectarian divisions ensured that Catholic schemes benefitted from greater autonomy and less scrutiny than their Protestant counterparts. Rather, the priority of Catholic leaders in Britain was to ensure that Protestant emigrating institutions were kept at bay. These concerns led to the creation of the Catholic Emigration Society founded in 1927, which aimed to complement the work of the Catholic Emigration Association 1904 and to deter Catholics from emigrating with Protestant or secular emigration societies.[34]

For Protestant emigration institutions therefore, children's 'letters of gratitude' were important and powerful ways to promote the success of child emigration schemes and were used widely by Manchester Refuge in their fundraising campaigns. This strategy seems to have been an established practice of other emigrating societies: Edward Brenton, founder of the Children's Friend Society, included heavily edited letters from children emigrated by the charity to South Africa in his account of the society's work in the 1830s, whilst the London Ragged School Union encouraged their emigrants to write letters that were subsequently read aloud at meetings in the 1860s.[35] Similarly, letters were fundamental to Manchester Refuge's claims to legitimacy, which became a crucial factor in the increasingly competitive late-Victorian charity market. As Sarah Roddy, Julie-Marie Strange, and Bertrand Taithe argue, accountability was central 'to the self-narrative of the institutions themselves. To be transparent was to be open and popular, clearly connected to the rich and powerful, which calling on the generosity of the greater number.'[36]

This need was certainly present through the annual meetings held by Manchester Refuge and Birt's Sheltering Home, which were used to celebrate their achievements, report on their finances, and drum up support for the future. The children's letters took centre stage. In 1884, Birt 'read several letters received from children sent out to Canada, all of whom expressed their contentedness and happiness in their new sphere of life.'[37] Similarly in 1893, the annual report for Manchester Refuge was read aloud at the meeting and also 'contained several letters from children who have been emigrated during the past few years.'[38] In 1900, the Manchester Refuge's annual meeting included a speech from their guest Lord Aberdeen, who had been governor general of Canada from 1893 to 1898. The *Manchester Guardian* reported that 'after reading letters from two emigrants from the homes, his Lordship said this work was eminently patriotic and practical.'[39] In 1901 at Manchester Town Hall, the Bishop of Hereford attended the annual meeting of the Manchester Refuge to celebrate the landmark of 'over 1000 children' emigrating from the institution to Canada. The chairman claimed that 'they constantly received from them letters of gratitude and thankfulness, many enclosing subscriptions to the Refuge funds – (hear hear).'[40] The double whammy of happy emigrant children who were thankful enough to praise their experiences and donate to ensure other 'friendless' children would be sent to Canada offered the Refuge a powerful advert for their work.

Perhaps more crucial was the role the children's letters played in challenging objections to the work of child emigration schemes. These letters became particularly important during disputes between institutions, which often arose due to the explicit anti-Catholicism from Protestant philanthropists that led Catholic institutions to call into question claims by Protestant institutions that they provided non-denominational care.[41] In Liverpool, Birt faced notable criticism from Catholic institutions who accused her of proselytising children in her care. A case in 1881 attracted significant local attention when Birt was accused by Richard Yates, secretary of the Liverpool Catholic Children's Protection Society (now Nugent Care), of removing a teenage boy from the Catholic section of an industrial school to her own Protestant institution, where, Yates alleged, he was 'shipped off to space.'[42] Birt responded to these accusations by writing to several Liverpool newspapers to state that she had followed procedure: 'In receiving and despatching this boy to Canada we acted according to our usual rule. After having satisfied ourselves of the utterly destitute condition of his only legal guardian, we gave him the benefit of the institution. As to his religious persuasion his own mother stated he was a Protestant, and signed a paper to that effect, and in this matter we are responsible to no other than the boy's mother.'[43] Six weeks later, as Birt set sail back to Liverpool from a visit to Canada, she sent several letters she alleged were written by the boy to the local press 'to show your readers a very bright contrast' to the way he had been depicted in the press previously. To his mother he had apparently written, 'I like living here because master and mistress are kind to me; and I drive the horses sometimes and I can milk the cows,' and to his old teacher in the Sheltering home, he stated, 'I am in a comfortable home. I sing for the master and mistress and they are pleased with me.'[44]

Yates was not convinced by the idyll presented in this correspondence and wrote to both the *Echo* and the *Daily Post* to accuse Birt of forgery: 'these letters would have been creditable to a fairly advanced, rather than an inveterate truant lad.' Claiming the boy 'cannot write, and that, therefore, the letters which would be accepted as the boy's own production, were of foreign manufacture.'[45] We cannot know the circumstances under which these letters were produced and whether the boy wrote them independently, or at all. What they do tell us, however, is that the emigrant child's letter – real or fabricated – represented important evidence for the emigrating institution when they sought to legitimise their policy.

Birt especially relied on letters that she claimed had been written by her emigrant children in the decade following the 1875 Doyle Report, which she needed to counter concerns about the risks of abuse. In 1883, Birt wrote to the *Liverpool Mercury* as she was about to depart to Canada with thirty boys, 'whose cheers have rung in our ears at the thought of so speedy an emancipation from what to them was such a dark future.' Birt claimed one boy was to join his brother, who had recently written to his mother about his new life in Canada, saying 'I can get all the milk I can drink and lots of eggs, which I like.' Birt also included another letter from a boy who had been abused by his stepfather and who had been living on the streets: 'I have not been so grateful to you for your kindness to me as I should have been, but I hope to do better for the future. I like Nova Scotia a great deal better than Liverpool, and can but feel thankful to think that I had the luck to be with such nice people … I thank you for the interest you have taken in my welfare, both practical and temporal … Please pray for me dear lady, and accept my best wishes for your welfare.'[46] The letters's emphasis on eating well and being with 'nice people' was no accident, as Birt wished to counter the allegations of the Doyle Report that emigrant children were being abused and forced to endure inhumane conditions. Letters were also a way for Birt to demonstrate that her institution proactively maintained relationships with emigrant children to reassure critics that they were confident that the farm and work placements were not exploitative or abusive. At the 1897 annual meeting, Birt 'read many extracts from letters showing how well the children were doing with their foster parents in Canada, and how fond their foster parents were of them.'[47] Again, the very deliberate use of these letters as a form of propaganda to facilitate donations and to challenge criticisms of child emigration, reflected the perceived epistolary authority of émigré child's voice – albeit when it suited the emigrating institution.

In Manchester, letters from emigrant children were used prominently from 1904, perhaps influenced by Birt's well-established strategy, as Manchester Refuge defended their practices and policies. At the thirty-fifth annual meeting of the Manchester Refuge in 1905, for instance, they celebrated the departure of fifty-two boys to Canada. Thomas Ackroyd, the secretary of the Refuge, made a speech that defended child emigration and emphasised their system of keeping in touch, as he 'desired to dispel the idea which evidently existed in the minds of some people that the children were badly treated.'[48] Ackroyd was referring to a period of significant hostility towards the Refuge and its role in child emigration policy that played out in the pages of the *Manchester Guardian*. As an influential mouthpiece for middle-class debate, the *Manchester Guardian* became central to increasingly divisive discussions between key philanthropic organisations around child welfare, particularly in the 1890s and 1900s, which emerged in response to evolving ideas about the role of the state and the alleviation of poverty.[49] These shifting and contested approaches towards child welfare facilitated a hostile conflict between some members of the Chorlton Board of Guardians, particularly Catherine Garrett, and the Manchester Refuge, led by Thomas Ackroyd. One of the key triggers was a letter published by the *Manchester Guardian* in November 1904 from a Harry Willing, who claimed to be a former Manchester resident now living in Ontario and working for one of their local newspapers. Willing claimed he was 'greatly struck with the number of homeless children sent out from Manchester in the care of the various homes, and with the miserable manner these poor little homeless ones are treated. They are neglected, do not get a proper education, and are made to slave from sunrise to sunset, and are thrashed for the least offences … in nearly every instance I have followed up I find ill-usage and neglect. I do implore the people of Manchester not to send their children out until they are able to look after themselves.'[50]

Ackroyd responded furiously and wrote to the *Manchester Guardian* in time for publication the next day. Rebutting the claims made by Willing the previous day, Ackroyd emphasised that their own investigations and those of the Dominion Government inspectors had revealed emigrant children were well-treated. Most importantly, however, 'the letters from which our boys and girls constantly send us' demonstrated they were 'most kindly treated and in every way helped by the farmers and their families.' Demanding that Willing send him the names and addresses of the children he referred to, Ackroyd emphasised that 'our knowledge of the whole subject leads us to declare most emphatically that the children are not neglected, ill-treated, and turned into slaves.'[51] Willing's allegations were serious and potentially very damaging, threatening to derail twenty-five years work by the Manchester Refuge.

The war waged on in the pages of the *Manchester Guardian*. A fortnight later, another correspondent, 'H.W.', claimed to have spent three years amongst the farming communities of Western Ontario and had made 'a special study of the treatment of the children sent out from England by various charitable organisations.' The letter alleged several 'isolated cases of cruelty' but suggested the larger offences were the farmers ignoring the education clause of the emigration schemes, keeping children working rather than allowing them to attend school as had been agreed. However, the correspondent noted, 'two years ago a "home" boy I knew committed suicide. I am confident that he knew no worse cruelty than this eternal loneliness in thought and sympathics. And many more are being slowly stifled to death by this same reason.'[52] In the same edition, a correspondent named H. Smith wrote from Canada after seeing the recent debate between Willing and Ackroyd reprinted in the local Ontario press. Smith outlined numerous instances of abused emigrant children, including a young boy, 'a living picture of misery,' who was beaten by the farmer. Smith maintained the abuse of Home children was widely known about in Ontario, writing 'many a time has my heart ached for these poor children, and Mr Editor, so would yours, and so would any person who had a heart to ache.'[53]

In retaliation, the Manchester Refuge contacted the Dominion Inspector of British Immigrant Children and Receiving Homes, George Bogue Smart, and sent him a copy of Willing's letter. A keen proponent of child emigration with strong ties to the North West England institutions, Smart's post had been created in 1900 by the Canadian government in order to address the increasing negative public opinion of child emigration schemes following the Doyle Report. Smart visited Willing, who apparently admitted that he had not known of any specific children or spoken to any farmers and that 'he only meant to imply that his knowledge was superficial and the letter was written as a protest against sending young children to Canada.' However, Smart claimed he had spoken to some emigrant children, including one young teenage girl in service, who 'is happy and contented and receiving good treatment from her mistress and the family.' Similarly, one emigrant boy 'has worked in the neighbourhood for five years, and said the farmers around there were not the class that would ill-treat a child. He had always received kind and considerate usage.'[54] Relentless, Ackroyd mobilised correspondence from the superintendent of Ontario's department for neglected and dependent children and sent an extract to the *Manchester Guardian* that stated he was 'amazed to note the kindness and affection shown by the Canadian people for these boys and girls from the old land … Canada is undoubtedly the land of promise.'[55] The debate as played out in the letters pages of the *Manchester Guardian* demonstrated the importance of the emigrant children's letters as testimony of the success and safety of the emigration scheme.

The letters between emigrant children and the home institutions were increasingly identified as an important method of regulating the policy and implementation of child emigration. Writing to the *Manchester Guardian* in 1905, Ackroyd explained that 'as far as possible we on this side keep in touch with the children, and are constantly receiving from them letters full of gratitude for having sent them to the new country and in this way giving them a fresh start in life.'[56] These 'letters of gratitude' became more fundamental to the tactics employed by those in favour of child emigration and the central evidence that it was an ethical and effective form of child welfare. In 1907 a Miss Miles, a Poor Law Guardian, wrote to defend child emigration after visiting Canada and returning 'fully convinced that un sending over children to Canada we were acting most wisely and well and for their good.' She stated that the children she met were 'treated with great consideration and so satisfied were they that not one of them wanted to return to their old life in England.' However, her testimony was supported by the children themselves and she emphasised, 'many of the children write voluntarily to their old schoolmasters and fellow-schoolers in enthusiastic terms of their life in Canada.'[57] According to the emigrating institutions, children's letters were portrayed as the most legitimate evidence that the scheme worked, followed by the government inspectors and philanthropists who had been in Canada, with critics of the scheme, like Willing, firmly at the bottom.

The debates around the ethics of child emigration did not wane in the years prior to the First World War however, perhaps reflecting the impact of Liberal welfare reforms and broader anxieties about the need to remedy the perceived 'degeneracy' of working-class children.[58] In Manchester, criticism of the scheme was led by Catherine Garrett of the Chorlton Board of Guardians, who became one of the most vocal opponents of child emigration in the North West. Significantly, Garrett also invested the power of letters, and wrote to the *Manchester Guardian* in March 1908 to claim she had 'received letters from both well-to-do and working men in Canada, and have been interviewed by others who have all been there, all asking me to go on and at all costs stop the practice of sending these children.' Attacking the validity of Ackroyd's use of the children's letters, she scornfully wrote, 'Letters saying they are "happy." Yes! But prove that these letters are not written under supervision, or even, has been done, by the employers themselves.'[59] This was a potentially dangerous accusation by Garrett as it was, and still is, impossible to know how freely children were allowed to write their own letters and whether they were coached or censored.

In response to Garrett's letter, a supporter of child emigration wrote to the *Manchester Guardian* in 1908 and suggested that 'the most enthusiastic and effective emigration agents are the children who are already out in Canada, and these children write regularly to their old companions telling of the good times experienced and urging those left behind to join them.'[60] Ackroyd responded to Garrett in a letter to the *Manchester Guardian* in which he stressed the importance of removing children to Canada away from 'relatives who are very undesirable … who will deliberately coerce or persuade the youth or girl to return to the old environment and exploit them for their own advantage.' Ackroyd claimed that most children did not want to return to Manchester from Canada and stated, 'we have just received a letter and photograph of a boy who went out three years ago. He is happy and writes: "I like the place fine." He came to us nine years ago from dreadful surroundings; indeed his mother sold him for a shilling to a woman in a bad house.'[61] Ackroyd here emphasised the need for children to be removed from their families in order to be fully reformed, which, as we have seen earlier, underpinned the policy of child emigration.

Garrett and another member of the Chorlton Board of Guardians, William Skivington, spent the next few years energetically campaigning against child emigration schemes and, like Ackroyd, letters became key to their methods of attack. In April 1910, the Department of Emigration of the Government of Canada requested that Garrett justified her claims about the alleged ill-treatment of Home children in Canada. Garrett held a meeting to say publicly that she stood by her claims and Skivington 'quoted from letters received about children sent to Canada by the

Guardians … a child of seven was employed doing "chores" (errands and odd jobs), and the terms there were board and clothing … In another case a child of twelve was to be returned to the Home because he could not milk and was too slow. The child went to school when it could get there, and was "sacked" because it could not do sufficient work.'[62] For Garrett, these letters were especially powerful because they illustrated the use of very young children for work who received no education or religious instruction. Ackroyd again challenged Garrett's accusations, particularly to emphasise that young children were not made to work and were 'lovingly cared for.' Again, the children's correspondence was central to his defence: 'every year letters come to us from many old boys and girls now happily settled and doing well, and I know some of the Guardians themselves encourage their boys and girls to write to them, and in this way keep up the connection with their children.'[63]

The legitimacy of these emigrant voices and their ability to testify about their experiences was central to the debates. In 1911, a meeting of the Board of Guardians discussed a letter from the Manchester Refuge in response to Garrett's complaints, but she felt they did not address her concerns. She told the meeting that 'only recently an Ontario newspaper reported that one lad was found with his feet so badly frozen that it was probable both feet would have to be amputated. The lad's back was covered with red and blue welts … emigration was merely a rate-saving policy.' However, Garrett was challenged by another board member named Miss Hertz, who argued that children were treated well 'and every week she received letters from emigrated children who expressed satisfaction with their surroundings.'[64] Again, this debate highlights how the children's letters were deemed to be more valuable to the defence of child emigration and more authentic in attesting to the welfare of child emigrants than a newspaper report in the Ontario press. As we shall see, many of the surviving letters from emigrant children took on the language of the emigration societies. Nevertheless, their voices still emerged in the correspondence, despite their increasing importance as a method of legitimising and promoting child emigration. As we shall see, although press coverage of the letters focussed on discussing the material conditions experienced by emigrated children, their correspondence also reveals important affective bonds between them and their home institutions that were overlooked within these public battles over child welfare.

LETTERS FROM THE LAND OF PLENTY

Emigrating institutions strongly encouraged children to write to them and, as we saw above, this correspondence became a fundamental defense against criticisms of child emigration policy. As Soares notes, letters written by children in institutions was responsive: 'important events such as birthdays and Christmas usually prompted contact, including the sending of cards and presents to institutionalized children.'[65] Many of the letters that have survived from emigrant children from the Manchester Refuge appear to have been a response to correspondence from the emigration home at Christmas, such as sixteen-year-old Alice, who had emigrated in 1906 and wrote to the home six years later: 'my dear friends I received your Christmas letter and was very glad to hear from you ... I have not forgotten you oh no I think of you often do you know I pray for you.'[66] The warmth of Alice's response conveyed her happiness to hear from the institution, a place that must have felt like a distant memory as she tried to keep warm in the depths of the Ontario winter. Her letter contrasts with the annual reports undertaken by Marchmont homes that emphasised Alice's volatility and noted the tensions between her and her employers in domestic service.[67] This kind of correspondence probably represented a rare link with emigrant children's own past as children like Alice had notably peripatetic and disrupted lives. Mair suggests that forgetting and remembering were key themes of letters written by children to emigrating institutions, as 'to forget those in England or be forgotten yourself signified estrangement from your English past and the loss of personal history.'[68] Correspondence with their institutions must have helped such children to maintain their sense of self as they navigated challenging working conditions, difficult employers, and social isolation in a world that must have felt so different from the North West of England.

As we saw in the first section however, the institutions had had more strategic motivations for maintaining this correspondence. In 1899 Mrs Wallace, warden at Marchmont, awarded eleven-year-old Kate a book as a prize for the best written letter. Kate had emigrated earlier that year and her winning letter offered a detailed and positive account of her journey from Marchmont to her foster home, where she was in charge of looking after a young baby, milking cows, and tending to hens and pigs. Kate described her new surroundings excitedly and asked after her friends and the staff at Marchmont, ending the letter 'LOVE TO ALL.'[69] Children like Kate were rewarded for providing the home institutions with positive, reassuring narratives about life in Canada. As Swartz argues, 'agency should be read not only through deliberate acts of rebellion, but also through children's (active) choice to consent or comply when their needs and those of adults aligned.'[70] The prize is symbolic of the broader ways in which children who provided happy reports of their placements were treated favourably by institutional staff and we can speculate that Kate's letter, along with others with a similarly positive narrative, were welcomed as ways to calm fears about moving to Canada and to encourage support for the scheme amongst resident children. In 1899, a letter from one seventeen-year-old boy stated, 'I have no desire now to come back to England, although I felt lonesome enough at first, There is lots of work to do here and plenty of good homes for boys.'[71] These letters must have provided powerful testimony as the institution garnered support from benefactors, silenced their critics, and built excitement amongst the children waiting to emigrate. Joe Ayre, born in Liverpool in 1910, wrote his memoir, *The Socialist*, in 1978 and described his experience growing up in poverty before being emigrated to Canada from Mrs Birt's Sheltering Home aged twelve. He narrates his impatience waiting to be chosen for departure and his frustration watching other boys leave ahead of him. When two more parties of children left for Canada in 1922, 'I started to wonder if I would ever be sent' and, after asking Matron, 'I was told that I would be sent to Canada when I was ready and not before.'[72] We can speculate how hearing these letters from their friends, and in Joe's case from his beloved older brother Bill, went a long way to persuade children that a new life really was waiting for them across the Atlantic.

The majority of the surviving correspondence drew on the home institute's propaganda and missionary zeal about the transformatory powers of emigration and presented. Many of the letters stressed the comfort of their new homes, such as one by a boy who had emigrated in April 1903 and, one month later, wrote 'I am very happy at my new home.' His letter described his farm work and testified, 'I have got a very nice and warm bed to sleep in every night.'[73] Eager to please the institution, children tended to claim that they enjoyed a more luxurious life than that they had left behind. Christmas featured heavily in correspondence – partly because of timing following the annual letters and Christmas tokens many institutions sent to their Home children, and partly also because it was an opportunity for children to share their new and comparatively opulent experiences. One such correspondent was Florence, who wrote to Mrs Birt in December 1893 to tell her that 'I like my place very much' and that 'we have had a Christmas tree and it was very nice.' Listing her cache of presents, which included books, a collar, an apron, three handkerchiefs, orange, apples, and sweets, Florence expressed that 'I have enjoy [*sic*] a Happy Christmas.'[74] Similarly, in 1913 Mabel wrote to the Manchester Refuge that 'I think of you all when I go to bed,' but keenly described her recent Christmas, 'I got quite a number of things last Christmas, I got gold locket and chain from Mrs Earle.' Mabel's enthusiasm may have reflected a desire to portray herself as successful and displays an awareness that her f Christmas was likely to be in marked contrast to those she experienced before emigration.[75] These positive depictions of their new lives also served to maintain connections between the children and the staff at their previous institutions, which has been described as a form of social capital for those with little else in the way of relationships with others.[76]

Child correspondents often stressed the quantity and quality of the food they ate and emphasised being well fed: one boy stated that Canada 'is a fine country to live. We get lots of watermelons and apples here now.'[77] Again, the children may have understood that emphasising their exotic and plentiful diet in Canada would act as a powerful symbol of their success to those they left behind. Ayre described life at Mrs Birt's home as being very strict and recalled 'the diet in the home was Spartan to say the least.'[78] It is not difficult to imagine the envy of those who remained in Liverpool or Manchester listening to these letters such as that written by Thomas, who happily described the contrast between his life in Canada and that which he life behind, writing 'I spent a jolly good Christmas over here and a glad new year and we have lots of nice things to eat over here. Now I often think of the half starved children in England when I am sitting down to my meals and I think why don't they all try to come out to the land of plenty.'[79] It is perhaps unsurprising that these children measured their happiness in terms of how full their stomachs were. Thomas, for instance, was admitted to the Manchester Refuge aged just seven after his unmarried mother was committed to an asylum. Yet these letters would have functioned as important testimonies to those children awaiting emigration and in support of the institution's fundraising propaganda, which, as Thomas described, presented Canada as the 'land of plenty.'

Letters also drew on the language and imagery of the fundraising material in more direct ways and the children portrayed their new lives in Canada as bringing personal and physical transformation. Several of the correspondents equated Canada with physical growth, such as Lizzie who wrote to Mrs Birt in 1895 to reassure her that her sister 'has grown greatly and is getting very fat.'[80] In 1911, one sixteen-year-old boy, who had emigrated the previous year, wrote, 'I like this country very much and I do not see why any boy or girl who comes out here should not get on well. It has done me a lot of good I am fatter and stronger than when I left England and I think it is the best thing I ever did was to come out here.'[81] The emphasis on their good health was especially common and Mabel, eighteen, claimed 'I have not had a day [of] sickness since I came to Canada I thank all the friends in the Home for sending me to Canada.'[82]

Others stressed the impact of Canadian life on their moral health, again mirroring the institution's propaganda that had presented British cities as agents of corruption and immorality. One girl wrote to Mrs Birt in 1897 to tell her about her experiences at Sunday School and her plans to join the Christian Endeavour Society, stressing that 'I am trusting in God to lead me through life's journey and help me to do what's right to my employers.'[83] Victor, who emigrated in 1910, described in his letter to the Manchester Refuge how temperance had been introduced in his town of Omemee. He explained that there was 'of course no whiskey which is the ruination of any man how takes it it [*sic*] did to one man here he was going home intockated [*sic*] when he fell of [*sic*] the sleighs and horse went on for about two hundred yards then one dropped dead when they found them the other died and the man was dead when they found him.'[84] This emphasis on Canada as place of religiosity and moral superiority reinforced the separation with the children's life in the North West. As Ayres's memoir attests, religious instruction was the main focus of the education at Mrs Birt's home in Liverpool, and 'if you failed your examination in Scripture you could be confined to the isolation ward where without any distraction and very little to eat you soon improved your knowledge of the Scriptures.'[85] Drawing attention to their moral and physical transformation was a way for the children to please their home institutions which, as we shall see, could be used as a bargaining chip to obtain information or assistance that they required.

Alongside food and health, the children's letters, like those from British migrants to the Commonwealth more generally, also tended to highlight Canadian weather, particularly the cold, harsh winters. In 1912, for instance, John wrote, 'we have had a very bad winter. It isn't anywhere near as cold in England as it is here, the snow has been very bad, in some places where it drifted it is nearly half as high as the house and we have great fun riding down the snow banks with hand sleighs.' The letter goes on to detail the hot summers and John's enjoyment of fishing in boats on the local lakes, before falling into familiar rhetoric that highlighted the 'land of plenty.' John wrote, ' I only wish some of the lads that don't want to come to see what the country is like and I don't think they would want to stay and more I think it is a far better place than … places in Britain.'[86] John's letter is typical of the ways in which migrant children used their new experiences to try to make sense of their own past. As with correspondence written by children emigrated elsewhere in the British Empire through earlier schemes, letters like John's 'actively contributed to a narrative' about life in the colonies.[87] This kind of correspondence helped to endorse and maintain emigration policies because emigrated children themselves, inadvertently or not, helped to maintain the system.

Letters show that children also saw the landscape of Canada as being associated with adventure and opportunity as well as with work and food. Its exoticism, particularly in terms of the dramatic weather and fecund summers, emerged as a powerful counterpoint to life in the North West. Archie described the duck-hunting season when 'you can hear the bang of the drum till late at night,' and the local community who made baskets and 'are very skilful with a canoe.' Between questions about the boys he knew at the Refuge, Archie recounts being invited to try the canoe 'but went over the rapids like an arrow,' and he landed in the water.[88] It is not difficult to imagine how the 'Refuge boys' might have responded to Archie's stories, which evoked popular motifs associated with boys' literature that emphasised adventure, risk and encounters with indigenous people of the Empire.[89] These letters reinforced the difference between the boys' new world and the one they left behind and the emphasis on adventure and exoticism allowed the children to fashion a selfhood that would be respected, and perhaps even envied, by the 'Refuge boys' left behind in a cold, grey, drizzly Manchester.

The children also picked up and repeated the institutions' discourse in ways that helped them make sense of the changes they were experiencing. Letter-writing may therefore have provided a rare opportunity for self-reflection. Annie wrote to Leonard Shaw at the Manchester Refuge to let him know that 'I have such a good home', with her master and mistress and to reassure him that 'I do try to please them, I do try to do as you told me in your kind letter. I am so happy ... I love them dearly. I hope all the other girls have got such good homes and are trying to learn and (be) good girls.'[90] Thomas emphasised the language of improvement and directly attributed the institution and its fundraisers for improving his life. He wrote, 'I thank you very much for getting me such a nice home in Canada and also the ladies and gentlemen who try to help to keep the home up and give money for us to come out to Canada.' Again drawing on the institution's fundraising rhetoric, he stated that the children who remained in the Refuge 'don't know what a treat it is to come out to the land of plenty', and he encouraged the Home to emigrate more boys because they 'are doing no good over there.'[91] The direct influence of the propaganda is so clear in Thomas's letter that it raises the question whether he was coerced into writing it, although he may simply have wanted to please his host family as his file includes a letter from his Canadian master asking Wallace to find Thomas a new home because he was dissatisfied with him. The letter dated 25 August 1908 stated that Thomas was suffering from asthma bronchitis and described him as 'a delicate boy, thinks Canada does not suit him.'[92] Thomas's ill-health meant that he was simply not of use to any farmer and unable to pay his own way in Canada. Since emigration relied on the premise of the children as useful citizens, Marchmont returned Thomas to England, where he died almost immediately in Salford's Hope Hospital of Consumption in November 1908. For Thomas, therefore, his enthusiasm for the 'land of plenty' masked a much darker reality and even its bountiful food was not enough to provide him with the transformation he was promised. Nor is it difficult to imagine the disappointment emigrant children felt when the Canada they experienced did not reflect the propaganda they had digested or the letters from friends that they had enjoyed. Joe Ayre's memoir describes how his first experiences on arriving at the receiving home Marchmont in Belleville, Ontario, did not live up to expectation: 'to my utter disappointment this place was just the same as Miss Birt's Home in Liverpool, the same drab buildings, the dormitory, the dining room the food, the discipline, everything exactly the same.'[93] Once the children reached Canada, it was almost impossible for them to leave their posts willingly until they were of age and there was no acknowledgement from any of the emigration societies that they ever felt they had oversold life in Canada.

The children's willingness to draw on the rhetoric of the emigration societies also reflected their connection to the institutions they had emigrated from, which, for some of them, represented home and family life. As Jane Hamlett's study of material culture in institutions shows, even patients in asylums could develop bonds of friendship and attachment as, like the children in refuge homes, they were constantly in each other's company and social spaces within asylums fostered sociability and even a sense of 'home.'[94] In place of parents – and the absence of references to parents in nearly all the letters is remarkable – the home institution, which most children had lived in for several years before moving to Canada, was the closest thing to home they had. Such as one teenage boy who wrote to the Refuge in 1906, four years after his emigration, asking for a picture of the boys he had lived with, explaining, 'I should like to get one of the dear old refuge if I could.'[95] Similarly, in 1911 another boy wrote that 'I am sure I have not forgot the good home and the good times I had in it,' having written an earlier letter thanking the Refuge master for sending him a picture of his class, depicting them winning a shield.[96] Michael Roper and Matthews-Jones stress the self-consciousness of working-class soldiers' writing style in the First World War, particularly to middle-class correspondents.[97] Yet the children, perhaps because of their age but arguably also because of their affective bonds with their home institutions, demonstrated little self-consciousness in their writings.

The bonds between child and institution emerged clearly when the emigrated children heard about the death of those they knew in the institution, such as James in January 1901 who heard that Mrs Wallace, matron of Marchmont Homes and wife of Reverend Robert Wallace, had died. James hoped that Mrs Wallace was in heaven, recalling her as 'a kind lady' to himself and his brother.[98] Similarly in 1900, Archibald, aged eighteen, was sorry to hear of the death of Albert, his friend from the institution, but pleased that they had sent him a photograph, as it 'was a very good one,' sending two dollars to pay for a wreath at the grave.[99] Leonore Davidoff's study of sibling relationships uses the idea of the 'long family' to address the important, and often complex, web of relationships that dominated across the long nineteenth century. As Davidoff suggests, we need to expand our understanding of family beyond immediate blood relations, as children build relationships dependant on the person they interact with rather than the relevancy of their kin.[100]

The sense of home offered by the Refuge persisted for these children into adulthood. On a brief trip home from Canada, having left the Refuge in 1912, Charles wrote to the home to ask for assistance. His letter described 'the goodness, tenderness and love always shown the boys and girls,' by Mr and Mrs Wood of the institution. Charles explained he had fallen in love in Britain and wanted to return to Canada with his new wife, but she had a child, which he wanted the Refuge to take. Appealing to what he understood as their long-term investment in his future, he asked, 'can you do anything for me and my future welfare. It will prevent me from getting ahead ... Had it been my child it would all be rather different. The child is a little backward. Would it be possible for the home in Cheetham Hill to look after it?'[101] This letter is interesting in that it reveals his trust and confidence in the Home in wanting to help him achieve his long-term success and looks to them, in place of family, to take the child. However, it also suggests a detachment from his wife's child and emotionless attitude to 'it.' His language suggests both that he continued to see the institution as having a family role but also hints at the longer-term implications that institutional life and emigration had on such children.

In place of blood siblings, those from the institution acted as important substitutes and even the superintendents of the homes could provide emotional support as surrogate family. In 1907, Thomas, implored the matron of the Refuge to write, explaining 'I hope you will kindly write back to me for it I have no other friends I just have you as me you're the only one I have in England or the world that's why I think so much of both of you.'[102] Similarly in 1911, Wilfred described his life in Canada to Mr and Mrs Binns, who ran the Emigration Training Home in Manchester. Wilfred explained the very infrequent correspondence he had with family made him grateful that he could write to his old home. 'It does me good to have someone to write to now I am out here, as I get very lonesome sometimes,' Wilfred confessed.[103] Loneliness and isolation remained a persistent problem for emigrant children, particularly because the farms they worked on could be very remote. One teenage girl was returned to Marchmont Home in 1913, due to 'strange behaviour, she was becoming mentally unbalanced.' Her problems followed a letter she had sent to Marchmont a year earlier that had complained about her loneliness and as she was not around any other young people.[104] The greatest challenge for these children was not necessarily the move to Canada but surviving outside of the institutional life they knew, and particularly being away from children they had formed relationships with.

'I HAVE NOT HEARD FROM MY PEOPLE FOR A LONG TIME.'

The intimate tones of the letters and the children's assertions of affection for the institution might well have been expedient and the child writers demonstrated an awareness of knowing what to say to the emigration homes in order to receive information or action that they required. As other examples of letter-writing from ordinary individuals to those in expert or official roles have demonstrated, correspondents exchanged information in order for the assistance they hoped to obtain.[105] Emigrant Florence reassured Mrs Birt 'I am doing better than in my other place. I can knit very well now too.' After emphasising that she was playing her role as dutiful émigré, she explained her reason for writing was because she was concerned about her family as 'I have not heard from my people for a long time and I am getting very uneasy about them.' Florence's letter interspersed her reiterations that she was diligently learning to make cakes and bread 'so I will make a fine housekeeper' and her affection for Mrs Birt's home and the last Christmas she had spent there, 'I do believe it was the best I ever spent we had for about six hours the greatest fun we ever had …' with her concerns for her brother who had been sent to the US. She explained, 'I was very anxious about George,' and 'would you kindly let me know what George [*sic*] address is for I am very anxious about him thank you for your kindness.'[106] This formulaic approach – moving between endorsements of the policy of emigration, affection for the home institution, and requests for help or information, especially regarding siblings – was a very common feature of the children's letters. Victor, the boy so keen to detail his commitment to temperance, included a plea: 'PS *Please help my mother*' at the end of his letter.[107] It reflected the value letters had as one of the few – perhaps only – method of complaint, resistance, or compliance that emigrant children possessed and were often methods of all three at once. Although very few letters made explicit accusations of abuse or ill-treatment, letter-writers had ways of coding or inferring problems and could utilise the propagandist language of the emigration institutions, like Alice did, in order to seek action or help.

One of the key reasons children wrote letters was to obtain information or access to their siblings or other family members. Returning to Victor, his letter dutifully expressed his affection for the institution and explained that 'I would also like to see the familiar faces and the old homes as I do get kind of homesick.' Victor's motivation for writing however, was to state his concern about his mother: 'she as [*sic*] been to you three times to try and get my little brother in the Emigration Home as she is well hard up.' Victor also pressed the institution then to send his brother over to Canada, 'I for one will repay you' before emphasising again his fondness for the refuge, 'I enjoyed a merry Christmas but not as good as last year I wished I had been back at the Old home on that day.'[108] Victor moved between telling the institution what he thought they wanted to hear and requesting the help he required. Similarly, Maggie's 1898 letter to Mrs Birt began with a description of her successful new life in Montreal. 'I am very glad to tell you Mrs Birt that I am very happy and I am in a very good home the lady I am living with is very kind to me and I always do my very best to please her.' Before moving on to her request for help: 'Mrs Birt I want to ask you if my Mother lives in the same place that she used to,' and explained she had written 'I have wrote a good many letters two [*sic*] her' at her last known address, but Maggie had not heard from her for two years. Maggie signed off with further evidence of her life as a dutiful émigré. 'I go to Church and Sunday school every Sunday. I will close in sending my love to you and all the Dear Children in the home.'[109] The formulaic structure of these letters suggests that emigrant children understood the best ways to get the institution on their side; perhaps they passed on advice to each other or maybe they were just aware of what the staff at these institutions liked to hear.

Information or help for siblings seem to have been the most common reasons for emigrant children to write to the homes. Most letters display scant regard for parents, who were often entirely absent from the correspondence. Soares has drawn attention to the ways in which parents of children under the care of the Waifs and Strays society would complain if they had not received letters from them and stresses that children's ability to correspond rested on the support of institutional staff members.[110] However, our analysis of letters written by children emigrated to Canada from the North West, shows that for many, parents were a distant memory, perhaps in consequence of the policies that severed their relationships. The key relationships emigrant children wished to maintain were those with their siblings, who they had often spent years with at the same institution. Joe Ayre provided an account of his very difficult childhood in his memoir and highlighted the adversity he endured after his mother died and his father remarried. Although he had several siblings he was notably close to his brother Bill, and they ended up at Mrs Birt's Home together after running away from their violent and abusive stepmother. Of the many hardships Joe endured, it was the separation from his brother, who emigrated to Canada three years ahead of him, that is presented in his memoir as the most traumatic: 'I missed Bill terribly.'[111]

Joe was not exceptional. Many letters stress frantic concern for brothers and sisters, such as that of Percy, who wrote to Ackroyd, Superintendent at Manchester in 1907, desperate for news of his brother. 'I hope you will make further enquiries about my brother Frank,' he wrote, 'I knew that he was not getting proper care … I hope and trust you will do all you can for Frank.'[112] A note on Percy's report shows Frank was very ill with pneumonia, which explains why he was not a candidate for emigration. Yet Percy remained undeterred, writing again in December 1909, 'I wish I was one of the boys for Christmas so I could go home and see my folks … I have a brother in Salford some place and if you will do me a favour and take him to the home I will send money to fetch him out here as I hear he is not getting used right.'[113] Percy's letter reveals his powerlessness and reliance on the Refuge to help him. It is challenging to know how far cases like Percy's were typical or if emigrant children were largely successful in bringing siblings over. The institutions strongly refuted claims that they purposefully kept siblings apart, and Ackroyd told the *Manchester Guardian* in 1910 that 'we make it a point to place brothers and sisters very near to each other and have not the slightest difficulty in doing this.'[114] Nevertheless, most of the surviving letters imply that requests for siblings to be located nearby were rarely successful.

Joe Ayre's memoir describes the disappointment he experienced when he was not placed near his brother Bill. 'I had been told I would be placed on a farm near my Brother and I was anxious to see him' but when he received instructions to travel to a farm in the Springbrook area and asked how far that was from Bill's placement, Matron 'said she didn't know I had a Brother and that I would have to go where I was told.'[115] After a year working on a farm, Joe wrote to the Home authorities to ask if he could be moved nearer to Bill, because

'I longed to see him, we had been through so much together.' When he did not receive a reply from the institution, Joe wrote to the Department of Immigration in Ottawa. This seemed to have some impact since he recalled that, shortly afterwards, 'I received a letter from the Home in Belville reprimanding me for writing to Ottawa and also informing me that they were trying to locate me nearer to Bill.'[116] Sure enough, Joe suddenly received instructions to get on a train to a farm that was much closer to his brother, where they had an emotional reunion after being apart for three years.

We do not know what Joe wrote in his letter to the Department of Immigration, but the swift action suggests that institutions were spurred to act when they were aware of possible intervention by a government agency. His memoir provides a moving description of being reunited with Bill: 'I will never forget arriving at that farm my Brother Bill come flying out of the Delahunt's house and we hugged each other and tears of sheer happiness ran down our cheeks. All the longing and separation had served to strengthen the bond that was forged when we lived as urchins in the gutters of Liverpool.'[117] The letter was Joe's only possible course of action, and its success suggests that émigré children did have some limited recourse that could be deployed with evidence of some successes.

For Joe, his renewed contact with Bill helped him navigate the difficulties he faced as a farm labourer working in demanding conditions: 'the one thing that sustained me was that I could talk my problems over with Bill.'[118] Other letters also evidence how the presence of siblings helped children adjust to their new lives in Canada. Kate's first letter complains about her loneliness without her younger sister, Jenny, or her friends from the Home. Her second letter two months later reports that 'I am so glad to say that Jenny and I have got lovely homes we go to see each other very often and we have both got a little boy to mind.' Kate also attended to a baby who 'is such a dear little thing, she will follow me wherever I go.' Kate was able to replicate the large kinship network she experienced in the institution, which had helped her adapt and develop emotional resilience, writing 'it is so nice living over here, at first I was so lonesome I did not like living over here and always wanted to come back.' For children who had spent so much time in institutions, kinship was crucial to their emotional survival, particularly when coping with the experience of emigration, but that was not limited to blood relatives. As we saw above, many of the boys were keen to hear from the others they had lived with in the institution and hoped to maintain some kind of connection with them, as the bonds between them replicated the family life that had been severed when they entered residential care.

The angry letter received by Mrs Birt from Leonora in August 1900 also related to the separation of siblings. The rage it contained suggested that Mrs Birt was not just held responsible by Leonora for the departure of her sister but was a figurehead to whom she could complain about what she saw as the wider injustices of the emigration system.[119] For Leonora, Mrs Birt's treatment of her sister reflected what she considered to be an overly money-minded approach to children in Canada. She wrote: 'She could have stayed here well enough … but you thought the 10$ would be of use to you, and you offered to take her over, as a paltry excuse to get the money … I shall never forget your unkindness as long as I live.' The letter does not explain why Birt received money for returning Leonora's sister home, but other correspondence shows that Canadian authorities had refused to keep her in an asylum there due to cost. A letter dated from May 1900 from a medical practitioner to Birt explained that the asylum had requested Leonora's sister be returned to England, having diagnosed her as a 'degenerate and incurable,' and suggested that it would be 'unfair to burden the Province with her support for the rest of her life.'[120] It was usual policy for sick or infirm children to be returned home, as we have seen, because a central tenet of child emigration policy was that the child should not be a burden on the Canadian state. Leonora's letter highlights the sheer heartache caused by sibling separation and her use of language to protest against this mirrored the criticisms of child emigration more generally, accusing Birt of greed and a lack of concern for children's welfare. Leonora claimed her sister had to travel 'on an old express wagon with her trunk, and her *paralysed*,' and continued, 'it is a wonder you are not ashamed of yourself to treat one whom God has afflicted with such unkindness and inhumanity. I hope you will enjoy spending the money, and that you will be thinking of her at the same time.' Leonora also repeated a common accusation that emigrating institutions and adoptive families did not clothe children appropriately in Canada, writing that 'she and her brother had to buy her underwear and a trunk and hat out of their own earnings. Again, Leonora mirrored wider accusations about neglect and the overwork of migrant children, claiming, 'If you had looked after your legal part as well as you looked after the bit of money, it would have suited all parties concerned better. There is one thing I want you never to forget as long as you live, that is Dr B. blames you for this early insanity. You should have noticed that she was not a strong girl, and given to fitting, and therefore you should have had her placed in an easy place in the city with plenty of amusements to keep her spirits lively but she was put in a place with continual work and no pleasure. And the strain was too much for her mind to bear.'[121]

Like the more positive letters, Leonora's drew on the wider language around child emigration policy. It is unlikely that Leonora's letter had much impact, and her sister would almost certainly have never been able to return to Canada, but the letter shows she understood how to assert her complaints at a time of helplessness. This letter stands out amongst the generally positive correspondence from children to the Home institutions, but it is hard to believe that Leonora was the only emigrant child to write such an impassioned complaint. However, Leonora's letter indicates that she felt she had little to lose, and many of the other correspondents sought help whilst they still needed to please their emigrating institution. It also suggests that children were aware of the language that criticised child emigration as much as they were aware of the emigration society's own publicity material that extoled its virtues so enthusiastically and, crucially, understood how to harness this negative rhetoric when needed.

As Leonora's correspondence reveals, letters were one of the few ways for migrant children to protest against their treatment. Several children, usually boys, wrote to their former wardens to complain about their treatment in foster homes. In 1907, Thomas complained about his master and mistress, who he accused of telling 'storeys [*sic*] about me.' He was denied appropriate winter garments, he explained, 'now I am in a bad shape for clothes and the bad winter on the snow up to the trees its so cold over here.'[122] Yet the wardens at Marchmont were quick to write to Ackroyd in Manchester to dispel Thomas's claims, arguing that Thomas was untruthful. 'He is a peculiar lad and I think he has the idea that his kind friends will send him money when he wants it and thinks of going home to see them,' they wrote. Thomas's problems, they suggested, lay in his own lack of commitment to his new life in Canada since 'he has a good home if he will only settle down and get his mind off the old life in Manchester.'[123] By drawing on the language of a new beginning, the wardens implied that Thomas's problems were not with his new home but due to his reluctance to embrace the 'opportunity' emigration presented him.

Nor was Thomas the only child to have their complaints discredited and their own character blamed instead. Walter was another one. He ran away after complaining about the physical punishment he received at the hands of one of his masters. However, the report by Marchmont described Walter as 'a very troublesome boy ... He cannot be trusted to do any work and is very saucy.'[124] Walter eventually went on the run and worked his way round Canada, moving quickly if his old institution tried to find him, even as an adult. These examples indicate that the emigration societies marginalised the voices of children who challenged their rhetoric and promoted and celebrated those that endorsed their message. They point to a reciprocal relationship between the propaganda produced by the institutions and the voice of the child, which the institution was not afraid to silence if it did not support their message about the redemptive power of emigration.

CONCLUSION

The letters help uncover the ways in which children responded to, resisted, and shaped their own experiences of emigration. Although these letters became central to the campaigns both for and against child emigration policy, the voice of the child was not silenced completely. Rather, the letters here provide an important opportunity to hear the ways in which the emigrant child shaped and reported their experiences of life in Canada. From their descriptions of Christmas, food, and weather, we can retrieve some sense of their feelings and responses to the new world they found themselves. Nor do the letters shy away from the challenges and hardships of emigrant life for these children; from missing siblings or their home institutions to struggling to access help, the letters help uncover the many challenges these children faced.

Perhaps one of the most notable aspects of the correspondence is how it challenges so many of the characterisations of the friendless, lost, and deprived children that suffused the language of proponents and critics of emigration alike. Whether or not children were happy in Canada, the letters show that these young correspondents could articulate a range of responses including excitement, loss, home sickness, and hope about their life across the Atlantic. Like Barron and Langhamer's reading of children's essays for Mass-Observation, emigrant children's letters 'reveal the emotional practices through which children negotiated their own place within the world.'[125] These letters demonstrated a startling willingness to engage with the authorities that had emigrated them. At the same time, the letters provided a form of emotional practice that allowed the children to express their feelings in return for help or to attempt to elicit a specific response from their home institution. As anthropologist Monique Scheer writes, 'because people know that emotions do things in social contexts, they use them as means of exchange.'[126] Emigrant children demonstrated a strong awareness of what emotions the emigrating societies wanted to see and used this knowledge expediently in the hope of improving their own émigré experiences.

As we have seen, children's letters were used particularly by Protestant emigration institutions and reflected their greater vulnerability than Catholic institutions to criticisms from the local population. Both Louisa Birt and the Manchester Refuge drew on the letters to defend their practices against hostility between the 1880s and 1910s. The letters helped counter claims of proselytization, exploitation, and the ill-treatment of children amid evolving concepts about child protection and the state provision of welfare. Like their attitudes towards children's ability to consent to emigration, institutions laid claim to knowing how far the narratives within children's letters could be held up as being authentic. In writing back to the 'dear old Refuge,' these letters captured a moment of contested ideas of child welfare, the use of emigration and the rights and abilities of children to speak. The weight which both critics and supporters placed on these letters to either endorse or undermine child emigration policy suggests we need to reassess attitudes to working-class children's writings.

As others have noted, the post-Second World War period marked a significant shift in approaches to the status of children and in encouraging new forms of self-expression during childhood.[127] However, although the emigrating institutions only wanted their emigrants to produce narratives that celebrated their new lives in Canada, by encouraging to write back to their Home institution they facilitated rich forms of expression that allowed the children to reflect on, respond to, shape, and challenge their experiences of emigration. Whether they were happy to express their gratitude for emigration, like Lizzie, or their anger at being separated from their sibling, like Leonora, letters provided emigrant children with a valuable method to articulate the very contradictory and complex feelings they felt whilst adjusting to their new lives. Their rich accounts tell us about more than just the food or weather in Canada and uncover some sense of how these 'friendless and forsaken' children navigated the challenges of life in the 'land of plenty' in ways that were not always convenient to either the critics or proponents of child emigration.

4

Rescue or Reward?

> The cost of outfitting and emigrating a child to Canada amounts to about $50 or $60. This expenditure is claimed to be about one-tenth of the actual cost of maintaining the child in an institution. In contributing so generously towards the emigration of necessitous and unbefriended children, the people of Great Britain are actuated first by a Christian and humanitarian spirit, and secondly by a duty to the state.
>
> G. Bogue Smart, Chief Inspector of British Immigrant Children and Receiving Homes, 'Juvenile Immigration,' (31 March 1907)[1]

Combing through the extensive archives of emigration correspondence, reports on the running of Homes, and discussions about children sent to Canada, it is striking how one topic dominates the files at both a local, national, and international level: *money*. Fundraising, the cost of feeding and outfitting children with appropriate clothes, the salaries of emigration agents, and the payment of bonuses on children emigrated (a reward mechanism introduced in 1875 to encourage the sending over of ever-larger parties of children by the Department of Agriculture) formed the primary bureaucratic concern of those engaged in the child emigration system from the 1860s until its suspension in the mid-1930s.[2] Mr G. Bogue Smart oversaw the inspection of British migrant children from 1903 on behalf of the Canadian government. As the quotation above suggests, in published reports and publicity materials officials such as Smart saw little contradiction in aligning the religious justification for emigrating impoverished children to Canada with an economic rationale; a distinctive form of 'moral economy' in which the cost of removing children from their country of origin was explicitly tied to collective material gain as well as the ethical and spiritual reward of 'rescue.'[3] Indeed, with the smooth patter of a salesman, the aptly-named Smart made a virtue of the way the Christian impetus to save children from poverty could be accompanied by the larger financial savings to the taxpayer and the state. Offering readers the surprisingly cheap cost of emigration at just 'about $50 or $60 … one tenth the actual cost of maintaining a child in an institution,' the report assured readers that Christian duty to aid the poor and promote the economic prosperity of Great Britain need not be irreconcilable. This was a particularly astute claim in 1907, when the use of the workhouse as a panacea to poverty was firmly in decline, but unemployment insurance, old age pensions, free school meals, and a minimum wage were just being introduced by the Edwardian Liberal government – and debates about their fiscal benefits were still contentious.[4]

Of course, it is (and was) impossible to calculate the total saving to the state created by the child emigration system. Not only do figures vary about the total number of children emigrated to Canada and other British colonial territories during the pre- and post- Second World War periods, but differences in local rates and individual institutional expenditure per child render such an attempt futile. Nonetheless, following the money is still an important and useful exercise for historians where histories of charitable, religious and/or state endeavour are concerned, as scholars Sarah Roddy, Julie-Marie Strange, and Bertrand Taithe have persuasively argued. Certainly, as this chapter will show, the financial behaviour of child emigration agencies in North West England underscored the significant confluence of interests between Christian organisations and the evolution of a modern capitalist society that characterised the Victorian and Edwardian philanthropic marketplace.[5]

Utilising surviving ledgers and correspondence between shipping, emigration, and government agents, this chapter traces the circulation of financial transactions and bonus payments on emigrated children. It uses this evidence to understand their surprisingly business-like operations, a key part of the routinisation of child emigration as an everyday occurrence. The sums of money involved tended to be relatively modest, and there is no suggestion here that the child emigration system made a profit. If the endless flow of desperate letters written by the managers and administrators of the children's Homes are to be believed, these institutions consistently operated at a loss and in the face of uncertainty over funding (whilst publishing chirpy annual reports extolling the professionalism of their work and unwavering investment in preparing children for Canada, furnishing them with an education, and sustaining a robust network of aftercare visitors). This chapter argues that the transactional nature of the system, and calculations of children's worth to the Canadian agricultural economy versus their likely burden on the taxpayer should they remain in England, reinforced their status as economic units within the emigration system (a status often difficult to fully reconcile with institutions' rhetoric of rescue).

Officials' notion of children as primarily economic units was an observation first made by historian Joy Parr in her classic 1980 work on child emigration schemes to Canada. As Parr notes, middle-class officials assumed that working-class families conceptualised their domestic relationships as 'a domain of economic imperative rather than sustained affection' especially once children were capable of earning a living.[6] By contrast, it is worth noting that there is extensive evidence that Victorian working-class homes were filled with love and affection, and that emotional attachment to children was fiercely held by both mothers and fathers – despite the stereotype of the often absent, beer-swilling, disciplinarian patriarch of this period.[7] Working-class parents' consent or effective submission to emigration of their child by charitable institutions was therefore expected to be forthcoming owing to the practical, economic considerations that scarcity forced them to make. As the 1902 Report of Father Berry's Homes stated, 'those who have left their children dependent for a period on public charity cannot claim them back again as a right,' reflecting both legal reality (see chapter 2) and middle-class prejudice against the poor.[8] Ironically, however, there was no attempt to change this estimation of a child's 'worth' by emigration officials. Parr asserts that children's placements in Canada were determined by economic criteria rather than meeting the emotional needs of host families, and as seen in Smart's quote above, emigration was often presented as being mainly for the economic benefit of both nations. This was part of the project of nation-and empire-building that was supposed to compensate working-class families for the loss of their children not in terms of emotional distress, but to offset their expectation that their children's earnings would have contributed to their own family's prosperity.[9]

We can better understand why children were thought about this way by analysing the payments and bonuses issued to emigrating institutions and shipping agents, which will form the first section of this chapter. Historians have, perhaps, been reluctant to conduct a financial audit of the emigration system due to the incomplete and inconsistent nature of the data. Mentions of financial exchanges appeared occasionally in correspondence between officials, were cited as examples in reports, or were recorded in account books, cash books, and finance journals (as in the Nugent Care collection) but – frustratingly – only for certain years. Similarly, institutions' grandiose statements of thanks to local patrons on their donation of particularly large sums of money sometimes featured in the pages of marketing ephemera; yet without corresponding ledgers in the archive it is not usually possible to establish whether these sums represented a bail-out in times of dire need, or the steadily accumulating wealth of a prosperous emigration society. However, it is still possible to use even fragmentary extant data to gain an understanding of the 'moral economy' that emerged around charitable donations and expenditure – an economy that was, perhaps, more useful to burnish the reputations of its benefactors than improve the prosperity of migrant children.[10]

This is particularly important when looking at the culture around child rescue and charity work in the cities of North West England during the Victorian and Edwardian periods. 'The Liverpool charity market was crowded and competitive,' Roddy, Strange and Taithe observe, noting how religious and business leaders in the city collaborated to launch investigations against newer charities, especially when founded by those not already connected with the city's elite.[11] Similarly, to become a 'Manchester Man' – one of the city's (male) social and political leaders – one had to be a 'charity leader' like Oliver Heywood, a banker, justice of the peace, and High Sheriff of Lancashire noted for his association with twenty-seven charities.[12] Within the North West, therefore, the amount and frequency of financial transactions between emigrating institutions, local businesses (especially shipping) and governments on both sides of the Atlantic acted as a register of the embeddedness of those relationships. Evidence of these transactions, however intermittent, enables us to identify the place of emigration schemes within the regional economy.

Children's reaction to their 'status' as prospective servants and farm labourers – somewhat like units of currency – will also be explored in this section. Many children who were emigrated to Canada eventually displayed an awareness of the financial exchanges attached to their emigration, and that their labour afforded them leverage to change their circumstances. One might suppose that a level of cynicism about their perceived 'value' would have been a necessary, even healthy response to the situation. Separated from their birth families and brought up in contractual limbo as both adoptees and 'employees' in a strange country, these children became more freewheeling in their dealings with farmers and other employers in negotiating wages and taking their labour elsewhere, as this chapter will show. By using their initiative and making new contracts with employers independently of the Homes from which they had been emigrated, such children took a pragmatic approach to surviving and improving their quality of life. Simultaneously, these actions asserted a measure of control over their circumstances that was largely absent in the years immediately following institutionalisation in England and during the emigration process.

Fraud (or the suspicion thereof) involving claims for the double payment of bonuses on emigrated children and attempts to claim bonuses on ineligible children (or even non-existent children), are the subject of the second section of this chapter. Questions over the morality and fiscal responsibility of emigration agents, including the priests and nuns working as managers and superintendents of Catholic Emigration Society Homes, created conflict and mistrust about the respective religious, political, and economic motives for child emigration among officials. It is therefore highly significant that these incidents did nothing to discontinue, or even interrupt, child emigration schemes or change the institutional actors involved. Similarly, the relationship between the resilience of the child emigration system and the financial opportunities it presented can also be seen in the stringent criteria that determined which children were eligible for bonus payments. Devised by the Canadian Department of Agriculture, these criteria demonstrated how monetary incentives to emigration were another tactic deployed in a eugenicist effort to optimise the health and moral character of those to be emigrated. Thus, analysing the financial 'scaffolding' of the child emigration system is integral to appreciate the diverse agendas it sustained on both sides of the Atlantic in this era, beyond the mere exchange of payments.

THE ECONOMY OF EMIGRATION

> Dear Sir,
> I am in receipt of your letter of apology for not seeing me on 5th inst. I confess I was exceedingly annoyed – two letters addressed to your self and both unanswered and two fruitless journeys … was enough to try anyone, to say nothing about the withdrawal of the $6 bonus and the addition of the $20 tax upon the children when landing at Halifax – I wanted to see some member of the Ontario Government about not so much my work as what may eventually be made governmental work between England and Canada, in the connection with poor children. I think I might venture to say – that for every $10 Canada voted to such a work, the English government would give from $50 to $100. The best men – on both sides of the Atlantic – are convinced that my scheme of juvenile emigration is the wisest and the best for the transplanting of our working peoples and many young people marry and settle so readily all over the country that I can really see no end to the openings for them.
>
> Letter from Maria Rye to Hon. Mr. Hardy (11 February 1880)[13]

There is no denying that by 1880, Maria Rye had become an extraordinarily confident businesswoman. Having been the first philanthropist to send a large party of children to Canada in October 1869 – a group of 100 girls aged between five and eleven, seventy of whom were from Liverpool industrial schools (though she was then based in London) – Rye was, as scholars Roger Kershaw and Janet Sacks note, a 'pioneer' of child emigration schemes. She had also demonstrated a remarkably entrepreneurial approach to fundraising. Awarded a grant of $500 by the Dominion Government to sponsor her child emigration proposal in 1868, in March 1869 Rye had a letter published in *The Times* calling for public contributions to the work, which appears to have met with success.[14] A little over a decade later, Rye evidently expected rather more deferential treatment from emigration officials in Canada than she had lately been receiving. Having her letters ignored, her attempts at face-to-face meetings dodged, and a new $20 tax imposed upon the children she had emigrated, Rye not only refused to take the hint, but expressed her 'annoyance' at this behaviour and proposed an ambitious new package of financial support for her emigration activities from both governments. We do not know the full context to Rye's treatment here; as chapter 1 explored, Rye had clashed with Canadian officials in 1877 over her unwillingness to assume responsibility when girls emigrated under her guardianship were sexually assaulted, and her standards of care for children were also heavily criticised in the Doyle Report of 1875.[15] Thus, by 1880 she was a decidedly controversial figure – rendering her willingness to claim to speak on behalf of the English government all the more striking.

Yet Rye was also an experienced negotiator and publicist of the economic advantages of the work, who (her letter reveals) had already secured some preferential treatment from the Dominion government in the past. The reference to a $6 per child bonus is (as far as the authors of this book are aware) unique; in 1875, the Department of Agriculture had introduced a $2 bonus on children emigrated from England, but there is no reference to a further $4 sum being extended to any other emigration agents. Rye's confident assurances of the political backing for future emigration schemes may also have derived from her relationship with the London and Liverpool elite. Lord Shaftesbury had presided over a meeting of the National Association for the Promotion of Social Science in 1870, at which Rye gave a speech claiming she could achieve dramatic savings for London's ratepayers by emigrating pauper children at a cost of $10 a head. This was followed swiftly, as Kershaw and Sacks note, by a lecture given by Dr Hayward at the Liverpool Literary and Philosophical Society arguing that Rye had 'already saved the Liverpool ratepayers £5,000, which would have been the cost of maintaining the children she had taken to Canada.'[16] Rye's cause was also patronised by the famed Liverpool philanthropist, businessman, and Liberal politician William Rathbone, who undertook to pay the £70 annual salary of Miss Still, Rye's assistant, although he threatened to withdraw it in 1877 unless proper inspections of the children's placements in Canada were carried out.[17] With such a history of endorsements, Rye's behaviour exemplified the enterprising attitude towards charity as a market-driven domain that, as Roddy, Strange, and Taithe observe, typified the late Victorian charity 'market' in Britain.[18]

However, the response to Rye's letter was curt. Her correspondent 'the Hon. Mr. Hardy' was likely to have been Arthur Sturgis Hardy, a lawyer and prominent Ontario politician (later premier and attorney general) who worked as Provincial Secretary in 1880 and features in much of the emigration correspondence.[19] Explaining that he had spent the morning of Rye's missed visit 'as Chairman of the Committee on Municipal Law and on another committee' – adding archly 'as indeed I am every morning Parliament is in session' – Hardy was politely discouraging towards Rye's suggestions: 'If I had had the pleasure of seeing you, I very much fear that I should not have been able to assure you that the Government would restore the $6 per head allowance to children, concerning which it is probable you desired to see me. The policy of the Government upon that question was fixed a year ago, and it would not be possible to reverse it as soon, whatever may be the result hereafter.'[20]

It is possible that, as a woman, Rye's unguarded expression of irritation and casual display of her financial acumen in her letter contributed to Hardy's dismissal of her proposal. Despite the increasing political role of women in both countries as agitators for social reform, philanthropic agents, and administrators of the poor law, local government and charitable entrepreneurs remained male-dominated at the start of the 1880s.[21] Further, Rye's orchestration of political support between Liverpool, London and the empire bore similarities with social reformer Josephine Butler's successful campaign to repeal the Contagious Diseases Acts, an incubator of the women's suffrage movement.[22] Rye herself never expressed interest in the movement, as her biographer Marion Diamond notes, but she did believe in the equal treatment of women under the law 'and that single women like her should be less disadvantaged by convention or the law in their efforts to achieve financial independence.'[23] Whilst there is nothing to *explicitly* suggest that Rye's gender or her assertive tone of correspondence played a role in Hardy squashing her bid for an augmented financial package, it is an important dimension to consider (a similarly gendered response to correspondence over the payment of bonuses can be inferred in letters sent between the Reverend Mother Evangelist O'Keeffe and Department of Agriculture officials, analysed in the second section of this chapter).

The interaction between Hardy and Rye offers a good example of the consistently multi-layered, sometimes tense exchanges over the economy of child emigration between emigration agents and government officials. Unpacking the layers of hidden meaning beneath these negotiations illustrates that the economy of child emigration schemes was never a straightforward set of transactions, nor did all emigration agents acquire equal monetary support from the system. Factors including agents' character, track record, gender, and sheer number of children emigrated per agent/institution/locale all affected the sums involved. While bonus payments on children tended to remain static at $2 per child before the First World War, different levels of patronage of Homes and the circumstances of child poverty locally created great variations in institutions' financial health. For this reason, it was also difficult to maintain a consistent financial policy around child emigration. Potentially, parity of financial reward for emigration schemes would have ensured that all agents operated under the same conditions, and all children might therefore have benefitted from the stability of prosperous Homes or been adequately equipped with relevant training and appropriate clothes on arrival in Canada (the lack of which sometimes reinforced their stigmatisation as unwanted paupers and likely criminals). This uncertainty also underpinned suspicions that certain Homes were attempting to defraud the bonus system, as will be seen presently.

Indeed, children's homes and charitable institutions did not work particularly hard to navigate the juxtaposition between the moral rhetoric of their work and its baser economic benefits. The value of children's labour in the Canadian agricultural market, it was argued, far exceeded the cost of emigration at an institutional level, a fact that was used as leverage to ensure political support for child emigration in both countries. As the 1902 Report of the Father Berry's Homes urged, 'We found the Canadian Government most sympathetic with the work of Child Emigration, and most willing to assist us in every way. Seeing however, the number of children that have been emigrated by charitable societies, amounting, as already said, to at least one in 150 of the total population, is it unreasonable to hope that some day the Government may see its way to encourage it by some further financial help? Canada wants population; the Charitable Societies are supplying that want to a great extent.'[24]

Sustaining their cost-benefit analysis of child emigration, the 1903 Report of the Homes similarly claimed that emigrating an impoverished child was likely to save domestic communities a projected spend, through taxes, of £2,250 per child on their maintenance in the workhouse over twenty years, and a further £3200 on a likely ten years' incarceration in prison.[25] By contrast, a child could labour for ten years on a Canadian farm at a modest wage of between one and three dollars per month (in the early 1900s), increasing to between ten and sixteen dollars per month by 1929, payment which the Catholic Emigration Society offered to 'bank' for the first three years to motivate a child to stay and ensure 'An industrious boy can amass a very goodly sum, which is a nest egg for him on attaining independence.'[26] Emigration thus prospectively secured financial prosperity for successive generations of 'worthy' emigrants: those who worked hard without complaint, who could thereby achieve independence from institutions and, implicitly, eradicate the stain of their childhood family origins.

Emigration offered a win for all involved. Creating a powerful imaginary economy of decades of unquantifiable savings to the British ratepayer and simultaneous boosts to the Canadian market, it would also 'weed out' the less racially desirable British children. By couching emigration in a language of 'survival of the fittest,' emigration agents capitalized on the imperial discourse of the physical health and strength of those children accepted to enter the emigration system. But why not send children into the English agricultural market? Unlike Canada, England had long been wrestling with agricultural depression by the late-nineteenth century. Wages in the English agricultural sector had been in sharp decline since the 1870s, as farm labour was supplanted by the rise of manufacturing industries, drawing workers to the towns, and the price of grain was affected by global food supplies and increased competition from cheaper producers.[27] The rapidly deteriorating situation prompted a new wave of trade unionism, culminating in farmer Joseph Arch (1826–1919) establishing the National Agricultural Labourers Union in 1872, which boasted over 86,200 members by 1874. Its success was short-lived, however. Historians George Boyer and Timothy Hatton note that Arch's efforts only raised agricultural wages temporarily until the collapse of unionism in 1876, having had a negligible effect in the long-term.[28] And, notably, unions became increasingly vocal in their support for state-sponsored emigration schemes as the only means of resolving the labour crisis. Poignantly, Arch's own son emigrated to Canada c. 1888.[29]

By the Edwardian period, therefore, the notion of sending children to imperial territories as farm labourers rather than keeping them at home became more obvious as a beneficial outcome of emigration, and the policy was supported more broadly by the Empire Settlement Act 1922. The traffic of claims and payments helps identify the intensification and periodisation of emigration activity, manifested in the pattern of claims across different institutions. For example, the quarterly Treasury Grants of £189 issued for emigration purposes to the

Boys' Refuge between 1910 and 1913 decreased to £168 between 1913 and 1917, indicating the impact of the First World War.[30] Emergency financial incentives were created to respond to the global conflict and from 1915, the Department of Agriculture agreed to provide a grant 'of $250.00 to those Homes which bring out 100 children and $500.00 to those Homes which bring out 200 children.'[31] These emergency incentives afford a point of reference for analysing the recovery of child emigration schemes post war, expressed in sums of $1,500 to the Catholic Emigration Association in 1920, and declining to between £326 and £370 per quarter granted by the Home Office to the St George's Industrial School for emigration between 1928 and 1929.[32] The latter payments suggest the resilience of state sponsorship of Catholic emigrating societies, maintained despite the imminent temporary suspension of child emigration in 1930.

Economic logic even prevailed in the face of the system's demise, ostensibly caused, according to the Catholic Emigration Society, by its expense rather than by the concerted campaign by the Canadian Council on Child Welfare led by Charlotte Whitman that led to its moratorium.[33] As the Society's internal report of 1930–31 stated bluntly, 'As regards the work of emigration, there is no emigration due to economic conditions abroad as well as at home,' apparently referring to the global depression caused by the Wall Street Crash of 1929. Even more starkly, the report suggested its stakeholders succumb to the inevitable rather than act to 'rescue' their own organisation, irrespective of its moral agenda: 'Actually economic pressure is more likely to solve the problem without any assistance from the North [an apparent reference to the Canadian branch of the Catholic Emigration Society], so the safer plan is to stand by and watch the Catholic Emigration Society die quietly.'[34]

Undeniably, many of the sums recorded in surviving financial ledgers and correspondence were mediocre (such as the two Treasury grants of £13.10 shillings in 1915 and £14.10 shillings in 1917 paid by the Home Office to the St Anne's Street Boys' Refuge to offset the expense of emigrating four children).[35] Given the effort involved in maintaining appropriate records, sustaining the emigration network overseas, and chasing grants through sending endless letters, the amounts involved appear scarcely worth the overall administrative workload (again attesting to the strength of the 'imaginary economy' referred to earlier). Even local businesses' involvement in the comparatively simple process of transportation demonstrates little obvious financial appeal. In 1885, the Allan Line steamers made a claim for £2,598.13s.6d ($12,646.88) on the children they had emigrated in eight different months between 1882 and 1884, an amount of such insignificance to them that they had overlooked it in their previous claim.[36] Still, the regularity of payments in the account books of emigrating agencies across Liverpool demonstrate the routinization of child emigration, as well as the commonplace nature of transactions between state and local institutions.[37] In this respect, unlike other forms of Victorian philanthropy, child emigration was not a free market in which deals could be cut with minimal state intervention or regulation (as Rye had discovered in her dealings with Hardy).[38] State oversight of child emigration schemes intensified incrementally through inspections (see chapter 1) and legislation (see chapter 2), finally matched by dual financial support following the Empire Settlement Act of 1922, when both governments agreed to 'make a joint grant of £14. 10s. for the transportation, etc., of each child. Agreements have also been entered into between the Imperial Government and the philanthropic Societies under which one half of the annual cost of the reception, after-care, etc., of the children is borne by the Imperial Government.'[39]

This joint commitment, though a late development in the early history of modern child emigration schemes, affords a revealing insight into the enduring strength of state support for the schemes. It also demonstrates that during the early 1920s, when Britain was in a state of economic recession following the First World War, the Imperial (British) government was willing to underwrite the child emigration system by bearing half the costs of its operations across both countries.[40] Thus, after six decades, emigration agents had engineered the level of state sponsorship for child emigration first suggested by Maria Rye in 1880.

Although financial exchanges expose the relationship between emigration agents and the state, written requests from farms and other employers to the Department of Agriculture for migrant children perhaps best encapsulate the tension between emigrating societies' public emphasis on welfare and children's fluctuating status as economic units and potential adoptees. Compare the following letters:

> (Toronto, 27 April 1878)
> Dear Sir,
> Looking over the Globe I saw the immigration department both males and females as domestic servants I do not wish one in particular as a servant but I wish to adopt a young girl the age of 15

or 16, a good strong healthy girl one that learns easy can go to school Autumn and Winter I only have one child & I wish to take one as my own church and school close by will have a good home as long as she wishes could I adopt one or on what conditions.[41]

(Toronto, 10 May 1886)
Dear Sir,
Will you kindly let me know when you expect the next shipment of immigrants, a friend of ours from Georgetown wants to get a girl to make herself useful about a farm house.[42]

The other half of this correspondence does not survive for historians to discover whether either request was fulfilled; both letters are, however, broadly representative of the content of hundreds of similar letters contained in the files. The first of the two letters represented an offer of family life, emotional support, and intellectual opportunity that epitomised the ideal outcomes for institutions' stated goals of removing children from their biological family into a better, adoptive one. The second letter represented an opportunity of paid employment, which could also have been characterised as fulfilling the same goals – although it is hard not to conclude that the second letter's injunction for 'a girl to make herself useful' reflected a complete disregard towards the child's emotional state.

Together, these letters serve to reveal that Canadian public impressions of the purpose of child emigration were inconsistent, with neither a clear definition of working-class children's social status, nor a sense of the nature and longevity of 'childhood' itself when migrant children were so explicitly required as labourers. Some children became acutely aware of this paradox. In 1904 Michael, aged eight, reportedly professed himself 'dissatisfied on the score of wages' despite earning three dollars per month as a farm labourer, the only comment on his experience of emigration that a visitor on behalf of the Father Berry's Homes was able to elicit from the child.[43] The same year Father Foley of Fallowfield, Manchester, writing for the emigration diary of Arthur Chilton Thomas, Manager of Father Berry's Homes, commented that boys became 'dissatisfied' if they were not given wages; whilst a letter Chilton Thomas transcribed from Dr Foley in 1905 agreed that 'some often try to "bolt" before the time limit [of employment] has expired' if children 'get too little wages.'[44] An even more assertive example was the case of John, who Chilton

Thomas characterized as 'sulky.' John had moved placements several times until arriving at the farm of a Mr Curran, who wished to pay John's wages to his receiving home rather than to John directly. As Chilton Thomas reported, the child promptly 'claimed the money and threatened to sue him.' Eventually Curran was made to pay the money to John in the presence of Chilton Thomas, who then forced the child to pay it into the bank.[45]

An awareness of their 'value' in the labour market provided certain children with a vocabulary for material complaint that could easily be established by visiting inspectors (unlike abuse). Coupled with running away on the grounds of inadequate wages, these actions provide further evidence of the strategies employed by emigrant children to exert their autonomy and financial acumen within a restrictive system, albeit in extreme circumstances. For older children, such measures were seemingly less necessary, as it was easier to emulate the forms of bargaining and agreement of contracts performed by adult labourers when looking for work elsewhere. For example, Walter was emigrated to Canada in 1900 by the Catholic Emigration Society, aged eleven (it is unclear where his original home in England was). In 1904, aged fifteen, he was discovered by Father Bans to have hired himself out to a Mr Duneen for two months, an act which so impressed Bans he instructed Duneen to pay Walter the money he had earned directly.[46] The incident suggests that Walter's demonstration of economic independence signalled a claim to adulthood, and possibly fully-realised masculinity, that even an interested emigration agent could not fail to ignore.

By contrast ignorance, or belated realisation, of one's economic 'worth' made for unnecessary suffering. Florence was interviewed by social worker Margaret Humphreys in Canada aged eighty-seven. She was emigrated from Newcastle aged twelve in 1913 by Barnardo's, so her case technically falls outside of the geographical scope of this book; it is important to cite, however, for the useful insight it affords into children's navigation of their economic status and how this was communicated informally amongst the children themselves. Florence recalled working as both housemaid and farm labourer in Fergus, Ontario, from the ages of fifteen to eighteen at a placement where the farmer beat her brutally and paid her just $3 a month. Finally, a friend and fellow migrant, Maud, explained to Florence that she was in fact now legally an adult with the freedom to move, helping her secure a $1 a day position as a maid in the city. As Florence commented: 'I was eighteen and legally I was free to go anywhere I wanted. But I did not know more than a kid of twelve, I had been kept shut in for so long ... I had a little tin trunk with my worldly belongings in it and I thought, "How am I going to get that out?" So finally I handed her [the farmer's wife] Maud's letter and she was furious, she thought she had me for life, cheap labour.'[47]

Though this case demonstrates the value of links between migrant children, maintained in Canada considered in chapter 4, Florence remained vulnerable. Lacking the money for a train ticket, it was only by the grace of her new employer sending the fare that she was able to make the journey from her abusive placement. This was a different kind of mobility to the more stigmatised removal of a child from a placement back to a Home as a result of mistreatment (or notions of the child's own ill-discipline and moral dangerousness) that was discussed in chapter 1. Knowing their worth was perhaps a surprising, yet valuable, sign of success for migrant children in a system predicated on blurring the boundaries between its moral and economic justifications.

MONEY OR MORALS?

On 20 December 1905, a discrepancy was identified in the payments to Father Berry's Homes.[48] The new auditor general of Canada, John Fraser (appointed after the controversial resignation of John Lorn McDougall in July of that year) wrote to C.H. Beddoe, Accountant at the Dept of the Interior, to complain that 'Under Immigration cheque No. 4082 of 1904–05, there is a payment to Father Berry's Homes, of Liverpool, for a bonus of $2 each on 144 pauper children. On examination I find that 110 of these were previously paid for by Immigration cheques No. 4090 of 1904–05 issued at Ottawa and No. 796 of 1903–04, issued in London. Of the remaining 34 there are the names of 20 who do not appear to have ever landed in this country. You will please have a refund made of the amount overpaid on this voucher.'[49] Fraser's letter would provoke a year of tense disputes between the Homes and emigration officials in London and Canada, as letters flew back and forth debating the number of overpayments (further inquiries appeared to reveal double payments on hundreds of children sent from the Homes since 1903).[50]

In amongst the tense exchanges, however, one silence is particularly noticeable: disturbingly, the fact that twenty (or more) children's names appeared in the records who had not arrived in Canada was never subject to further investigation, though mentioned in passing a number of times in the letters. Did these children exist? If so, where did they go? We may never know. This section explores how the shadow of financial fraud, and disputes over the correct payment of bonuses, represented a powerful force for destabilising the child emigration network. The political implications of financial scandal were so weighty that they eclipsed the issue of whether the Homes had distributed their income to adequately clothe and feed children in Canada, or even whether they had in fact 'invented' or lost children in the process.

Although concerns about Father Berry's Homes' finances originated in Canada, it is worth noting that the financial dealings of Liverpool-based Children's Homes were also subject to heightened local scrutiny during the early 1900s. This was largely due to the crusading agenda of another Liverpool philanthropist, Herbert Lee Jackson Jones (known as Lee Jones). Jones ran a charity, the Liverpool Food and Betterment Association (founded 1893, renamed the League of Welldoers in 1908), which sought to address chronic want in the North docklands area.[51] As Roddy, Strange, and Taithe describe, from 1905 Jones lobbied editors of the leading Liverpool newspapers to create a blacklist of charities in the city whose claims to child rescue were fraudulent and whose financial practices appeared suspect. Maintaining an active approach to shaming the city's shadier charity entrepreneurs for the next five years, he managed to get a few press editors to cease publishing advertising copy from those on his blacklist, despite a collaboration with Liverpool police to investigate several charities that resulted in no prosecutions.[52] Jones's motives in championing fiscal virtue were twofold: 'For Lee Jones, the exposure and policing of local organizations in the local press was pivotal to raising public awareness, not only of "discreditable" schemes but also of the very need to discriminate … By identifying what was wrong with other charities, Lee Jones implicitly stated what was right about his.' As this suggests, Jones's virtue-signalling about his own finances was bound up in his claims to the broader authenticity and morality of his cause, indicating the relative fragility of philanthropists' reputations in an era of minimal state regulation (nationally, fraudulent charity work was more commonly exposed by the Charity Organisation Society rather than by government inquiry).[53]

This context placed emigration societies in a unique position. By dint of working closely with government officials on both sides of the

Atlantic to sustain the traffic of children and adults to imperial territories, emigration societies were not exclusively reliant on their own internal auditing processes, notionally giving them greater credibility for managing their finances responsibly. Jones did not target the Catholic Emigration Society; we do not know if this was because he found no evidence to suggest financial mismanagement, or if its complex national, international, and regional structure made the prospect impossible for a single man busy running his own charity as well. He also depended upon the influence of the city's Catholic bishops. Along with the lord mayors of Liverpool, the Earl of Derby, and Princess Louise, the bishops lent their patronage to his League of Welldoers, vital since it was situated in Vauxhall, among Liverpool's largest Irish Catholic community.[54] Still, it is remarkable that even as the correspondence over the double payment of bonuses at Father Berry's Homes descended into acrimony throughout 1906, no mention of the affair seems to have reached the ears of Jones nor featured within the press in either country (there is also no surviving reference to it in the Nugent Care archives, if any existed).

The explanation for this silence may lie in the political stature of those who became involved, as well as the internal government quarrels the scandal piqued. In March 1906, W.D. Scott, Superintendent of Immigration, wrote to the high commissioner for Canada in London to summons the manager of Father Berry's Homes to discuss the matter. Scott urged that 'I would be glad to have a report in this connection and also to have Mr Arthur Chilton Thomas, St. Vincent de Paul's House, 105 Shaw St., Liverpool, communicated with as to why he accepted double payment and a demand made upon him for refund.'[55] Directing the accusation personally at Chilton Thomas was to prove a mistake. Just returned from a leave of absence abroad due to illness, Chilton Thomas promptly contacted W.T.R. Preston, the commissioner of emigration for Canada, who in turn wrote to his superior Donald Smith, high commissioner for immigration and 1st Baron Strathcona and Mount Royal. An eminent financier, Strathcona (as he was called) was instrumental in extending the bonus system to steamship agents and along with Preston had established the North Atlantic Trading Company to this end. Known for his liberal immigration policy, Strathcona was keen to expand the work (despite opposition from other ministers in Wilfred Laurier's government).[56] Preston was therefore preaching to the converted when he reported to Strathcona that Chilton Thomas could not find the payments but had explained the irregularity by producing a copy of a memorandum, a document 'discovered amongst the papers of the Society's office' that appeared to show the bonus payments had been sent to the wrong office in Montreal (rather than Liverpool). Noting that Chilton Thomas had offered to repay a sum of £20.8.4s ($99.36) (as opposed to the $260 originally demanded by Fraser), Preston opined: 'The explanation given as to why the double payment was accepted is to the effect that the payments, coming from a Government Department, were regarded as correct without question, and as their total did not equal the amounts claimed to be due, no suspicion existed that there was any possibility of duplicate payments.'[57]

Questioning the accuracy of accounting by the government, rather than the emigration society, unleashed a minor furore within the ranks of Canadian officialdom. Scott 'expressed dissatisfaction with the correspondence' and turned on Preston, asserting that he had 'failed to explain why payment was made without authority' and demanding another explanation.[58] Preston poured his outrage at this reply into another lengthy letter to Strathcona, in which he exclaimed 'I can hardly bring myself to believe that he [Scott] would put such words, so utterly at variance with the facts, in an official document.' He then proceeded to counter-accuse Scott of having authorised the double payment as part of an invoice for the sum of £112 on fifty-six children, producing an invoice 'signed in Mr. Scott's handwriting' as evidence.[59] Tensions between the two simmered until November, when Scott's assistant superintendent, Bruce Walker, wrote to him conceding that 'it appears that one of the duplicate payments was made by the Department at Ottawa direct to the Society's Homes in Montreal.' Crucially, it was not until this letter that case of the missing children's names reappeared, when Walker requested 'you will kindly furnish a list of the names of the 20 children who, it is stated, do not appear to have ever landed in Canada.'[60]

The incident of double bonus payments to Father Berry's Homes is highly suggestive. By criticising the fact that payments coming from a government department 'were regarded as correct without question,' Preston not only offended the sensibilities of his colleagues, but also struck a note of fallibility in the government's dealings with child emigration agents that inferred the need for external auditing. His mention of the 'amounts claimed to be due' referred to other letters sent by the Homes chasing the government for late or unpaid bonus payments during the previous year; another crucial way of insinuating that the clumsy bureaucracy of the state was ultimately responsible for the mess in which they found themselves.[61] Indeed, this would not be the first time Preston turned on his colleagues. In 1914 he published a book accusing Strathcona (with whom he eventually fell out of favour) of accruing his fortune through financial impropriety.[62] Wrangling over financial responsibility carried a bigger set of meanings than a simple attempt to correct an error in this era. As literary scholar Kristen Guest observes, popular late-Victorian plays increasingly dramatized middle-class male financiers' growing sense of a loss of control over the global marketplace. New legislation introducing limited liability from the 1850s to the 1870s had divorced financial transactions from older markers of masculinity such as personal reputation, private moral character, and public behaviour.[63] Preston's criticisms that the double payment of bonuses originated in the Government's own mismanagement, therefore, evoked older ideas entwining fiscal accuracy and reliability with masculinity – notably in the context of the state's importation of vulnerable children, a responsibility that closely mirrored patriarchal models of family .

For the Father Berry's Homes, there were no immediate consequences from the scandal beyond repayment of a token sum (insufficient to cover the full amount), which hardly amounted to a concession of guilt. Correspondence indicates that Fraser was still chasing a full refund in December 1906. In 1907, however, Cecil Arden (who acted in Canada as agent for the Catholic Emigration Association, including the Father Berry's Homes) was accused by the Catholic Emigration Association's senior clergy of repeated 'acts of dishonesty' in reference to his handling of the finances. This was particularly significant since until March 1907, Arden was chiefly responsible for processing the bonus claims on behalf of the various Homes attached to the Association (indeed, the cheques were often addressed to him personally, enabling him to cash them in his own name).[64] According to an enquiry by Fathers Pinnington and Hudson, Arden had 'used monies of the Association to pay personal accounts of himself and his relatives', spending $127 in total, an amount Arden was forced to sign an undertaking to repay. Secondly, Arden had employed his brother Darcy as a visitor and, most heinously, 'took his salary out of the children's wages he collected. No account of this was made on the monthly statement of accounts, and the reports made by Mr. Darcy Arden were signed by Mr. Cecil Arden. The amount of wages used by Mr. Darcy Arden was $236.30 (£49.4.7).'[65]

In this instance, the scandal that engrossed Arden appears to have been silenced in reverse. Although it appears in the Nugent Care correspondence, there is no mention of it in the Canadian archives, suggesting the Catholic Emigration Association were keen to avoid an embarrassing enquiry into one of their most prominent agents reaching the ears of Canadian officials (perhaps keeping the events of the previous year in mind). Only by juxtaposing both sets of archives from the two countries can we understand the cat-and-mouse-like game of attempting to preserve one's reputation for fiscal virtue, played variously by emigration agents and representatives of both governments. As such, child emigration schemes fell prey to the same underhand practices as the wider Victorian charitable marketplace which, despite its philanthropic and religious aspect, bred behaviours akin to those of wily businessmen and con artists among their power brokers.[66] Once again, the starkest absence in the Arden correspondence is the lack of reference to which children had their wages purloined, indicating how the children themselves must have been unaware of where their money went on collection. Within the financial machinations of the child emigration system, therefore, migrant children appeared to be least prioritised, instead being conceptualised merely as the tool with which to generate these monies. Arden's fraudulent behaviour offers an important case for illustrating the fragility of publicised claims that emigration ultimately secured children's financial independence, with agents acting merely as 'middlemen' to ensure their labour materialised in savings on achieving adulthood.

Children were, in fact, valued differently within the emigration system (in both a monetary and social sense) depending on what type of institution they were emigrated from. This rendered some children's future ability to use their economic worth as leverage to improve their circumstances even less certain. The stringent criteria that determined which children were eligible for bonus payments included a clause that children emigrated from industrial schools and workhouses were ineligible.[67] Devised by the Canadian Department of the Interior, this criterion demonstrated how monetary incentives to emigration were another tactic deployed in a eugenicist effort to optimise the health and moral character of those to be emigrated. By contrast, the dual imperatives of emigrating 'dangerous' poor children out of Britain and maintaining the flow of bonus payments meant that English emigration agents attempted to obscure the origins of the children they sent where they fell foul of the clause. In 1908, the Reverend Mother Evangelist O'Keeffe had taken over the running of the St George's Home in Ottawa, which received migrant children of the Catholic Emigration Association (predominantly from Liverpool and the North West, as well as Birmingham and London). For the next few years, O'Keeffe was engaged in a near-constant back-and-forth of correspondence with Superintendent of Immigration W.D. Scott relating to bonus payments, stemming from her resistance to the stipulation that they were not paid in full on all the migrant children who passed through the Home.[68] For example, on 7 July 1908, O'Keeffe wrote to Scott that 'I am in receipt of your letter of the 4th instant, re party of children per S.S. Tunisian, arriving at Quebec June 5th 1908. The children came out under the auspices of the Catholic Emigration Association, to this Home, but came from the certain Industrial Schools enumerated. The Medical Certificate was signed by the Medical Examiner of these Schools. I understand that this has been a regular occurrence for several years past, and am rather surprised that it has only now for the first time been taken notice of. Trusting that this explanation will be satisfactory.'[69]

It is difficult to ascertain whether O'Keeffe was being disingenuous in reporting her 'surprise' at the refusal to pay bonuses on children from industrial schools; her claim that this had been a common practice for 'several years past' served firstly to shift responsibility away from herself, and secondly to imply a historic lack of oversight on the part of the Canadian government. Either way, O'Keeffe was forced to concede ground on the issue and accept a reduced fee.[70] Yet an underlying mistrust of how O'Keeffe (and, by extension, the Catholic Emigration Association) calculated their claims and how they had spent the money awarded to them lingered, possibly as a direct result of O'Keeffe's attempt to obfuscate. During the First World War, O'Keeffe pointedly produced for the Canadian government long lists of boys migrated by the Society who enlisted to serve in the Canadian Expeditionary Forces, described as 'brave boys'.[71] Simultaneously, both she and Hudson sought to negotiate an increased grant for the St George's Homes over and above the $250 per 100 children emigrated offered in the context of the war, prompting an irritated reply from Scott in February 1917: 'The Department cannot very well offer a grant to your Society without making a similar grant to a considerable number of other Societies engaged in the same work', and noting that the matter had already been 'pretty thoroughly discussed'.[72]

The interactions between O'Keeffe and Scott hold echoes of the earlier friction between Maria Rye and officials, and it is worth entertaining the likelihood of a gendered dimension to the particular ire that Scott directed towards her given the events that followed. Turning the tables on O'Keeffe, between 1918 and 1919 Scott and his colleague G. Bogue Smart, inspector of British Emigrant children, launched an investigation into the payment of children's wages and the Homes' expenditure on the appropriate provision of clothing for children (an issue that had previously appeared in individual reports on children dressed inappropriately for Canadian winters, but had failed to be addressed at a structural level).[73] Smart reported on a boy he had visited whose clothes were 'unsatisfactory', 'discreditable', and 'wretched', hinting at the situation as abusive. In an extraordinary move, Smart opined '"This is another case in which a specified sum for clothing should be named by the Home and a cash payment of $5. per month in addition', adding menacingly, 'I will be glad to personally discuss this question with you when I call at St. George's Home.'[74] This allegation represented a new and unexpected economic burden for the Homes. As O'Keeffe replied, with an air of panic: 'we are not sure how much is spent on clothing, and we have no proof to give us an idea as to the amount expended each year. Also, what is the annual cost of clothing for a boy from 12 to 16 years, and for a girl of the same age?'[75]

Financial ledgers show that the Homes ended up putting up the costs. Lloyd's Outfitters, a Liverpool clothing company preferred by shipping agents that supplied caps and jackets for children emigrating, received regular payments of between £10 and £30 per month from St George's explicitly for providing these services between 1926 and 1929.[76] In fact, this brought them into line with the sums spent by other emigrating organisations; in December 1908, the Boys' Refuge Certified Industrial School in St Anne's Street, Liverpool paid an unspecified outfitters for 'emigration' the sum of £189.[77] It is difficult, however, to avoid the conclusion that raising the issue of children's clothing so late in the early history of emigration schemes, and with a particular focus on the St George's Home, manifested a subtle dig at the Reverend Mother O'Keeffe's level of 'care' for migrant children in a maternal sense; especially since those who 'adopted' the children into their families or for employment were contractually expected to treat them as their own in return for the children's labour – extending to the provision of suitable clothing.

These payments thus illustrate the way that political intervention into child emigration schemes served a multi-layered agenda. On the one hand, they continued to foster mutually beneficial commercial arrangements between emigrating Homes and local businesses, whilst also providing an avenue for undermining the opportunities for fraud via limiting the possibilities for surplus. On the other, the clothing of children was a matter of welfare, but also represented an ideal mechanism for questioning the claims to both moral and fiscal responsibility of suspect Homes – especially those whose managers were prone to questioning the government on their own accountancy.

CONCLUSION

The economy of child emigration schemes cannot be accurately quantified or calculated. This does not, however, diminish the value of interrogating the financial exchanges that took place historically, which offer a rich history of the way children's lives and labour were assessed – and, sadly, the way children's worth was often defined. Instances in which children understood their status in this manner paradoxically created moments of opportunity where they could assert their agency, and bargain for a change in their situation, albeit within the limits of their relationships to adults and frequent isolation. Such moments show how financial acumen was linked to constructs of attaining maturity and independence, even for the acutely vulnerable. Historians may only scratch the surface of how far government sponsorship of child emigration schemes made a meaningful contribution to the regional economy; we may also struggle to understand the extent to which local businesses were supported by the system. Yet the economic logic developed by certain children in order to survive tells its own story of the importance of the system's economic aspect.

Likewise, these transactions (and the correspondence they generated) afford significant insights into the relationships between emigration agents and the British and Canadian governments, as well as glimpses of the gendered discourses of financial entrepreneurship at the fin de siècle. Female emigration figures such as Maria Rye and the Reverend Mother Evangelist O'Keeffe attempted to deal with officials in a manner that often reads, in retrospect, as surprisingly assertive and financially astute. Neither woman enjoyed much success at augmenting the incomes of their agencies with this approach, although these moments of rebuttal should be contextualised against the fact that they were both entrepreneurs and managers who ran their 'businesses' for years despite this. It is hard to cheer on these achievements in light of the reported instances of maltreatment of migrant children, who were nominally in these women's 'care.' Instead, it is perhaps more useful to locate these examples within the broader point that child emigration schemes fostered another branch of the charitable 'marketplace' identified by Roddy, Strange, and Taithe, with associated forms of behaviour on the part of all the agents involved. Accordingly, the intermittent accusations of fraud and financial mismanagement within child emigration schemes do not seem to have deterred the Canadian government from using bonuses as incentives. Instances of fraudulent activity are more notable for their swift silencing, and a lack of concern for the children involved, than for any fundamental alterations to the economic operation of the system. In this light, we should view the economy of child emigration schemes as a cultural force, in which the imagined economic benefits to the taxpayer in both countries outweighed the principle of a truly 'moral' economy.

5

Aftermath

In 2017, a monument was erected in Toronto's Park Lawn Cemetery to commemorate seventy-five children whose remains had lain 'unmarked and virtually forgotten in a pair of mass graves.'[1] These children were 'Home Children' who were emigrated from Britain to Canada via the schemes we have explained in the preceding chapters. Their existence was found, by accident, four years previously by Lori Oschefski, the CEO of the British Home Children Advocacy and Research Association (BHCARA, now Home Children Canada), and her partner, Paul Jackson, after they followed up on rumours of a mass children's grave in the cemetery. The BHCARA led a crowd-sourced campaign to fund a monument to acknowledge the lives of these children. Some were teenage girls who had died in childbirth, others died from diseases or from neglect, and their treatment in death reflected the silences around the experiences of children emigrated to Canada. The discovery of these graves helped to bring greater public attention to the systematic emigration of children and encouraged advocates for Home Children to hope for greater acknowledgement of their experiences. As Oschefski explained: 'I believe there is a reason why these children were revealed to me ... When I discovered these graves, a purely serendipitous discovery, I knew instantly that through their lost voices, the story of the plight of our British Home Children must come to light in Canada.'[2] The positive response to Oschefski's crowdfunded appeal illustrates how the stories of British Home Children have taken an increasingly central place in Canadian public history across the past decade. For example, since 2017 Canada has celebrated British Home Child Day on 28 September, which from 2019 has included a beacon of light that sees notable public buildings and monuments across the country lit up in red, white, and blue, or yellow to mark the occasion.

Two days following British Home Child Day in Canada is the National Day for Truth and Reconciliation. A federal statutory holiday since 2021, it commemorates the difficult histories and continuing problems caused by the Indian residential school system and occurs alongside Orange Shirt Day, an Indigenous-led commemorative act to challenge the harms experienced by Indigenous children. The Indian residential school system was established in the 1870s and saw over 150,000 First Nations, Métis, and Inuit children attend more than 130 schools until the system ended in the 1990s. Like child emigration schemes, the system enforced Indigenous children away from their families and trained them for manual work (domestic labour for girls, farm work and technical skills for boys); religious instruction was prioritised over academic skills, meaning levels of attainment were low, and the system was influenced by the introduction of industrial schools in Canada that allowed the removal of children from poor or 'immoral' homes. Most residential schools were run by religious organisations, the Catholic Church being the largest operator with around 60 per cent of institutionalised children under its charge. They aimed to Christianize children and represented 'an assault on Aboriginal culture, language, spiritual beliefs, and practices'.[3] The system aimed to eradicate indigenous culture by forcibly removing children from their families to reside at schools where they were separated from siblings, would be punished for speaking their native languages, and experienced very difficult conditions: 'Survivors recall being beaten and strapped; some students were shackled to their beds; some had needles shoved in their tongues for speaking their native languages'.[4]

As with British Home Children, survivors of the Indian residential school system and their families continue to campaign for acknowledgement of the harms caused to them. Recent discoveries suggest the existence of mass graves on the sites of former residential schools. Most notably, in 2021 a survey conducted with a radar by anthropologist Sarah Beaulieu identified the possibility of 215 unmarked graves on the grounds of Kamloops Indian Residential School in British Columbia. Once the largest residential school in Canada, with up to 500 students, Kamloops was run by the Catholic Church between 1890 and 1969 before being taken over by federal government until its closure in 1978. Following the findings of a child's rib bone and tooth, Beaulieu recommended that forensic excavation was required for confirmation. Tk'emlúps te Secwépemc Chief Rosanne Casimir told the *Toronto Star* that her mother and grandmother had talked of abuse at the school, and that the community had fought to find out what had happened to the many children known to have gone missing whilst in residence there: 'It's a harsh reality and it's our truths. It's our history and it's something we've always had to fight to prove.'[5] The potential findings reflected the poor living conditions and abuse that occurred in residential schools: the 1907 Bryce Report responded to concerns about high levels of illness and disease in residential schools found tuberculosis and other diseases were rife. Bryce circulated surveys to principals, and of those who responded, found of those children enrolled between 1888 and 1905, 'nearly 25 per cent are dead, of one school with an absolutely accurate statement, 69 per cent of ex pupils are dead, and that everywhere the almost invariable cause of death given is tuberculosis.'[6]

Beaulieu's initial findings were met with horror and dismay both in Canada and in the wider world: Prime Minister Justin Trudeau announced that all Canadian flags at federal buildings would be lowed to half-mast in honour of the tragedy unearthed. In addition, Canada Day celebrations in Victoria were cancelled, and across the country there were rallies and vigils. The practice began of placing children's shoes and toys outside Catholic churches, which were also targeted by violence and vandalism for their role in the residential school system. In June 2021, a statue of Egerton Ryerson, known for his prominent role in establishing the system, situated at the centre of the campus of Ryerson University (now named Toronto Metropolitan University) was graffitied, toppled, and thrown into Toronto Harbour. In Ottawa, the federal government pledged $320 million to support the search of residential schools and to assist survivors and their families. Beaulieu's findings also led China to call for an investigation into human rights violations against the Indigenous people in Canada at the UN Human Rights Tribunal in June 2021 and in July 2022, Pope Francis made a formal apology for the Church's role in the residential school system during a visit to Canada. Further potential mass graves have since been located: in June 2021, the Cowessess First Nation in Saskatchewan announced that 751 unmarked graves had been identified at the site of Marieval Indian Residential School; in July 2021, the Penelakut Tribe in British Columbia reported that 160 undocumented or unmarked graves had been found in the grounds of the Kuper Island Industrial School; and in January 2023, Star Blanket Cree Nation in Saskatchewan announced the discovery of the jawbone belonging to a young child and over 2,000 areas that they wished to investigate further relating to the Qu'Appelle Indian Residential School.

However, whereas Home Children Canada was able to unveil a crowd-funded monument after identifying the deceased children and could highlight the lost voices they represented, the response to the potential findings at Kamloops has sometimes been criticised or denounced as 'fake news', particularly by media with national-populist and culture-warrior tendencies.[7] In January 2022, Jacques Rouillard, emeritus professor of history at the University of Montreal, denied the genocide of Indigenous people and suggested that the speculation around mass deaths at residential schools emerged from administrative errors made by the Truth and Reconciliation Commission. Rouillard claimed that as no remains had actually been found, 'Imaginary stories and emotion have outweighed the pursuit of truth. On the road to reconciliation, isn't the best way to seek and tell the whole truth rather than deliberately create sensational myths?'[8] Tom Flanagan, professor emeritus of political science at the University of Calgary described Kamloops as 'the biggest fake news story in Canadian history' and 'a moral panic.'[9] Articles in *Spiked Online*, *Unherd*, and *The Spectator* all claimed the findings at Kamloops had been misinterpreted, exaggerated, or overblown, and were fuelled by hysterical media coverage. Flanagan suggested in *Unherd* that 'the indigenous industry has an obvious financial stake in driving the story: As long as the dollars flow, expect more stories about unmarked graves, yet no excavations to test the truth of the stories.'[10]

The different responses to the graves found at Toronto's Park Lawn Cemetery and the potential remains at Kamloops and at other sites of residential schools reflects the ongoing disparities between Canadian perceptions of British Home children and their descendants – seen as worthy, assimilable, and co-operative – in comparison to First Nations children, who remain stigmatized as unassimilable, neglected, or deviant. Consequently, First Nations children remain the focus of state intervention and of welfare policies that focus on the removal of children from their homes and families: recent statistics show that Indigenous children comprise 52 per cent of children in government care in Canada, despite just being 4.4 per cent of the total population.[11] The racial discrimination experienced by First Nations children was recently recognised by the Federal Court, who have approved a $23 billion settlement agreement in compensation for inequalities in child welfare and family services.[12]

The popular memory of child emigration has been underpinned and reinforced in recent years by a large body of popular and fictionalised histories of British Home Children that endorse the powerful model of the white, British emigrant child as assumable. They emphasise stoic, self-sacrificial individuals who overcame any abuse or hard living conditions in the same way they triumphed over the severe Canadian winters. One such is Cecilia Jowett, who has become a figurehead for those seeking to promote the experiences of British Home Children.[13] Jowett epitomises the 'good immigrant' narrative: she was emigrated in 1907 aged five and became a nurse in an extremely remote part of Ontario, where she tended to other settlers living in very harsh conditions. Her memoir, published in 1954, has become perhaps the best-known account by a British Home Child. In it she claims to have won 'a battle against circumstances and it really began, I believe, when I was five years old.'[14] Jowett probably became so popular because she strongly reinforces Canadian narratives of progress and citizenship. However, the challenges members of the public face in accessing sources – one we have tried to address throughout our undertaking of this project – has meant that much of our history British Home Children has focussed on those emigrated via Barnardo's homes, who were usually born in London or the South-East of England, and particularly on those that stayed in Canada and built successful careers and home lives there, including Cecilia Jowett. Our emphasis on the institutions situated in the North-West of England has privileged different archival sources and perspectives that challenge these dominant narratives and indicate, as well as positive narratives, the ambivalence, difficult, traumatic and conflicted experiences of child migrants.

This chapter compares the representation of child emigration in popular culture with testimonies by well-known individuals such as Cecilia Jowett and those of lesser-known memoirists from the North West. Unfortunately there are very few autobiographies by those who were emigrated as children, a product perhaps of the secrecy and shame that so many continued to take with them into adulthood. Most life writings are biographies that have been written by family members wanting to record and make sense of the lives of older relatives. A welcome exception is the memoir of Joe Ayre, *The Socialist*, written in 1978 and has been preserved by the Burnett Collection of Working Class Autobiographies at Brunel University. Ayre's autobiography shows that the experience of child emigration shaped a sense of self in both positive and negative ways; it also demonstrates that the public history of child emigration needs to incorporate a broader range of stories and experiences, especially those that do not fit the dominant story. Ayre's autobiography is a rare opportunity to view the experience of child emigration within an individual's wider life. Historian Julie-Marie Strange stresses the value of autobiographical sources in providing adult identities and perspectives in the construction of life stories, arguing 'this is not a weakness of autobiography; it is its great strength. Autobiography is a deliberate composition, with emphasis on particular events and characters, written in a chosen genre with particular stylistic modes and edited for coherence.'[15]

Autobiographical and biographical texts provide us with an insight into how, as adults, those emigrated as children sought to understand and made sense of their experience and, for those who stayed, especially reinforced their citizenship as worthy Canadians. Placing historical novels next to a range of retrospective testimonies from child emigrants, we see that the narrative of the good immigrant has become integral to public histories of British Home Children. However, a comparison with a broader range of perspectives and accounts illustrates the trauma, ambivalence, and ongoing dislocation, as well as adventure and excitement, experienced by those emigrated as children. It suggests a more flexible narrative around the public history of child emigration can capture these ambiguous experiences in order to empower those who seek to understand those who remain marginalised from history.

THE CONTRASTING PUBLIC HISTORIES OF CHILD EMIGRATION AND THE INDIAN RESIDENTIAL SCHOOL SYSTEM

The successful campaign to build a monument to commemorate British children emigrated to Canada reflects the important work undertaken by campaigners such as Oschefski and Home Children Canada, often with the support of descendants of Home Children, in uncovering the history of child emigration schemes. Although the policy of emigrating children to Canada only ceased in the 1930s, there was little public acknowledgement of the schemes on either side of the Atlantic. As we noted in the introduction, this silence was only addressed following investigative work by social worker Margaret Humphreys in 1987 which exposed the abuse suffered by many children emigrated to Commonwealth countries and led to the establishment of the Child Migrants Trust. This exposé also facilitated greater attention from broadcasters and filmmakers. The 1987 film *Heaven on Earth*, written by Margaret Atwood and Peter Pearson, depicted the experiences of emigrated British children in the 1910s, and along with the 1992 miniseries *The Leaving of Liverpool*, about child migrants to Australia, helped to fuel greater interest in emigrated British children. Humphreys's book *Empty Cradles* was published in 1995 and dramatized in 2010 as the film *Oranges and Sunshine*. The film brought increased public understanding of child emigration, which forced both the British and the Canadian governments to act. The Canadian government declared 2010 to be the 'Year of the British Home Child' and released a commemorative stamp and the British Prime Minister Gordon Brown apologised for the abuse suffered by children emigrated to Commonwealth countries.

The increased pressure on governments on both sides of the Atlantic to address the history of child emigration policy was largely driven by public sentiment rather than by the institutions responsible or the British or Canadian national states. Public interest has intensified in both countries since the early 2000s as the children of emigrants have lost their parents, approach old age themselves, and embraced the genealogy and family history.[16] Oschefski has become one of the best-known campaigners after becoming involved in child emigration history and advocacy after her mother, then aged eighty-six, revealed that she was migrated as a child by the Salvation Army, leading Oschefski to find out that her grandfather was emigrated by Barnardo's, and that she had a total of thirteen British Home Children in her family.[17] Yet descendants of those emigrated as children continue to face significant barriers to finding out about their ancestors. Following the unveiling of the 2017 monument, one correspondent to the *Toronto Star* welcomed the press coverage of the 'forgotten dead' and acknowledged that 'many of us want to know to whom we are related but our birth right is denied. Even the simplest fact is elusive.' They noted that one British agency requested a fee of $200 to disclose the locations of their grandmother's farm placements so that 'Beside the abuse and death these young indentured servants suffered, is the severance of all they knew and how that legacy continues.'[18]

However because of the work of committed advocates such as Oschefski and members of the BHCARA, there is far greater awareness of the history of child emigration, particularly by means of well-resourced websites that offer free information and sources aimed at family historians and descendants of home children.[19] Their achievements in bringing this knowledge to light have ensured that British Home Children have a more prominent role in public history in recent years, such as the 'beacon of light' tribute in 2019 for the scheme's 150th anniversary that saw the illumination of iconic landmarks such as Niagara Falls and Toronto's CN Tower.[20] There has also been some interest in Britain where an exhibition titled 'On their own: Britain's child migrants' was featured at Merseyside Maritime Museum between October 2014 and 2015, and London's Museum of Childhood from October 2015 to June 2016.[21] Yet the story of British Home Children remains less central to British public history, perhaps because more recent episodes of emigration to Australia and South Africa featured more prominently in Humphreys's book. She notes in that text that she notes that she purposefully chose to shift her investigative work away from Canada after realising those emigrated were of advanced elderly age.[22]

Greater public acknowledgement of the abuses caused by the Indian residential school system has followed a similar chronology and has also relied on the campaign work of survivors and their descendants, especially former students who made abuse claims against the government in the 1990s and early 2000s. This activism led to the Indian Residential Schools Settlement Agreement in 2006, according to which the government agreed to pay compensation to all former students and established the Truth and Reconciliation Commission of Canada (TRC) to document the harms caused by residential schools. The TRC acknowledged the 'cultural genocide' perpetuated by the residential school and charted the harsh living conditions many children endured, citing inadequate food, clothing, heating, and poor medical care. A 2012 TRC report quoted survivor George Manuel, who attended the Kamloops school c. 1930s, 'hunger is both the first and the last thing I can remember about that school … Every Indian student smelled of hunger.'[23] Activists continue to campaign for greater acknowledgement of the sexual, physical, and psychological abuse that was prevalent. Peake Hall, a residential school that stood on the territory of Tseshaht First Nation, was considered one of the worst in the country and produced 'stories whose basis still keeps survivors awake at night, in fear, shame and dread.'[24] Ray Guno, a sixty-four-year-old Nisga'a from Terrace, a survivor of Peake Hall, participated in a ceremony held by Tseshaht Nation when the school was demolished and told researchers that 'Ten guys I know, some of them my closest buddies, died in the 50s. Not from natural causes, but from sexual, emotional and physical abuses.'[25] His testimony illustrates the significant harms that persist due to colonization; Indigenous peoples in Canada suffer from greater problems of ill health than other citizens as a result of the long-term damage caused by residential schools.[26]

Yet despite the increasing acknowledgement in Canada of the negative consequences of child emigration policies and the Indian residential school system, the commemoration of the harms caused against Indigenous children remains particularly contentious. Scholar Veldon Coburn, Anishinaabe and a member of the Algonquins of Pikwàkanagàn, notes the problematic politics of memory shaping 'who and what gets memorialized in Canada' particularly as 'part of the national myth of Canada' is the idea that it was an 'empty land without any people or present when settler communities arrived. These issues make it especially challenging for Canada to deal with the possibility of children's abuse and deaths at residential schools because it is an 'ugly history for the supposed … new world.'[27] Consequently residential school survivors and their descendants have articulated their frustration with the way their trauma has been represented. Michelle Daigle, a Mushkegowuk woman whose parents, grandparents, and great-grandparents experienced residential schools, described the anger she felt when the release of the final TRC report in 2015 created 'a spectacle of reconciliation' in Canada. Explaining how she was bombarded with media images of trauma and of white settler guilt, Daigle notes that the concept of reconciliation obscured the continued harms Indigenous families were subjected to, because 'the state's fetishization of Indigenous suffering tied to the *history* of residential schools masked the ongoing truths of the colonial present.'[28] Indigenous communities have highlighted the inadequacy of the financial compensation they have received as a way to repair the damage inflicted by residential schools and have criticised other forms of state-organised processes as doing 'little reunify and regenerate families and communities dispersed and dislocated by the trauma of these schools.'[29] Instead, communities have undertaken alternative forms of seeking justice such as storytelling, ceremonies on sites where schools had stood, and other community-driven methods to challenge the state-centred vision of reconciliation.

These tensions reflect the political role of public history in Canada more generally, especially in the context of global debates and anxieties about immigration, racism, and citizenship. The increased prominence of British Home Children in popular culture, public history, and heritage is both a product of generational interest in family history and a reflection of an impetus to reshape the public narrative of child emigration in ways that support the Canadian national story, perhaps in response to the ongoing trauma caused by the residential school system. As Canadian legal scholar Sherene H. Razack explains, central to the national mythology is the belief that 'Canada is a kinder, gentler and more pristine land. Significantly, the ultimate proof of the country's national character lies in its treatment of immigrants.'[30] Razack notes the impetus to bolster Canadian identity emerged prominently in the 1990s, and produced regressive regulations and tighter border controls to exclude undocumented or 'deviant' migrants.

Attempts to present Canada as a benevolent nation have therefore welcomed and made room for the history of child emigration in recent years because their experiences can be articulated in ways that endorse the idea that immigrants are welcome in Canada. Ivy Sucee, who describes herself as the 'proud daughter' of a Home Child and the founder and president of the Hazelbrae Barnardo Home Memorial Group in Ontario, states in her foreword to Rose McCormick Brandon's *Promises of Home*, a collection of biographies of Home Children, that 'a number of books have been written on how poorly the children were treated. But, seldom has the good side of their lives been written about or talked about. There was a good side ... The Home Children worked extremely hard. But, over the many years I've been speaking to Home Children and their descendants, I've found many who experienced fair treatment.'[31] This positive emphasis is part of a wider aspiration by their relatives to highlight their contributions as Canadian citizens and to present the experiences of British Home Children through narratives that distinguish the good and worthy emigrant from those deemed criminal or illegal. As Brandon states in her author's note to *Promises of Home*: 'It's time to cry over the abuses they suffered, to applaud their successes and to say, as a nation, "thank you."'[32] The collection of biographies in *Promises of Home* all emphasise a commitment to hard work and demonstrate the achievement of happy, worthwhile lives after the émigré has submitted to the value of hard work and self-sacrifice. One such was Ada Lamb Stinson

(1903–2004), who sailed via Liverpool to Quebec in 1913, where she became a music teacher. Ada is quoted in old age as saying, 'I feel that I was very lucky to get in a home like I did. I was taught to help others. I'm very thankful for all those years and now I'm one hundred.'[33] By emphasising fulfilment through a commitment to the Canadian nation, accounts such as this are attempting to change the otherwise negative image that so many British Home Children suffered.

The construction of these life stories reflects and reinforces national accounts more broadly. As editors Nicole Neatby and Peter Hodgins explain in the introduction to their collection of essays on Canadian public history, narratives 'typically followed a "colony to nation" storyline in which Canada's past is recounted as one of unbounded, incremental, and progressive success.'[34] They note that there was a renewed promotion of 'a unifying Canadian memory' from the 1990s as 'the best defence against the divisive narrations to come out of "popular memories" – more specifically, those of marginalized or silenced citizens.'[35] Yet, as we have seen, these tensions have intensified following the final TRC report in 2015, which formally acknowledged cultural genocide against Canada's Aboriginal peoples through the Indian residential school system.[36] Art historian Stephanie Anderson highlights the neglect of Indigenous peoples in Canadian museums and archives, but argues that often when exhibitions do recognise the harms experienced by Indigenous peoples, they use the narrative of reconciliation, 'thereby appropriating and weaving historically harmful policies and Aboriginal resilience into national storylines of social justice.'[37] The tension around the increased acknowledgement of the harms caused against Canada's Indigenous peoples and the cultures of national heritage are important in understanding the way that the British Home children are presented. Again, Razack argues that the 'forgetting or disavowal of bodies of colour in the national story secures specific material arrangements and simultaneously shapes dominant subjects' understanding of themselves as entitled and as good.'[38] The silences around the experiences of Indigenous people need further consideration, particularly, as Canadian legal historian Laura J. Kwak argues, 'anti-immigration discourses have expanded to include the figure of the "good immigrant."'[39] This narrative has become especially powerful in recent decades in light of broader anxieties about immigration and stricter border controls in Canada and alongside the increased public acceptance of the harms caused to Canada's Indigenous peoples.

These narratives around good citizenship have been reinforced through the representations of child emigration schemes in popular culture, which, in turn, shapes its public history. In recent years there has been a proliferation of novels, primarily by Canadian female authors, that take the experience of child emigration as its central theme. Mostly aimed at a female readership, they offer storylines of hope and hardiness and often centre on stoic female protagonists, usually of Irish heritage (a nod to their whiteness), who reluctantly turn to deviant or criminal behaviours due to the death or destitution of their parents. The central characters are forced into residential institutions and subsequently emigrated to Canada, usually without the knowledge or consent of any surviving parents, where they bravely endure neglect and hardship until they are rewarded with their own domestic happiness. The belief that historical fiction provides a convincing portrayal of the past and its provision of an 'emotional journey' for readers is key to its success as a genre. Novelist Hilary Mantel stated in her 2017 BBC Reith lectures that readers of historical fiction are not looking for facts, but are 'actively requesting a subjective interpretation.'[40] The purpose of historical fiction, suggests Mantel, is 'to recreate the texture of lived experience: to activate the senses, and to deepen the reader's engagement through feeling.'[41] Novels focussing on British Home Children foreground emotional connections between readers and their characters and by providing opportunities to experience loss and redemption may also provide some emotional connection between descendants of migrant children and their relatives. Historical fiction may be 'a form of sentimental communion with the dead'[42] or, as Margaret Atwood suggests, it can be 'like questioning your dead great-grandparents.'[43] Storylines that encourage readers to feel the protagonist's losses, hardships, and happy ending can shape how they understand history. The influence of such novels on the public memory of child emigration schemes needs further investigation.

Historical novels have contributed to the Canadian narrative of child migration, which Razack explains as 'a practice that is highly dependent on the construct of the good immigrant who establishes Canada's essential goodness.'[44] As Tracey Loughran suggests, 'historical novels can exploit gaps in the historical record' and 'can fulfil an important political function in imagining dissident histories, or bringing alternative perspectives on the past to new audiences.'[45] That is, historical novels have contributed to the popular desire to know more about the experiences of child emigrants where official records have been scant or access to archives has been difficult. There has been an active process by advocates for British Home Children to help produce historical novels that reflect and reproduce dominant narratives of child emigration. Some of the best known were written with input from or in consultation with Canadian-based British Home Child networks. These include as Genevieve Graham's *The Forgotten Home Child* (2020) and Carrie Turansky's two books: *No Ocean Too Wide* (2019) and its sequel *No Journey Too Far* (2021).[46] Oschefski endorsed Graham's *The Forgotten Home Child*, for which she acted as a historical consultant, describing it as a 'skilfully written portrayal of a Home Child's experience that typified so many. The absence of any sugar coating makes this story come to life and brings a level of reality that is often lacking – an emotional journey well worth reading.'[47] Similarly, Oschefski stated that *No Ocean Too Wide* was 'an important historical lesson for her readers.'[48]

As we shall see, these novels conform to the heroic image of female lead characters of white ethnicity and working-class British backgrounds, who typically triumph over the hardships of emigration as children to find fulfilment in adulthood as dutiful and morally superior wives and mothers in Canada. In doing so, such fiction tries to make sense of the child emigration system and its role in the Canadian nation, but also risks homogenizing the varied and disruptive experiences of child emigration. These narratives are also mirrored in some autobiographical accounts and memoirs, which also demonstrate that citizenship was heavily gendered: female emigrants deliberately sought to distance themselves from accusations of sexual immorality and impropriety which tainted the experiences of many emigrant children in Canada into adulthood.

THE INVISIBLE BRIDGE

Both historical novels and memoirs draw on and engage with the ideology and imagery disseminated by emigrating institutions in both positive and negative ways. Born in Liverpool in 1910, Joe Ayre was sent to Mrs Birt's Sheltering Home in 1920 after running away with his brother from his violent, alcoholic stepmother. As we saw in chapter 3, Joe was emigrated to Canada in May 1923, where he was eventually reunited with his beloved brother Bill. Joe continued to live a peripatetic life after he was liberated from the emigration scheme, with periods spent unemployed and homeless in Canada and back in Liverpool punctuated by casual labouring and farm work. Joe's memoir makes clear his contempt for those in power, and he hints that he felt hoodwinked about why he had been placed in the Home, reflecting that: 'in later years I found out that Miss Birt the founder of the Home was a rich philanthropist who founded the home thinking she was helping waifs and strays, but in fact this institution was being used to attempt to reduce the amount of juvenile delinquency and to get kids like us off the streets and out of sight. Also to prepare us for immigration to the Colonies to provide the farmers with cheap labor.'[49]

In contrast, Cecilia Jowett claimed that when she was reunited with family, 'my aunt expressed her sorrow and regret that my father had neglected to tell the family about his children and our removal to Dr Barnardo's Orphanage, Today I do not regret it – I'm glad of it – else how could I write my small tribute to so great a world benefactor as Dr Barnardo?'[50] Both memoirists gesture at being grateful to the founders of their institutions, but Joe was explicit in denouncing the scheme as a form of exploitation that specifically targeted poor children. His narrative is suggestive of conflicted feelings, whereas Cecilia only stressed her gratitude to her 'benefactor'.

We see Jowett's sentiments mirrored in historical novels such as Graham's *The Forgotten Home Child*, in which the lead character, Winny, depicted in old age looking back to being emigrated as a young girl, is positive about Dr Barnardo, who had died before she entered one of his institutions. Winny explains that 'his plan to send children to Canada was supposed to be a good one. This country was young and it needed people, and England was overwhelmed by poor children with no foreseeable future. A win-win situation, you'd call it these days.' However she goes on to note that the lack of inspectors allowed 'a lot of people [to take] terrible advantage of the children in their care.'[51] On the other hand, another emigrated child character in the novel says, 'London's so crowded there's no room to breathe, and we was dirty, ragged waifs living off what we could steal. Somebody had to figure out what to do with us. As much as we hated it, the orphanage and Barnardo's fed us and took care of us, but they ran out of room. By sending us over here we reckon they thought they was doing the right thing for everyone. London gets cleaned up, the farmers here get help, and we get to live a better life.'[52] In contrast, Turansky's *No Ocean Too Wide* includes the character of a lawyer, Henry, sent to Canada to investigate the child emigration system, who acknowledges that, 'those who started it had good intentions, and probably most still do. But it's grown so large, and with the number of children emigrating, it's easy to see how some would slip through the cracks and come to a bad end.'[53]

In Naomi Finley's *The Forsaken Children*, sixteen-year-old Hazel is first seen living in a shack within a poor area of Liverpool 1921, where 'lying in sewage and puddles from last night's rain, an emaciated girl wept over her mother's body … The chittering and squeaking of rats drew my attention to the rodents picking at a child's carcass.' Whereas in Canada, 'I inhaled the air, not contaminated with the sewage and decay of Liverpool's slums but redolent with the scent of blooming summer flowers and fresh-cut grass.'[54] The common thread between these novels and memoirs by such as Jowett and Ayre is that they strived to explain the system as one that had aimed to rehabilitate, rather than punish, children. These authors were all writing in post-war Britain and North America: a time that saw the emergence of ideas about childhood as discrete life cycle alongside new child-centred approaches to education and citizenship.[55] The idea of separating children so dramatically from their families and putting them to hard physical work jars so significantly with these ideas about childhood that these authors interpret them as methods of reform and rehabilitation in order to make sense of the system. The acknowledgement that abuse did happen, with the caveat that it was almost inevitable in light of the sheer number of children emigrated, helps to explain the system in ways acceptable to contemporary audiences.

Popular narratives of child emigration emphasise the sense of rupture wrought by emigration, and the loneliness and isolation of children setting off to Canada. Cecilia Jowett's memoir makes the rather melodramatic recollection of being 'the lonely little five-year-old girl who came out from England so long ago, with just a ticket pinned to her coat by way of family. She was a small girl with a large determination. A strange world lay all about her, and in it she walked alone.'[56] Joe Ayre's account is quite different, as he noted his familiarity with the ship and recalled the sense of excitement he felt: 'What an adventure this was. I knew the ship as I had seen it many times there were few ships that came into Liverpool that we didn't know, but I never thought I would sail in one.'[57] Joe's account implies that he was at ease on the ship, perhaps because of his eagerness to be reunited with his brother as we saw in chapter 3, or because of his age: at twelve, he was considerably older than Cecelia. It also suggests that for children like

Joe, whose memoir tells us that he and his brother had roamed the city of Liverpool unsupervised from an early age, independence and self-sufficiency were not neccessarily new, or a dramatic break in their experiences. His testimony provides an interesting counterpoint to the conceptualisation of these children as victims of circumstance by demonstrating some children's agency and determination in shaping their own lives. For children in Liverpool especially, where the port and its ships suffused everyday urban life and where the training ship *Indefatigable*, which prepared boys for life at sea, sat prominently on the Mersey, the idea of setting sail was by no means unusual. Joe's uncle and Dad had been sailors and Joe, like many local children, understood the way of life on a ship. This perspective helps to us to understand Joe's ability to embrace the hospitality offered to him on board: 'The crew of the ship seemed to go out of their way to make the voyage enjoyable especially for the kids from Liverpool, for most of the crew it was their home port. The food was fabulous, eggs, bacon and pancakes and Maple Syrup and fresh fruit for breakfast, five courses at lunch and from soup to nuts for dinner. I ate like a hog. The crew organised games for the kids and I remember how good they were with the kids of the Europeans whose language they didn't know.'[58]

Children like Joe, and many others in port cities such as Liverpool, were so accustomed with tales of life at sea and too seeing the ships themselves that the voyage to Canada was not necessarily associated with loneliness or a sense of rupture with their home. And despite Cecilia's sense of loss, even regret, she remembered the journey as a 'tremendous adventure … the beautiful, scintillating icebergs, not too far away for us to see the colours caused by the sun on the ice, a whale blowing early one morning, the great green billows of angry water, and the friendly sea-birds along the route.'[59] The journey's dramatic distinction from life in Britain was presented by memoirists as a pivotal moment of transformation away from their old lives. By drawing on the language of adventure, these young travellers, like the children writing back to Britain from Canada in chapter 3, reproduced some of the missionary zeal of emigration institutions that emphasised the transformational powers of removing children from their old lives.

This sense of rupture appears repeatedly in child emigration novels, which often depict the separation from siblings or from living parents. Tanya Cooper's *Doll in the Woodpile* (2019) is based on the true story of Edith Farr, emigrated to Canada in 1908 aged eight after her destitute mother could no longer care for her. The novel emphasises

Edith's sense of loss as she departed for Canada, with Edith scorning the idea of a 'golden bridge' between Britain and Canada: 'I'm sure we would have confessed that this voyage did not feel as if there was any golden bridge beneath our feet, but rather an abyss of indescribable loneliness and longing for the wretched life we had left.'[60] Turansky's *No Ocean Too Wide* vividly depicts the powerlessness of families when children were taken into institutions through the story of three younger children sent to Canada whilst their mother is hospitalised and an older sister is away in service. One of the emigrated children, Katie, is sent to an isolated farm where she 'slept in the barn loft with the bats and mice ... working all day and never hearing a kind word.'[61] Katie is shown to deal with this loneliness – made worse because she remained separated from her three siblings – by forging a close bond with the farmer's abused dog, Charger. As Katie was near to death from pneumonia, the dog 'lay down beside her and rested his head on her arm with a sigh. Comforting warmth flowed through her. She was not alone' and 'every time she woke, she found him there beside her like a silent guardian, giving her assurance and peace.'[62] These kinds of bonds with animals appear regularly in child emigration novels. Another example is Cat, who 'did her part' in helping to care for a gravely injured emigrant farmhand 'by curling up tight between his shoulder and his neck.'[63] Claudia Soares has discussed how important pets were for children in institutions and for alternative forms of family life beyond that of the nuclear family, noting that 'animals offered some of the most significant bonds of childhood and young adult life for some children, and these relationships were likely to have been as affecting as ties with other friends, family, and kin.'[64]

In child emigration novels, bonds between animals and children help to counter the dominant themes of isolation and loneliness, reassuring the reader that lone children were still cared for. Cecilia Jowett gives an especially moving account of her relationship with her dog, Prince, whom she owned as an adult whilst nursing in remote areas of Canada. In fact, this is depicted as the only close relationship she had in her life. The penultimate two paragraphs of her memoir are devoted to describing Prince's death aged fifteen, in which she says that he was 'at all times my comfort in loneliness, and he waited for and welcomed me home at all times.'[65] Cecilia's account endorses Strange's, in which she argues that pets 'contributed to the lived experience of the working-class home with their tactile, material bodies and affective behaviours.'[66] Jowett, like the characters in fictionalised accounts of child emigration, is shown to have found a form of 'home' through a close bond with a pet, whilst their lives otherwise remained uncertain and unfixed. Here pets are positioned as a way of making – or in Lucinda Matthews-Jones's words – of 'unmaking' home – as an affective and imagined space in an otherwise turbulent and unsettled time.[67]

NARRATIVES OF ABUSE AND REDEMPTION

Most of the novels and popular representations of child emigrants in Canada highlight their tough working conditions, often at the hands of abusive and violent farmers. The film *Heaven and Earth* depicts a vicious clash between two teenage farm workers and their cruel boss after they complain about their poor treatment, and Lynn L. Clark's ghost story, *The Home Child*, depicts a haunting by the wife of an abusive farmer who had buried an emigrant teenage boy on the farm after he had drowned trying to escape the abuse he was suffering.[68] Graham's *The Forgotten Home Child* also describes a violent farmer that the protagonist, Jack, is placed with: 'the stick he used to punish them at will was always in plain sight. In the first couple of days, Jack had accidentally spilled a bucket of fresh milk, and Warren had descended on him with that stick. He'd borne those bruises for a week.'[69] Farmer Warren is shown to commit such a violent attack that he causes the death of another Home Child. This kind of abuse was seen in the tragic case of Charles Bradbury, a young farmhand who had been emigrated by Barnardo's and was found dead in 1897 in a burned-down barn, having had his throat slit.[70] Stories of violence and abuse also appear in autobiographical sources such as Joe Ayre's memoir, which described how his happiness at moving to a placement near his brother Bill was tempered by the abuse he received at the hands of his new boss, who 'was a big powerful man and no matter how much work I done he was never satisfied. I was very small for my age but he expected me to perform work that a fully grown man would only be capable of doing, and he often kicked me up the arse in a fit of temper.'[71]

Violence and abuse are widely accepted as part of the experiences of British Home children and feature heavily in child emigration novels. In Finley's *The Forsaken Children*, when Hazel arrives at the receiving home in Canada, she encounters Clara, a girl returned from the home she had been placed at because 'her flesh is seared with the marks of the hot poker the missus punished her with if she spotted so much as a speck of food on the clean dishes.'[72] In Graham's *The Forgotten Home Child*, a wealthy and influential farmer, Master Renshaw, is known for his violence, with one emigrant child explaining, 'He comes off as a friendly sort, but he's cruel with his Home Boys. He's locked them up without food for days, tied them outside in the winter. He's just rotten.'[73] Sometimes in these novels, cross-species love between Home Children and animals is contrasted with animals' treatment by abusive farmers. For example, in Finley's *The Forsaken Children*, sixteen-year-old Hazel is sent to live with the abusive Mrs Gagnon, who had already starved another teenage Home Child to death. One of the young farmhands abused at the hands of Mrs Gagnon notes that she once killed the family dog: She 'used to kick him for no reason at all. He was skeered [scared] of her, just like the rest of us.' One day, the boy explains, Mrs Gagnon was angry with husband because the farm crops were selling badly and she saw dog sleeping and fetched her shotgun. The dog was 'napping in the sun … shot him dead; she did it for no cause at all. Called him a lazy good for nothing.'[74]

This story reinforces Mrs Gagnon's psychopathic cruelty and the powerlessness of emigrant children, who were vulnerable to the moods and violence of those they were homed with. On the other hand, such storylines reinforce the humanity of British Home Children, who share food with and care for each other as well as the children they look after. For example, in *The Forsaken Children*, 'the baby needed his mother and sought one in Hazel.'[75] Cecilia Jowett's memoir spends little time describing her life as a child emigrant, so we learn almost nothing about her placements other than she 'slept under a gable roof' where a squirrel would come to feed; she looked after a baby; and 'washed the dishes and dusted; went to school; was loved, and made a nuisance of myself at times, I fear,' but maintained her focus on finding her family and 'to help suffering people.'[76] By hinting at her perseverance amid hard domestic work, Cecilia emphasised her narrative of stoicism and redemption, reinforcing her identity as a successful emigrant who became a worthy Canadian citizen.

Very commonly, narratives present the first placement children experienced as abusive, but following institutional processes, they are given a much more pleasant employer who treats them with kindness and generosity. For example, Gloria V. Phillips's *A Pilgrim Passing Through*, based on her family history, tells the story of Gottlob who is emigrated to Canada in 1901 after his widowed father remarries. During his first placement, the farmer treats Gottlob very poorly and makes him sleep in a freezing shed but, we are told, 'it had taken many letters home and several visits from the agent before word finally arrived that Gottlob would be moved to another farm.'[77] His next placement is with a couple who had lost their three children and feed and clothe Gottlob very well, treating him like a family member. Some novels narrate encounters between emigrant children and their adoptive families as moving from neglect to acceptance, as the emigrant child proves their commitment to transformation from errant waif to worthy Canadian citizen. In Graham's *The Forgotten Home Child*, Winny is at first beaten for asking for new boots, whipped for falling asleep in the day, and only eats if she gets to the leftovers before they are fed to the dogs. However, her mistress eventually allows Winny to attend school, where she thrives, and even supports her financially when she trains to become a nurse: '"I'm sure you are aware that when you first arrived here, I had rather low expectations. But despite my prejudices, you proved me wrong. You're wearing a sweater made from yarn you made. You can milk a cow with your eyes closed and practically juggle eggs. You're no longer the confused little girl I picked up at the train station almost two years ago but a smart, capable young woman on her way to becoming a nurse." She swallowed hard, and Winny felt the woman's fingers tighten around her own. "I know I wasn't easy on you. I know I was unfair – I see that now – and I'm sorry."'[78] Again, this pattern supports Canadian national narratives, in which the good immigrant is in opposition to 'the bad immigrant who forces otherwise generous people into taking stern disciplinary measures.'[79] According to this model, abuse is as an acceptable form of treatment for newly arrived children, who were considered inherently deviant and criminal until they demonstrated their commitment to the nation through hard work and patience.

Despite the emphasis on redemption, memoirs frequently stress how emigrated children were made to feel tainted by assumptions made by the Canadians. Joe Ayre recalled, 'I think they assumed I was illegitimate' and when he explained he had a family 'I think they thought I was lying, at least they seemed very much surprised.'[80] Cecelia Jowett includes this unpleasant experience as part of her narrative of stoicism and reconciliation, explaining her experiences as a nurse: '"Oh I'd never take a child like that into my home," I have heard the ladies say, "You never know how they will turn out." And there was

I, a graduate nurse, in their homes, rendering skilled assistance, perhaps saving or helping to save a life. Yet they didn't dream that I was one of "those children" once.'[81] In other accounts, emigrants continued to carry internalised shame into adulthood. Walter Gibson Goulding (1908–2014) stated 'it took me a long time to tell my two sons I was a Home Boy. I was ashamed to tell them. I hid my life so they wouldn't know they had an orphan boy for a father. But here I am know, God's given gift and I don't want to forget that.'[82] Joe notes that the discrimination felt constant: 'For a long time I was considered an outsider, and was referred to as that English Bastard' and whereas most boys his age would spend Sunday afternoons in swimming, 'it was sometime before I was accepted and allowed to swim at the water hole.'[83] He also depicts the violence emigrant boys were subjected by local farmers, explaining that 'they resented us because of the small wages we were obliged to work for, most of the farmers sons were big husky men and us lads being smaller usually got the worst of it.'[84]

Joe's account gives some sense of the relentless hostility British Home children experienced and how challenging it was to develop connections and relationships given the stigma attached to emigration. These themes also emerge in novels such as *The Forgotten Home Child* in which Jack, having escaped his abusive farm placement and drifting through Canada, is shocked by encountering so many others in the same situation. In one scene, Jack is so stunned by the news he doesn't notice the crust of bread Toby is offering to him. "I haven't seen many." "Aye, well." He gave Jack a cheeky grin and kept the crust for himself. "We don't go around talking about it, do we? 'Good morning, sir, the name's Toby and I'm a useless piece of garbage. How are you?' I dunno about you, mate, but I'm not fond of the subject."'[85] In *The Forsaken Children*, Charlotte refuses to tell her fiancé about her identity as a British Home Child, explaining 'I have spent my whole life being embarrassed about who I was – not wanted by anyone, made to feel dirty and no good. I've tried to forget where I came from and who I was because they ingrained it in me.'[86]

STIGMA AND SHAME

Popular representations of emigrant children have also reinforced the belief that they were associated with immorality and sexual promiscuity. The film *Heaven and Earth* includes a scene where two Canadian women discuss whether one of the emigrant girls, Megan, is pregnant, with one commenting pointedly, 'well of course the Home girls *are* like that.'[87] Interestingly, Margaret Atwood distanced herself from the film after a scene relating to sexual abuse was inserted against her wishes, explaining that 'It didn't seem to fit … 'It was more like a 20th century idea. Now those [Home] girls were raped, but it was usually by the farmer where they were placed. We had lots of stories like that, but we didn't have any like the type shown, with schoolboys.'[88] Atwood's observations expose the tensions between what viewers may have expected to see in the film – an illicit sexual relationship between two young emigrants – and what Atwood understood to be more historically accurate – the rape of a young woman at the hands of the farmer where they had been placed.

This incident gives some sense of how the alleged sexual immorality of emigrants had become entrenched in Canadian popular culture by the 1980s, despite it being far more likely that young women and girls were at risk from where they were placed. We also see the connotations of sexual immorality in fictionalised accounts such as *Doll in the Woodpile*, where Edith says 'there was an *us* and there was a *them*. And as long as I was in *their* home; or *their* school; or *their* church; I would always be a dirty little Home Child.'[89] This book includes a scene where a group of Home Children are taunted by local children as 'the girls whose mothers must have come from the brothels.'[90] The ill-treatment of emigrant girls is a common theme in novels; for example, when Hazel is told she is a 'street whore' and that 'you gutter rats should be thankful we open our homes to you. Nothing but thieves and whores.'[91]

Sexual abuse is addressed in child emigration novels but it tends to be shown alongside the suicide of victims. Graham's *The Forgotten Home Child* includes the tragic suicide of Mary when she is returned to her rapist, Master Renshaw, after having been made to give up her child fathered by him.[92] Similarly, in Finley's *The Forsaken Children*, Clara commits suicide after being abused by the farmer she is housed with. Whilst waiting to be sent to an asylum, she is returned to the receiving home, where she is described as tearfully ranting to herself, 'Worthless. Whore. Street trash.'[93] Fictional depictions of suicide by female characters, particularly by those considered to be 'fallen women,' is often understood by literary scholars as offering a form of redemption. As Margaret Higonnet asserts, 'rape has been affiliated with the breakdown of a woman's identity' and so 'suicide serves magically to purge the assaulted body, in a sense displacing responsibility for the violation.'[94] The trope of suicide following rape, therefore, helps to reconcile the innocence of emigrant girls in such novels by not letting them grow up.

We know that emigrated girls, many of whom were living in isolated farms or working alone for farming families, were raped and sexually abused, but their vulnerability could be overlooked as they were seen as already debased by the Canadians they encountered. Barbara Young's account of trying to untangle the truth about her grandmother's life as a British Home Child describes how her grandmother confided that she had been abused, but provided scant details. Young subsequently located her grandmother's records, which revealed she had received a lot of inspections during her first placement, inferring that there had been problems, and Young speculated that her grandmother probably had a child when she was aged about fourteen or fifteen.[95] This silence around her grandmother's life gives some sense of how women were shamed into keeping quiet about sexual violence. This topic, which remains erased from the popular memory of British Home Children, is never fully addressed by child emigration novels.

Consequently, for women who had been child emigrants, success tended to be associated with becoming respectable wives and mothers. Nellie Page Delaney (1897–1983) was emigrated after she woke up aged four to find her mother had died. She then spent several years begging on the streets with her blind uncle. One of her daughters testified that 'I'm proud of my mother because in spite of her challenges, she showed kindness to others. In her situation, many women would've become bitter, but she didn't. Without any role models to pattern her life after, she became a wonderful wife and mother.'[96] Similarly, Young notes, 'the grandmother I remember was a hardworking, capable woman and extremely clean in personal hygiene as well as her household. Careful with money, she waited until she could afford an item, then made it last. She was a good cook, who always used the best fresh ingredients. Most of all, she was very kind, although not demonstrative, to those she loved.'[97]

This narrative is particularly mirrored in child emigration novels such as *Doll in the Woodpile*, where Edith marries a fellow Home Child, Ernest, and they have eleven children who 'repaid to me every bit of love – and more so – than I ever game to them.'[98] Such stoic, self-sacrificing maternal figures dominated working-class models of domesticity and, crucially, distanced emigrant women from the inferences of sexual immorality. The novels tend to portray some kind of domestic fulfilment for the main female characters, who often find love and financial stability with more affluent men. In Finley's *The Forsaken Children*, Charlotte marries the wealthy Frederick, causing her sister to stress 'how lucky I was to capture the attention of a man like Frederick, with the means to care for me'.[99]

However, persistent connotations of sexual immorality and illegitimacy ensured that emigrant children hide their status even when they appeared to have made successful lives and careers for themselves. Peter Pearson, the producer of *Heaven on Earth*, began researching Home Children in the late 1970s and advertised in newspapers for survivors to come forward. He received around 750 letters, but noted that 'A lot of them wrote me to say, "this is the first time anybody knows this, that I am one of the children. My own children don't know and my grandchildren don't know." And often their spouses didn't know either. "They were very mortified by it."'[100] This secrecy reflected the ongoing discrimination many Home Children continued to experience as adults. For instance, Ada Lamb never told her children that she was a Home Child and refused to let them look inside her wooden trunk, symbolic of her emigration. As we saw earlier, Ada grew up to become a successful music teacher and is described as a 'community-minded woman' but continued to be treated as a lower-class citizen in later life. *Promises of Home* explains that her adopted parents wanted her to inherit their farm, but their relatives were furious: 'She was, they said, a mere Home Child with no right to inherit the Reburn property. The courts agreed and awarded the farm to the relatives.'[101] This xenophobia persisted throughout the emigrant child's life. George Higgins (1911–1981), who emigrated in 1920 aged nine, eventually inherited the farm he worked on and became fluent in French, 'but never felt completely accepted by the community. In old age, he said with sadness, "They still call me *the immigrant*."'[102]

It is also plausible that the stigma impacted children even when they returned to Britain. In 1936, when Joe Ayre returned to Liverpool and applied to the Public Assistance Board for unemployment relief, he was refused help and told to enter an institution instead. Joe explained that 'I became furious I had some choice words for the Chairman and his committee. The institution they wanted me to go to at one time had been the Workhouse, it was now a place for the aged and the infirm.'[103] The decision was only overturned by a magistrate who was baffled that the Board had chosen the more expensive option over outdoor relief (the payment of a small amount of money for the alleviation of poverty). However what was not said, that we can only infer from this unusual scenario, was that Joe's status as an emigrated child probably caused his poorer treatment from the Public Assistance Board.

Cecilia's memoir, in which she strongly reinforced her sense of belonging and Canadian citizenship, differs from the foregoing accounts. On her visit back to Britain as an adult, for instance, we are told that 'It was not easy to leave my old friends and patients, and as the train sped along I could hear the words of one man whom I had nursed through pneumonia, "God! Miss Jowett, we need you here, we will give you all the potatoes you need if you'll stay here."'[104] For Cecilia, good citizenship lay in her identity as a nurse who had undertaken work in remote parts of Canada with extreme winters. Cecilia presented herself as a success story of child emigration: 'I could not contemplate staying in England. I did not really like it as well as Canada.'[105] Her powerful account helps to explain why she has become such a figurehead for the descendants of British Home Children, who seek to draw attention to the positive contributions these emigrants made to Canada.

At the same time, there are tensions within these sources that show that emigrant children struggled to feel at home in either Canada or back in Britain, and which indicate how the destabilizing process of emigration had an impact on their identity that persisted into adulthood. Despite Cecilia's confident assertions that she would both 'make a place for myself in the great, cold world' and surround herself with family, she struggled to forge the relationship that she wanted with her brother Ernest.[106] After training as a nurse, Cecilia moved to a remote part of Ontario to be near her adult brother, who had also been emigrated as a child. They struggled to adjust to life together, and her memoir notes, 'I fear the earnestness of my housekeeping endeavours were a little too much for him at times' and as Ernest spent more time with other men at a camp, 'I was left to my own thoughts for many hours at a time.'[107] Joe Ayre enjoyed a happy relationship with his brother Bill, making significant financial sacrifices to ensure Bill got the medical treatment he needed. One of his sisters, Edie, aged twenty-two, joined them through a domestic service association and he remained clearly amused thinking back to her arrival, when 'she couldn't believe her own eyes' as Bill and Joe turned up as 'two typical farm workers dressed in bib and brace overalls and driving a horse and buggy. When the horse broke into a good fast trot she hung on for dear life scared out of her wits.'[108] On returning to Liverpool in the 1930s, Joe found his British citizenship was in doubt when he was detained by police and threatened with deportation because he had no passport: 'I was questioned by a surly old immigration officer who told me I had no right to land without a passport and that he could have me detained by the police. I told him he could do as he liked that I was born in Liverpool and I intended to land there come what may.'[109] He was only admitted when the police confirmed his identity with Barnardo's.

This was not an unusual scenario and adult emigrants could find themselves with little documentation. William James Lemmon (1908–1993) found it impossible to discover any information about his own background and required Barnardo's create a birth certificate for him, choosing a date of birth at random.[110] Young also puzzled at the lack of documentation her grandmother had , which led Young 'on a merry chase' when she tried to research her grandmother's life.[111] Young's account points to the ongoing sense of loss her grandmother experienced: 'her rooms were like those of a boarder, a transient who had few possessions, with no memorabilia of a family, such as could be found around our house' and describes how difficult her grandmother found it when she moved into foster family care in advanced age: 'dislocated again.'[112]

CONCLUSION

This chapter has explored the public history of child emigration. It has only relatively recently been acknowledged in the history and heritage of Canada and Britain, gaining prominence in Canada since the early 2000s. The work of British Home Child networks and local history groups in Canada has drawn attention to the experiences of the tens of thousands of destitute, abandoned, and orphaned children emigrated to Canada in the late nineteenth and early twentieth centuries. They have provided invaluable resources and support for the descendants of British Home Children seeking to learn more about family members. These networks have been crucial in seeking to challenge the negative stereotypes associating emigrated children with criminality and sexual immorality by bringing to light the contributions British Home Children made to Canadian public life as adults, and by revealing the difficult or even abusive experiences of children in the care of host families. These narratives are disseminated through the ceremonial and commemorative work of these networks, and also through the wealth of historical novels taking child emigration as their theme. Whilst promoting the history of child emigration history, however, they have sometimes overlooked the challenges that British Home Children experienced into adulthood, and reinforced the narrow and idealised image of the 'good immigrant' as a white, stoic, and self-sacrificing.

Comparing historical novels with autobiographical sources suggests that we need to provide a more nuanced public history of British Home Children. The figure of Cecilia Jowett, dedicated to caring for others in the most remote parts of Canada with only a dog for company, has taken a central role in the public history of child emigration. Similarly, historical novels reinforce the idea that most girls became dedicated caregivers in adulthood. Yet we know that other emigrants continued to experience isolation, dislocation, and difficulties in adult life. The public history of child emigration needs to acknowledge and incorporate the fractured and contradictory experiences and recollections that so many emigrated children seem to have. Finally, we need to examine the experience of emigrant children from Britain in relation to the important findings of the TRC of 2015, particularly the continued harms caused to Indigenous peoples through the Indian residential school system. The system of child emigration to Canada has recently been described as a 'very effective and intentionally placed cog in the machinery of capitalist, racialized settler colonial expansion.'[113] But the traumas caused by both forms of intervention should not be pitted against each other. Rather, a more inclusive and diverse history of British Home Children can help to deal with other troubling and difficult episodes in the past. There is a pressing need to bring to light the trauma and abuse experienced by migrant and other marginalised children.

Conclusion

EM: 'Would you mind telling me again the story about how you got the trunk?'

DK: 'OK so I was in Halifax, in the military at that time, and I was chasing this around, and I found out that he went to this Stevenson's place in Kinburn, now I didn't even know where Kinburn was, and I went to the phone book and I aimed for I guess Kinburn, and I guess looked it up, and I found there was only one Stevenson listed in the phone book. I phoned them, and it was Elmer, the son. And he said "oh yeah, we have his trunk out in the barn." And they'd had it about 50 years by this time, and I went there, well my mother and I went there after my dad died so this would be say, [19]80, 81 maybe, something like that, and we got the trunk, and in there there was a tie, and you know a little bit of clothes, not much, but there was a bunch of old letters, and a lot of photographs, and that picture of my dad I showed you, that's one of the pictures that were in there, and I had them all developed – some were negatives, I had them all developed, and the letters talked about his brother, like letters he got from his brother, mainly from him I think its only from his older brother, and they were just general information like where the other kids were.'[1]

Shortly after his father's death, in 1981, Dennis Kelly and his mother visited the farm in Kinburn, Ontario, where his father had been placed as a teenage migrant from Liverpool. There, as he recounted nearly four decades later, they made a remarkable discovery. The Stevenson family had kept his father's trunk for fifty years: an astonishing find that would be the envy of most child migrants and their descendants. Offering mother and son, wife and descendant a material glimpse into the history of William Kelly's early life, the trunk was all the more important since William had been generally reluctant to talk about his childhood. The list of items in this trunk make for poignant reading. An old tie and a few clothes ('not much') afforded scant preparation for embarking on a new life in Canada, with its fierce summers and freezing winters. But more significantly, William had kept the letters and photographs that continued to connect him, however distantly, to the family from which he had originated – his brother – and the new family of fellow child migrants he had briefly acquired at the Liverpool Sheltering Homes during the 1920s.

'They were just general information like where the other kids were.' This brief description attests to the resourcefulness of child migrants in attempting to monitor each other's whereabouts, and safety, in their new country. It also underlines a practice and an ideology that is still difficult for us to understand today: how could tens of thousands of children, some just infants, have been forced to endure separation from their families only to then find themselves displaced from their institutional Homes' and friends on the other side of the world? This has been the central question at the heart of this book, prompting our efforts to analyse why the child emigration system flourished for so long in North West England during the period of 1860–1935. As we noted in the introduction, we began this project with a set of questions designed to help us explain the fates of the tens of thousands of children emigrated to Canada. Below, we summarise some of the answers we have offered.

(1) What were the primary reasons behind emigration schemes, and what were the priorities for child rescue work in the North West? What ensured the schemes' longevity – to what extent were they legitimised by social, cultural, political, economic, and/or legal structures at the time, and transnationally?

William Kelly's trunk reflects many of the answers to these questions. Donated by Dennis to the Merseyside Maritime Museum in Liverpool, it has since been on display as part of their exhibition on child emigration in the region.[2] As the online exhibition catalogue notes, 'This trunk was issued to William before departure. It contained a new set of winter and summer clothes, boots, handkerchiefs, needle and thread, a Bible and a copy of Pilgrim's Progress. All child migrants set out to their new lives with these few possessions.'[3] Furnished with only a few articles of practical use such as clothes, boots, and sewing materials to mend and maintain these items, child migrants were expected to be physically robust, thrifty, and resourceful. These were qualities that, as we have shown in this book (building on the insights of historian Ellen Boucher) were intrinsically linked to ideas of the British imperial racial stock.[4] Dispatched from Liverpool, a high-profile trading port, on an adventure to find their fortunes in the 'land of opportunity', working-class children's fates were represented by emigration agencies as admirable and enviable chances to contribute to the history and prosperity of the British Empire.

Crucially, it was proclaimed that such children could achieve religious and moral salvation only by leaving. This was communicated both through child emigration agencies' publicity leaflets and through the bible and the copy of John Bunyan's *Pilgrim's Progress* that children were given to take on their journey. The *Pilgrim's Progress* (1678) is an allegorical story of Christian faith in which 'the pilgrimage metaphor implies a final destination that is known, albeit obscurely, from the outset of the journey. According to this structure, a right path and a wrong path exist. The traveller's task is to discern the right path, the straight and narrow path of virtue, and to follow it without straying off into sin or temptation.'[5] Child migrants were to embark upon a test of character, faith, and morals by leaving for Canada, a challenge that was embraced by multidenominational child emigration organisations across Britain. Yet in Liverpool, which became the nexus for emigrating agencies, this ideology held particular resonance. As a city with a large Catholic population, whose social problems of poverty and crime were strongly associated with Irish immigration during the Victorian period, the notion of rescuing children from sinful parents and thereby preventing their likely descent into hell was a frequently stated goal of Catholic emigration innovators such as Father James Nugent. Indeed, the *Pilgrim's Progress* discouraged readers from looking backwards, since that would only serve to show the protagonist, Christian, the dangers he had already overcome.[6] Similarly, separation – in fact, severance – from parents, families, local community, and cities such as Liverpool and Manchester, was portrayed as vital to prevent children's turn to criminality.

(2) How was consent to emigration negotiated between parent, institution, child, and state? To what extent did children have agency to embrace, or resist, the experience of emigration and the putative new life it offered?

Charitable interventions in family life, underpinned by both religious organisations and state-funded industrial school, were significant in seeking to separate the child from the family in the child's alleged best interests. This separation was achieved first through institutionalisation, and subsequently legally, though the severing of the legal relationship between the child and the parent. Emigration represented the final, most practical stage of separation, through geographical distance. Effective severance of the child's relationship with any remaining birth family through emigration was seen as a desirable outcome, having significant effects on the regulation of children's status and relationships into the twentieth century. Removal of a child was (and remains) a key assertion of authority over the child, ostensibly seeking to secure a better outcome for them even if there was evidence that this was not likely to be achieved. This approach of regarding children as 'becomings' to be shaped, having regard to their undefined future and their capacity for productive citizenship, suffused the narrative surrounding child emigration, providing a significant spur to intervention.[7] This approach often ignored the child's current everyday 'being' including their remaining family (siblings in particular), their self-sufficiency, adaptability, and resilience. It underpinned the development of the law and policy in relation to child emigration, but also child protection more broadly. The battle over who held authority over the child to determine their future needs became central to this process.

Emigration of children as a form of welfare was achieved by charities that both exploited most working-class parents' inability to access the law to realise their parental rights and the lack of a legal framework to manage the encroachment of charity and state into the parent-child relationship.[8] At first, parents likely viewed charities as a godsend. Charities not only supported children exposed to harm and abuse within the family, but their welfare provision was also utilised by poor families. The use of charities as a form of welfare provision when in economic or other difficulty was important to many families' survival. However, attached to this strategy was the risk of judgment by the charitable institution of the child, the family, and their perceived needs. The lack of legal definition and lacuna in regulation over when intervention in family life was legitimate, or what forms of intervention were suitable, first enabled emigration and then left the child vulnerable to exploitative placement in Canada – even though some were lucky enough to find good homes and jobs there.

There was contemporary confusion over the status of children emigrated; that is, whether they were retained in Canada as contractual paid labour, or were adopted (see chapter 2). This too demonstrates the confused basis upon which authority was assumed over the child and consent obtained from the parent. It was not clear, even to those administering emigration schemes, whether children were to be found new families or merely found potential work placements. The concept of adoption was limited to simple *de facto* adoptions in England until the Adoption Act 1926, which permitted the legal assumption of parenthood by the adoptive parents and the removal of the birth parents' rights over the child.[9] The increasing regulation of circumstances through which parental authority could be removed meant that adoption too was legally formalised.[10] Legal adoption could then only be achieved with judicial oversight in order to ensure the welfare of the child, and required the informed consent of the birth parents, unless they were dead or had abandoned the child. Adoption in Canada is regulated on a provincial basis; it was first introduced in New Brunswick in 1878, and in all provinces of Canada by 1921.[11] The use of the term 'adoption' in placement arrangements was therefore ambiguous and informal and did not necessarily denote a care-based parent-child relationship.

Thus, despite the legal importance of parental rights during this period, the practical difficulties of challenging the processes leading to emigration of a child are best revealed by how few recorded instances exist of birth families' attempts to do so. One example, as we have written about elsewhere, was the case of Amelia Mason. In 1914, Liverpool Girls' Industrial School sought to emigrate the thirteen-year-old girl to Canada, having sought Amelia's consent from the Home Secretary under s.70, Children Act 1908. Complaints by the girl's father, extended family, and his MP, Stephen Walsh, eventually persuaded the Home Secretary to stop the emigration, but only because they were able to prove the child had an older 'respectable' brother (with no previous convictions for neglect), despite her father being labelled a drunk and a 'low blackguard.'[12] As in this case, preventing emigration required families to demonstrate extraordinary political networking, acumen, and financial capital, of which few were able to boast.

Another example of a successful refusal to emigrate, in 1881, was achieved by the courage of a boy named Daniel Lynch, who apparently acted alone. Lynch, of unspecified age, took the extraordinary step of defying the Local Board of Guardians, who noted that he 'assigns as his reason for refusing to go to Canada that he would rather not leave England and be separated from his sister who is in service in Hampshire.'[13] Lynch had managed to secure employment as a page with a wealthy patron in South Kensington, and it was this security with an upper-class sponsor, as well as Lynch's economic independence – betokening mature masculinity in the Victorian psychology of gender –that appear to have enabled him to refuse to consent to emigration. Lynch's resourcefulness was highly unusual, reinforcing the fact that securing children's informed consent was, in general, a token principle among emigration societies. Indeed, our project team have only discovered three such cases (including one failed attempt) in the thousands of records we have examined.

(3) Has the overwhelming scholarly emphasis on narratives of victimhood and abuse obscured the resilience and entrepreneurialism of children whose biological families were perceived as offering little emotional or practical support?

Child migrants began their lives in Canada under a cloud. The racialised language of the 'street arab' recurred frequently, and particularly in relation to children from England's industrial centres and Liverpool's label as the 'black spot on the Mersey.' To offset fears about racial decline among the working classes and to satisfy the cultural and political currency of white supremacy on both sides of the Atlantic, a system of selective emigration took place in which those selected to go to Canada and other British colonial territories were primarily white children who displayed no obvious signs of trauma, ill-health, or disability. Yet these 'Home Children' frequently discovered they could never escape the stigma of being portrayed as orphaned, abandoned, criminal, or sexually precocious. Treated as second-class citizens and sometimes physically and sexually abused, child migrants from the North West found that their ill-treatment was routinely ignored, or worse, actively institutionalised through the servile positions they were expected to embrace.

Bravely, children sought to make these experiences heard, even during a period when the language of abuse was alien, communicated in metaphor, or might actually further endanger children by revealing their knowledge of sexual matters. Surviving letters from child migrants to institutions and emigration agents articulated a mixture of emotions ranging from excitement to loss, home sickness, and hope for the future (often in the face of extreme adversity). Children cleverly navigated the expectation that they would only write home in positive terms, knowing their letters would serve as propaganda for the schemes, by using conversations about food or weather to reveal a deeper emotional state. Sometimes they risked violent punishments by misbehaving and running away, leaving members of the visiting clergy in the uncomfortable position of reporting children who were lost, neglected, and in need of further rescue – thereby undermining the whole rationale for the agencies' enterprise. Many revealed their trauma in later years through memoirs, autobiographies, novels, and art. In 2019, our project team collaborated with curator Sophie Dutton to provide historical context to an exhibition of works by acclaimed artist Madge Gill (1882–1961) at the William Morris Gallery in London. Gill, who was emigrated to Canada as a thirteen-year-old to work as a domestic servant, managed to save up her fare to travel back to England when she was eighteen. Gill's artworks became a vehicle for her to express the hardships she had experienced: ill-health, an unhappy marriage, and the loss of two children. They were created when (according to Gill) she was possessed by her spirit guide, whom she named 'Myrninerest'.[14] Rendered in incredible room-sized drawings, in knitting, and in fabric, Gill's works depicted 'the pale faces of discarnate and nameless women' swirling through space, externalizing her own sense of anonymity, mobility, and dissociation from society.

Such creativity afforded one of the few avenues for child migrants to express themselves, since they held little agency within the late-nineteenth and early-twentieth-century legal apparatus. As chapter 2 explored, the movement of children abroad created an unregulated and unmonitored space where there was opportunity for the exploitation and abuse of children without penalty or intervention. This was exactly the situation that the charitable intervention originally sought to correct in separating the child from the family, a hitherto unmonitored space. By preventing state intervention into family life whilst enabling local authorities, schools, and religious and philanthropic charities to remove children from their parents, the legal apparatus of emigration devolved responsibility for children's care onto a group of local officials. In turn, this practice ensured that in the urban centres of the North West, the powerful charitable marketplace could exert its full force in persuading working-class families that their children would live happier, more prosperous lives away from their care – and ultimately, with scant explicit consent, as part of entirely new families abroad.

(4) How far did money awarded through local patrons, and the payments of bonuses on numbers of children emigrated to shipping and emigration agents, underpin a commercial rationale for child emigration and create a distinctive economy of welfare in the North West region?

As other historians besides us have noted, children held an economic status within the emigration system. Although the Victorian period witnessed a new concept of childhood as a discrete life stage devoted to education and play, these experiences remained more frequently the privilege of the offspring of middle- and upper-class families.[15] Working-class children were economic units, expected to use their labour to offer financial support to their relatives and, ultimately, their nation and empire. As such, they were often dehumanised and expected to be grateful for the opportunity of gainful employment, under any circumstances. Sadly, child migrants appear to have realised this themselves. As chapter 4 illustrated, and in the case of Daniel Lynch above, debates over pay and a willingness to take their labour elsewhere most frequently gave children the chance to assert their worth and make decisions about their future. The administrative work of processing payments, securing bonuses on children emigrated, and disputes over financial fraud tended to characterise the bulk of conversations about the wider system.

Championed as a boon to the taxpayer in both countries, child emigration appeared perfectly designed to assuage fears of future generations being trapped in a cycle of unemployment at home, whilst driving the economic progress of Canada. It is therefore unsurprising that debates about welfare occurred only sporadically, whilst publicised instances of child abuse made little impact on the system's longevity. Admittedly, the economy of North West child emigration schemes was not a large one, but it sustained the operation of a local and national emigration business amongst a diverse range of institutions. From the shops that were commissioned to provide new sets of clothes for the children, to the fees paid in shipping costs, to the payments and bonuses collected by institutions, and finally, the disputed wages owed to children themselves, the child emigration system was an important cog in the region's charitable marketplace.

(5) What aspects of the original rationale for child emigration schemes can be seen to have endured in modern adoption law and twentieth-century child separation policies enacted towards other vulnerable groups?

As originally conceived in English law after 1926, adoption was intended to create a complete break between the birth parent(s) and child. This is known as a 'closed' adoption: one in which the child retains no contact with their birth family following adoption (now under the Adoption and Children Act 2002), and has been the form of adoption in England into the twenty-first century.[16] It is directly informed by emigration as a form of child protection and institutionalised care, providing a clear attempt to achieve this outcome through geographical distance. Closed adoptions were regarded as beneficial, providing for the development of a new family unit without the birth parent(s) relationship 'confusing' the child. This is not the practice in other jurisdictions which tend to provide for open adoptions, wherein the child retains contact with members of their birth family. The evidence suggests that for a child adopted from the care system, 'whose long-term needs cannot be met by returning to birth parents or relatives [they] need security, love, stability and to be "part of a family" – what has come to be known as a "sense of permanence" and belonging. However, they also need knowledge of their birth family and their personal and cultural history, and to be helped to come to an understanding of "why" they needed to leave their birth family and then become a member of another family.'[17]

It is this sense of belonging and the value attached to kinship networks that were so important to children emigrated to Canada, who in their correspondence sought information about siblings and staff at their former homes. Under section 51A of the Adoption and Children Act 2002, birth parents and other relatives can now apply for post-adoption contact with the child if the court gives leave. Organised contact can be direct (in person), or indirect (e.g. through letters). However, despite increasing evidence of the importance of contact for children's identity post-adoption, the English courts remain unwilling to allow contact, ordering only indirect contact with the birth family if any order is made at all.[18] Any contact should be supported, whether between children and their parent(s), and/or wider birth family (including for example, siblings, grandparents etc), and the adopted child should be given a full understanding of their life story.[19] Despite the modern potential for contact post-adoption, in practice there has been little to disrupt the narrative of enforced and complete separation from their birth family as being the best outcome for a child adopted from care. However, children themselves may now circumvent these restrictions by using social media to identify and contact birth family members, much as children on placement sought contact with their siblings and tried to maintain relationships through their correspondence from Canada.

Claims have also been made that modern English law has a system of forced adoptions, made without consent of the birth parent(s), which has obvious resonance with the removal of children abroad without parental consent.[20] The difficulties of assessing the risks posed to the child by their family relationships remain. Despite attempts through social work to embed a partnership between the state and parents to improve the circumstances of a child, separation of the child from the family is still central to child protection practice in England.[21] The Adoption and Children Act 2002 does allow for parental consent to the adoption to be dispensed with, but only in defined circumstances to secure the welfare of the child. The retention of the birth parent(s)' interest in what happens to the child is still important, despite the abrogation of the parental rights doctrine. It remains possible to place or adopt a child abroad, though the child now must have lived with the proposed adopters, normally in the UK, before they can be moved.[22] The movement and placement of children at risk of harm outside their home country, with or without their birth family, therefore remains a live global issue.[23] The difficulties of providing effectively for children who are taken into the care of the state (in some form) continue to represent some of the most challenging aspects of legal and social policy.

This book has sought to explore the aftermath of the child migrant system as depicted in both autobiographical and fictional form, and to investigate the lived reality of children within the child emigration system, so far as this remains possible. Access to these histories is necessary for two reasons. First, accessing records and information about how policies were created and individual decisions were reached, and the outcomes of such policies for the affected children, must be central to processes of accountability. The impact of charitable and state-condoned activities in separating children from their birth families is increasingly receiving examination in a range of contexts.[24] Maintenance of records, and their accessibility, are key to this process. Secondly, the campaigns and organisations associated with the history of child emigration, and advocacy on behalf of survivors, their families, and descendants, are embodiments of the importance of the history of family in creating current identities. The right to an identity is complex (and has been debated mainly in the context of determining biological or genetic origins e.g. on adoption, surrogacy, or secret births).[25] However, in 2006 (*Jaggi v Switzerland*) the European Court of Human Rights stated that: 'persons seeking to establish the identity of ascendants have a vital interest … in receiving information necessary to uncover the truth about an important aspect of their personal identity.'[26] The broader significance of the social history of an individual's family and the lived experience of their ancestors may also be central to individual identity, their sense of participation, and current citizenship.

Throughout this book, we have sought to demonstrate that the story of Britain's child migrants cannot be told simplistically in terms of 'heroes and villains,' nor 'survivors and victims.' For some children, the claims of emigration agents to provide them with an opportunity of a better life proved true; equally, not all child emigration agents and agencies were uncaring, with many showing a genuine determination to lift children out of poverty and remove them from families they viewed as unsafe.[27] To return to the wise words of Dennis Kelly, 'some of them had troubles also, of course. But some did rather well too.'[28] More significantly, child migrants were not passive actors in their own fates. In myriad ways, children endured, embraced, flourished, resisted, and reacted against their status as migrants. Here, it behoves us to return to William Kelly's trunk, and ask a simple question: how did it come to be left at Stevenson's farm?

EM: 'So what kind of home was it, like an agricultural farm, agricultural labour?'

DK: 'It was a farm, yeah. And I don't know how long he stayed there but in the early thirties he was on the move somewhere, and I think it was about maybe 1933 or 32, they were – him and his friend went to a dance, in Almonte, which is not far from Kinburn, and that was a Saturday night dance, and the next – they just kept right on going, they just never went back.'

EM: 'They never went back?'

DK: 'No.'[29]

William did not eschew the life of a farmer; indeed, he took the skills he had learned and made his way to Redbridge to work the harvests. There, he met Dennis's mother, got married in 1934, and built a house on the land her father gave them for a dollar. Later, following the birth of their children, William also ran the school bus for twenty years, and became the local postmaster. William Kelly's trunk, therefore, stands as the material embodiment of an act of courage and entrepreneurialism that symbolises the intergenerational reckoning with the history of child emigration and the work to understand the legacy of trauma and displacement experienced by many. Although this book has necessarily focussed on the lives of child migrants in their youth, seeking to understand how and why the system operated during the period 1860–1935 and its particular relevance to the history of North West England, it is the personal stories of the child migrants and their descendants that continues to be a source of inspiration.

Notes

INTRODUCTION

1 *Eighth Annual Report of the Father Berry's Homes* 1903, 6, Liverpool Hope University (henceforth LHU), NCA 005.
2 Patricia T. Rooke, R.L. Schnell, and Kenneth Bagnell respectively estimate the figure at 'more than 80,000,' whilst one of the earliest authors on the subject, Phyllis Harrison, estimated the number at 100,000. This figure is also referenced on the website of child emigration records on Libraries and Archives Canada, which states that 'between 1869 and 1932, over 100,000 children were sent from Britain to Canada through assisted juvenile emigration.' Rooke and Schnell, 'Imperial Philanthropy and Colonial Response,' 57; Bagnell, *The Little Immigrants*, 9; Harrison, ed., *The Home Children*, 17; 'Home Children, 1869–1932,' Libraries and Archives Canada.
3 Kohli, *The Golden Bridge*.
4 Ibid., 10.
5 Lynch, *Remembering Child Migration*, 42.
6 Belchem, *Merseypride*, 120.
7 See, for example, Parr, *Labouring Children*; Murdoch, *Imagined Orphans*; Rose, 'Raggedness and Respectability,' 136–50; Parker, *Uprooted*.
8 Harrison, ed., *The Home Children*; Bagnell, *The Little Immigrants*; Bean and Melville, *Lost Children of the Empire*; Humphreys, *Empty Cradles*.
9 The Prime Minister (Gordon Brown), 'Child Migration.'
10 Humphreys, *Empty Cradles*, 352, 372.
11 Ibid., 324.
12 Folkes, 'Moving beyond Shopping List Positionality.'
13 'Central Library Exhibition Marks 135 Years of Nugent,' Nugent Care, 22 November 2016.

14 'Nugent – 135 Years of Care,' Liverpool Hope University Library, 12 September 2016.
15 Koven, *Slumming*, 90.
16 Ibid., 88–139.
17 Kohli, *The Golden Bridge*, 379.
18 Ibid., 214.
19 Moss, Wildman, Lamont, and Kelly, 'Rethinking Child Welfare.'
20 Some records remain confidential under the Data Protection Act. The Finding Guide to the Nugent Care Archive at Liverpool Records Office can be accessed at the LRO, or by contacting: archives@liverpool.gov.uk.
21 'Retrieving Archives and Obtaining Birth Certificates,' Child Migrants Trust.
22 Swartz, 'Children In Between,' 78.
23 See British Isles Family History Society of Greater Ottawa, site hosted by Facebook, posts dated 21 May 2015 and 12 December 2019.
24 Lori Oschefski, 'About.'
25 Moss, 'Oral History interview with Dennis Kelly.' Reproduced here by kind permission of Dennis Kelly.
26 Lamb, '"Their Mother Is a Violent Drunken Woman",' 72.
27 Letter from Father Pinnington, Honorary Director, to Mr Yates, 21 October 1908, LRO: 364 Nugent Care Archives NUG 14/5.
28 Delap, '"Thus Does Man Prove His Fitness".'
29 *Father Berry's Homes, Third Annual Report and Balance Sheets*, 1894–95, 2, LHU: NCA 005.
30 Boucher, *Empire's Children*, 14.
31 Swartz, 'Children In Between,' 85.
32 Emigration Diary of Arthur Chilton Thomas (c. 1902–1906), entry dated 30 October 1904, LRO: 364 NUG/14/4.
33 University of Ottawa Law Library, Sessional Papers 17:59 Victoria A.1896, *Third Report of Work Under the Children's Protection Act of Ontario for the Year Ending December 31st, 1895* (Toronto, 1896), 47.
34 Ibid., 37–8.
35 Mukherjee, 'Indian Child Migration in the British Empire.'
36 Ayre, *The Socialist*, 21.
37 As reported in *Denton and Haughton Examiner*, 6 April 1889. On wider concerns about institutions proselytising children, see 'Proselytising in Boys' and Girls' Refuges,' *Manchester Guardian*, 16 March 1887; 'The Bishop of Salford on Proselytising in Workhouses,' *Manchester Courier*, 15 December 1896.
38 *Manchester Evening News*, 21 February 1887.

39 Shore, *Artful Dodgers*; Lamb, '"Their Mother Is a Violent Drunken Woman"', 51–8.
40 Soares, *A Home from Home?*
41 Lynch, *Remembering Child Migration*, 40.
42 Lamont, Moss, and Wildman, 'Reintegrating Agency.'
43 Bagnell, *The Little Immigrants*; Parr, *Labouring Children*; Kershaw and Sacks, *New Lives for Old*; Lynch, *Remembering*; Soares, *A Home from Home?*
44 Lynch, *Remembering Child Migration*, 12.
45 Independent Inquiry into Child Sexual Abuse, 'Child Migration Programmes: Investigation Report,' March 2018, HC954-II.
46 Wagner, *Children of the Empire*; Bean and Melville, *Lost Children of the Empire*; Constantine, 'The British Government'; Fink, 'Children of Empire'; Kershaw and Sacks, *New Lives for Old*; Parker, *Uprooted*; Boucher, *Empire's Children*.
47 Kershaw and Sacks, *New Lives for Old*, 35–6.
48 Dennis Kelly interview.
49 Soares, *A Home from Home?*
50 Home Children Canada, 'Our Story.'

CHAPTER ONE

1 The Very Reverend Canon Keating, 'Emigration Work in Canada,' in 'Emigration Diary of Chilton Thomas,' c. 1902, Liverpool Records Office (henceforth LRO), 364 NUG 14/4.
2 Letter to Father Cazeau from Bishop Lynch, February 1873, Archdiocese of Toronto Archives (henceforth ATA), AE0501.
3 Boucher, *Empire's Children*, 7; Rebecca Ward, 'An Alternative Approach to Child Rescue.'
4 Eekelaar, '"The Chief Glory"', 495–8; Lynch, *Remembering Child Migration*, 12.
5 Lynch, *Remembering Child Migration*, 11.
6 'Keating, William Frederick Rev.' Archive for the Roman Catholic Diocese of East Anglia
7 The Very Reverend Canon Keating, 'Emigration Work in Canada.'
8 Maxwell-Stuart and Oxley, 'Convicts and the Colonisation of Australia, 1788–1868.'
9 Bingham, Delap, Jackson, and Settle, 'Historical Child Sexual Abuse in England and Wales,' 416.

10 Davin, 'When Is a Child Not a Child?', 46; Hadley, 'Natives in a Strange Land', 413–14; Shore, *Artful Dodgers*, 132–47; Kershaw and Sacks, *New Lives for Old*, 13–15; Horn, *Young Offenders*, 67; Bates, 'From Suppression to Sponsorship', 509–10; Boucher, *Empire's Children*, 44.

11 Parr, *Labouring Children*, 88; see also chapter 4 on economy of schemes.

12 Letter to Father Cazeau from Bishop Lynch (February 1873), ATA: AE0501.

13 Eekelar, '"The Chief Glory"', 491.

14 Letter to Father Cazeau from Bishop Lynch (February 1873).

15 Independent Inquiry into Child Sexual Abuse, 'Child Migration Programmes: Investigation Report', (March 2018), 18–19, HC954-II.

16 Desrosiers, 'Raising the Age of Sexual Consent'.

17 Moss, Wildman, Lamont, and Kelly, 'Rethinking Child Welfare'.

18 Davin, 'When Is a Child Not a Child?', 51–2.

19 Frost, *Victorian Childhoods*, 143.

20 Ibid., 160.

21 Horn, *Young Offenders*, 158–61.

22 Heather Shore's magisterial *Artful Dodgers* devotes a full chapter to transportation and early reformation schemes involving emigration, which perhaps renders the absence of mention of the latter more surprising in other texts. See Horn and Shore (eds), *Becoming Delinquent*; Watkins and Godfrey, *Criminal Children*; Horn, *Young Offenders*, 96.

23 Davie, 'Criminal Man Revisited?', 4.

24 Friar Nugent Personal Notes Vol. 1, n.d., c. 1860, 2–3, LHU: Nugent Care Archive, Box 2.

25 Library and Archives Canada (henceforth LAC), RG25/198, Letter from F.P. Morley, Secretary of the Board of Trade for the City of Toronto, to Sir Wilfred Laurier, Premier of the Dominion, concerning the shipping of criminals from England to Canada, 24 March 1906; *Twentieth Report of Superintendent Neglected and Dependent Children of Ontario: Year Ending December 30th, 1912* (Toronto: L.K. Cameron, 1913), 14, UOLL.

26 *Child Welfare Acts as Amended to April 28, 1928, also Sections from the Criminal Code* (Toronto, 1928), 24, ATA: AE0524.

27 Belchem, *Irish, Catholic and Scouse*, 3.

28 Kay, *The Social Condition and Education*, 37.

29 Carpenter, *Our Convicts*, Vol. II, 344.

30 'Liverpool "Ripper" Crime', *Manchester Courier and Lancashire General Advertiser* (18 June 1909), 10.

31 Furnival, *Children of the Second Spring*, 241–2.

32 *Father Berry's Homes, Third Annual Report and Balance Sheets*, 1894–5, 2, LHU: NCA 005.

33 Wiener, *Reconstructing the Criminal*, 200–2.

34 Boucher, *Empire's Children*, 7.

35 *Sixth Annual Reports of the Homes for Catholic Friendless Youths*, 1897–1898, 28, LHU: NCA/005 Box 2.

36 Gillian Wagner, 'Barnardo, Thomas John (1845-1905), Oxford Dictionary of National Biography (23 September 2004), online at: https://doi.org/10.1093/ref:odnb/30600 [accessed 27 October 2023].

37 Appropriated as a marketing tool by a number of prominent domestic and international child rescue organisations including the Save the Children Fund, 'before and after' photographs' success can be measured in donations and the endurance of this strategy over time. However, as historians including Seth Koven have discussed, a public scandal engulfed Barnardo in 1877 when he was taken to court after being discovered to have posed children as workers in occupations in which they were never employed, and having torn their clothing to exaggerate neglect suffered on the part of their parents. Barnardo was acquitted, although he suffered enough criticism to claim no further photographs of the kind would be taken. Despite this, Laura Briggs notes that the stock images of humanitarian organisations into the later decades of the twentieth century still operated along these lines, problematically directing 'attention away from structural explanations for poverty, famine, and other disasters, including international, political, military and economic causes. [This strategy] mobilises ideologies of "rescue" while pointing away from addressing "causes."' Briggs, 'Mother, Child, Race, Nation,' 181; Hilton, 'Ken Loach and the Save the Children Film,' 366; Fehrenbach, 'Children and Other Civilians,' 165–99; Koven, *Slumming*, 129.

38 Baughan, '"Every Citizen of Empire Implored to Save the Children!",' 124; Nunn, 'Emotional Death,' 273–4.

39 Swain, 'Sweet Childhood Lost,' 202–8; Murdoch, *Imagined Orphans*, 130–1.

40 *Fourth Annual Reports of the Homes for Catholic Friendless Youths*, 1894–1895, 3, LHU: NCA/005 Box 2.

41 *Sixth Annual Reports of the Homes for Catholic Friendless Youths*, 1897–1898, 11 LHU: NCA/005 Box 2; *Ninth Annual Reports of the Father Berry's Homes*, 1901, 1, LHU: NCA/005 Box 2.

42 Myers, 'The Ambiguities of Aid and Agency,' 43.

43 Elementary Education Act 1880 (43 & 44 Vict, c.23); Snell, 'The Sunday-School Movement,' 140–1.

44 Wiener, *Reconstructing the Criminal*, 200–2.
45 Logan, 'A Suitable Person for Suitable Cases,' 133–4.
46 *Fourth Annual Reports of the Homes for Catholic Friendless Youths*, 1894–1895, 4, LHU: NCA/005 Box 2.
47 *Fifth Annual Report of the Homes for Catholic Friendless Youths*, 1896–1897, 3, LHU: NCA/005 Box 2; 'corner-man, n.' OED Online (Oxford: Oxford University Press, June 2016). As the entry notes, the *Daily News* of 10 April 1890 commented 'The ruffianism of Birmingham is unfortunately the ruffianism of the entire kingdom … If Birmingham has its claqueurs, Liverpool has its corner men.'
48 *Eleventh Annual Reports of the Father Berry's Homes*, 1903, 4–5, LHU: NCA/005 Box 2.
49 Boucher, *Empire's Children*, 14.
50 *Sixth Annual Reports of the Homes for Catholic Friendless Youths*, 1897–1898, 11, LHU: NCA/005 Box 2; *Seventh Annual Reports of the Homes for Catholic Friendless* Youths, 1899, 1, LHU: NCA/005 Box 2; *Ninth Annual Reports of the Father Berry's Homes*, 1901, 1, LHU: NCA/005 Box 2.
51 Swain, 'Sweet Childhood Lost,' 200; Smith, *The Government of Childhood*, 142.
52 *Seventh Annual Reports of the Homes for Catholic Friendless* Youths, 1899, 18, LHU: NCA/005 Box 2.
53 Ibid., 28.
54 *Eighth Annual Reports of the Homes for Catholic Friendless Youths*, 1900, 5, LHU: NCA/005 Box 2.
55 Davidoff, 'Gender and the "Great Divide",' 18.
56 Boyd, *Manliness and the Boys' Story Paper*, 15; Murdoch, *Imagined Orphans*, 131.
57 Murdoch, *Imagined Orphans*, 131; Tosh, *Manliness and Masculinities*, 177.
58 Boyd, *Manliness' and the Boys' Story Paper*, 131.
59 *Tenth Annual Reports of the Father Berry's Homes*, 1902; Arthur Chilton Thomas, 'Catholic Child Emigration to Canada', 4, LHU: NCA/005 Box 2
60 During 1902–04, following a report from the President of the Catholic Emigration Society, the Rev. Emanuel Bans, it became policy not to emigrate children under the age of twelve due to concerns about child exploitation within the labour market as well as the sexual vulnerability of pre-pubescent girls. Parker, *Uprooted*, 101–4.
61 Sessional Papers (No. 17), 62 Victoria, *Sixth Report of Work Under the Children's Protection Act Ontario for the Year Ending November 30th, 1898*, (Ottawa, 1898), 73–4, UOLL.
62 *Nineteenth Report of Superintendent of Neglected and Dependent Children*

of Ontario, Year Ending December 30th, 1911 (Toronto: L.K. Cameron, 1912), 94, UOLL.

63 'Liverpool Catholic Children's Aid Committee: Form of Application for the Emigration of a Child', c.1902, LRO: 364 NUG 14/6.

64 As Neil Davie argues, the theory of Criminal Anthropology propounded by Italian 'criminologist' Cesare Lombroso was highly influential in Britain, even though it was often ridiculed by the medico-psychiatric Establishment. Davie, 'Criminal Man Revisited?'.

65 'Liverpool Catholic Children's Aid Committee: Form of Application for the Emigration of a Child', c.1902, LRO: 364 NUG 14/6.

66 This logic applied more widely to female victims of rape in the Victorian era, who, in the process of explaining what had occurred to them, had to be careful to conceal any existing knowledge of sexual behaviours so that courts would regard them as purely innocent. See for example: Clark, *Women's Silence*, 46–52; D'Cruze, 'Sex, Violence, and Local Courts', 46–7; Bates, *Sexual Forensics*, 85.

67 *Salford Catholic Protection and Rescue Society: Emigration Branch, Chaplain's Visitation* Report, August and September 1890, 5, LRO: 364 NUG 14/9.

68 'Louisa' is the original name of the child; her case and the circumstances of her pregnancy are already a matter of open access public record via the Libraries and Archives Canada's Home Children Database, hence her name has not been anonymised beyond removing her surname. See Library and Archives Canada, 'Home Children Records (164656)'.

69 Letter from Rev. Hodnett to J.A. Donaldson, 10 December 1877, Archives of Ontario (henceforth AO): MS847/13.

70 Ibid.

71 Letter from Hodnett to D. Spence Esq., Immigration Office, 14 January 1878, AO: MS847/13.

72 Diamond, *Emigration and Empire*, 226.

73 Rose, *For the Sake of the Children*, 91–2.

74 See Humphreys, *Empty Cradles*.

75 Although scholars of child emigration have recorded many instances of abuse, understanding that a modern readership will recognise it as such, the thorny issue of how historical actors categorised these behaviours has been less explicitly discussed until the recent IICSA report, which concluded that the clear legal framework for prosecuting child sexual abuse from the 1880s should have provided ample conditions for its prevention (as noted above).

76 Boucher, *Empire's Children*, 24–5.
77 'Department of Agriculture: List of Pauper Children Reported Upon by W.J. Wills,' 1888, AO: RG2.
78 Ibid.
79 'Department of Agriculture: List of Pauper Children Reported Upon by R. MacPherson, 1888, AO: RG2.
80 Ibid.
81 Ibid.
82 Moss, Wildman, Lamont, and Kelly, 'Rethinking Child Welfare.'
83 *Salford Catholic Protection and Rescue Society: Emigration Branch, Chaplain's Visitation Report* (August and September 1890), Appendix 2, LRO: 364 NUG 14/9.
84 Ibid., 1.
85 Ibid., 4, 8; see also 11.
86 Ibid., 3.
87 Rev. Robert Rossall, 'Second Report of Children Emigrated to Canada' (31 October 1890), 5. LRO: 364 NUG 14/9,
88 *Salford Catholic Protection and Rescue Society: Emigration Branch, Chaplain's Visitation Report* (August and September 1890), Appendix 2, 1, LRO: 364 NUG 14/9.
89 Ibid., 16.
90 Ibid., 2.
91 Ibid., 15.
92 Strange, 'Tramp'; Cresswell, *The Tramp in America*.
93 Cresswell, *The Tramp in America*, 14.
94 *Salford Catholic Protection and Rescue Society: Emigration Branch, Chaplain's Visitation Report,* August and September 1890, Appendix 2, 1, LRO: 364 NUG 14/9.
95 *Nineteenth Report of Superintendent Neglected and Dependent Children of Ontario, Year Ending December 30th, 1911*, 101, UOLL.

CHAPTER TWO

1 'Report for 1880 of Miss Rye's Emigration Home for Destitute Little Girls: List of Children Received into the Home at Peckham during the year 1880, with their Placings out in Canada,' University of Liverpool Archives, D630-1-1-17.
2 Eekelaar, 'The Chief Glory,' 487–504.
3 Lamont, Moss, and Wildman, 'Who Cares?.'
4 Lynch, *UK Child Migration to Australia*, 25.

5 Lynch, *Remembering Child Migration*, 33.
6 British overseas settlement delegation to Canada, 1924, 'Report to the Secretary of State for the Colonies from the delegation appointed to obtain information regarding the system of child migration and settlement in Canada,' 4. Overseas Settlement Board, London School of Economics Archives, 1/sos/14.
7 Bondfield Delegation, British overseas settlement delegation to Canada, 1924. 'Report to the Secretary of State for the Colonies from the delegation appointed to obtain information regarding the system of child migration and settlement in Canada.' Overseas Settlement Board, London School of Economics Archives, 1/sos/14 Cmd.2285. See Lynch, *UK Child Migration to Australia*.
8 Cockburn, *Rethinking Children's Citizenship*, 98.
9 Ibid., 104.
10 See Behlmer, *Child Abuse and Moral Reform*.
11 Cockburn, *Rethinking Children's Citizenship*, 106.
12 Clapton, Cree, and Smith, 'Moral Panics and Social Work,' 197, 202.
13 'Autumn Appeal Miss Rye's Emigration Home for Destitute Little Girls 1876,' University of Liverpool Archives, D630-2-9-9.
14 Lynch, *Remembering Child Migration*, 32.
15 See Watkins, *Life Courses of Young Convicts*.
16 Annie Macpherson also pursued a similar emigration scheme for boys. See Parker, *Uprooted*, 10.
17 'Report for 1880 of Miss Rye's Emigration Home for Destitute Little Girls.'
18 Parker, *Uprooted*, 25–6.
19 Lamont, Moss, and Wildman, 'Who Cares?,' 45, 54.
20 'Fifth Annual Reports 1896–97: Homes for Catholic Friendless Youths.' Father Berry's Homes, LHUA: NCA 005.
21 s.62, Poor Law Amendment Act 1832.
22 See Parker, *Uprooted*.
23 Both the Nugent Trust and the Manchester and Salford Boys' and Girls' Refuges and Homes (now the Together Trust) exist as modern charities, fulfilling a range of roles for children including residential and community care. The Together Trust has completed extensive work to preserve and catalogue their historical work as part of the education aspect of their modern work, including the role that emigration played in their activities. See Together Trust, 'Our History.'
24 Together Trust, Emigration Files 1897.
25 *Ex parte Skinner*, 9 Moo 278.

26 *Re Agar-Ellis* (1883) 23 Ch D 317.
27 O'Halloran, *The Politics of Adoption*, 14.
28 *Barnardo v McHugh* [1891] AC 388. A divorced mother could acquire such rights by court order, though this was not a route open to working-class women even after the Matrimonial Causes Act 1857. See Cretney, *Family Law in the Twentieth Century*, 566.
29 *Talbot v Earl of Shrewsbury* (1840) 4 My&Cr 672.
30 Behlmer, *Child Abuse and Moral Reform*.
31 Cretney, *Family Law in the Twentieth Century*, 567.
32 Griffin, *Bread Winner*, 144.
33 *Re Agar-Ellis* 91883) Ch D 317.
34 Livesey, 'Reading for Character,' 43, 48.
35 Cretney, *Family Law in the Twentieth Century*, 567.
36 Ibid.
37 Vaccination Act 1853 made it compulsory for children to be vaccinated within the first three months of life.
38 Durbach, *Bodily Matters*, 56.
39 *R v Downes* (1875) 1 QBD 25, para 29.
40 Pimm-Smith, 'A New-born of Respectable Class,' 191.
41 Ibid., 199.
42 Murdoch, *Imagined Orphans*.
43 Pooley, 'Child Philanthropy.'
44 Lamb, '"Their Mother Is a Violent Drunken Woman".'
45 Soares, *A Home from Home?*, 101.
46 Ibid., 101.
47 Lamont, Moss, and Wildman, 'Who Cares?,' 63.
48 Soares, *A Home from Home?*, 116.
49 Pooley, 'Child Philanthropy,' 114.
50 The father had exclusive rights to determine questions of the child's upbringing which the mother, and even the court, could not interfere with. See Cretney, *Family Law*, 526.
51 *Barnardo v McHugh* [1891] AC 388. For a full account of the legal issues, see Lamont, Moss, and Wildman, 'Who Cares?,' 45–65.
52 Barnardo, 'Is Philanthropic Abduction Ever Justified? (1885), *Night and Day: A Monthly Record of Christian Missions and Practical Philanthropy*, 98.
53 s.3, Custody of Children Act 1891.
54 s.62, Poor Law Amendment Act 1834.
55 s.1, Poor Law Act 1889.
56 s.6(5), Prevention of Cruelty to Children Act 1894; subsequently s.21(6), Children Act 1908.

57 Godfrey, Cox, Shore, and Alker, *Young Criminal Lives*, 18.

58 s.9, Industrial Schools Act 1861. This was expanded further to include children whose parent(s) had been convicted of a felony under s.17, Industrial Schools Act 1866.

59 Godfrey, Cox, Shore, and Alker, *Young Criminal Lives*, 25.

60 Kidd, 'Civil Society or the State?,' 333.

61 s.1, Reformatory and Industrial Schools Act 1891. Subsequently, under s.70, Children Act 1908, the manager of an industrial school could dispose of a well conducted child by emigration 'as if the managers were his parents' with the consent of the Secretary of State and the child.

62 Report of the Departmental Committee on Reformatory and Industrial Schools, 1913, Cmd. 6838, 59.

63 Children emigrated at an early age saved considerable public funds: Liverpool Education Authority calculated a saving of £30,213 to the Treasury and £4,666 to the Local Authority. Report of the Departmental Committee on Reformatory and Industrial Schools, 1913, Cmd.6838, 59.

64 Report to the Secretary of State for the Home Department of the departmental committee on reformatory and industrial schools 1896, Cmd. 8204, 66.

65 s.3, Poor Law Amendment Act 1850.

66 s.70, Children Act 1908.

67 Letter from Mr Robert Parr, Director of NSPCC to Under-Secretary of State for the Home Office, 22 June 1910, NA HO45 10598 18863.

68 Letter from the Convent of the Golden Shepherd to the Liverpool Catholic Children's Aid Committee, 24 April 1903, 364 NUG-14-6 Emigration Correspondence, Liverpool Record Office.

69 Eekelaar, 'Victims or Threats?,' 68, 74.

70 Ferguson, 'Cleveland in History,' 152.

71 Soares, *A Home from Home?*, 107.

72 Father Berry's Homes, 'Ninth Annual Reports 1901: Father Berry's Homes,' LHU: NCA 005.

73 Lamb, '"Their Mother Is a Violent Drunken Woman".'

74 See, for example, Letter from GA Arthur Esq. Cokermouth to Secretary of State for the Home Department, 6 May 1910, NA HO45 10598 18863; where the decision to emigrate Grace Potts from a Barnardo's Home without the prior permission of her father was questioned.

75 Letter from Mr Robert Parr.

76 Under s.21(6), Children Act 1908.

77 Lamont, Moss, and Wildman, 'Who Cares?.'

78 'Report for 1880 of Miss Rye's Emigration Home for Destitute Little Girls,' 7.
79 Report to President of Local Government Board, by Andrew Doyle, Local Government Inspector, as to Emigration of Pauper Children to Canada, HC Paper 9, 1875, 11–12.
80 O'Halloran, *The Politics of Adoption*, 4.
81 Ibid., 10.
82 Report to President of Local Government Board, by Andrew Doyle.
83 See Lynch, *Remembering Child Migration*, 36–40.
84 Report to President of Local Government Board, by Andrew Doyle, 10.
85 Ibid., 13.
86 Ibid., 14.
87 Lynch, *Remembering Child Emigration*, 36.
88 'Pauper Children (emigration to Canada)': Reply of Mr Doyle to Miss Rye's Report on Emigration of Pauper Children to Canada,' 1877 HC 263, 13.
89 Ibid., 20.
90 Ibid., 27–8.
91 Ibid., 36.
92 Parker, *Uprooted*, 52. Guidance was eventually created by the Emigrants' Information Office; see 'Emigration of Children by Boards of Guardians: 1903,' Liverpool University Archives, d630-3-1-7.
93 'Pauper Children' 1.
94 (1890) 24 QBD 283.
95 'Pauper Children,' 5.
96 Maria Rye 'The Emigration of Infant Children to Canada: To the Hon. Sclater-Booth, President of the Local Government Board, December 1876,' Liverpool University Archives, D630-2-1-9.
97 First Report of the Select Committee of the Parliament of the Dominion of Canada on Immigration and Colonization,' Colonial Office, 1875, 15.
98 'Pauper Children,' 8.
99 See Article 1, Convention to Supress the Slave Trade and Slavery 1926, which reflects contemporaneous understandings of the concept of 'slavery' as ownership of the property of the enslaved person.
100 Lynch, *Remembering Child Emigration*, 37.
101 Fortieth Annual Report of the Local Government Board, 1910–1911, Part I: Administration of the Poor Law, the Unemployed Workmen Act, and the Old Age Pensions Act. 1911, Cmd. 5865, 28.

102 The reports had been conducted in 1909.

103 British overseas settlement delegation to Canada, 1924. Report to the Secretary of State for the Colonies from the delegation appointed to obtain information regarding the system of child migration and settlement in Canada. Cmd. 2285.

104 Lynch, *UK Child Migration to Australia*, 26.

105 Ibid., 139

106 Ibid., 4.

107 Ibid., 29.

108 Ibid., 13.

109 Ibid., 29.

110 Ibid., 10.

111 Ibid., 11.

112 Ibid., 47.

113 Ibid., 45.

114 Report to the Secretary of State for Dominion Affairs of the Inter-Departmental Committee on Migration Policy 1933–34, 49. Cmd. 4689.

115 Ibid.

116 s.4, Poor Law Amendment Act 1850; s.68 Poor Law Act 1930.

117 National Archives: MH57-67, Oct. 1935.

118 Ibid.

119 This was also the case in relation to subsequent child emigration schemes to Australia, leading Lynch to call this policy a failure; see Lynch, *UK Child Emigration to Australia*, 302.

CHAPTER THREE

1 Letter to Birt, 6 May 1899. Library and Archives Canada Birt letters MG28-1470 (hereafter MG28-1470).

2 Peters, *Victorian Orphans*; Boucher, *Empire's Children*; Parker, *Uprooted*; Kershaw and Sacks, *New Lives for Old*; Bean and Melville, *Lost Children*.

3 Letter, 16 July 1906. Archives of the Manchester and Salford Refuge (hereafter M189): M692.

4 Letter to Birt, 5 August 1900, MG28-1470.

5 Constantine, '"Dear Grace … Love Maidie"'; McCarthy, 'Personal Letters'; Gerber, 'The Immigrant Letter.'

6 Soares, *A Home from Home?*, 83–109; Swartz, 'Children's Experiences.'

7 Soares, *A Home from Home?*, 16.

8 Pooley and Taylor, 'Introduction,' 7.
9 Lamb, '"Their Mother Is a Violent Drunken Woman".'
10 Mair, *Religion and Relationship*, 175.
11 Swartz, 'Children In Between,' 84.
12 Gatrell, Ghoshal, Nowak, and Dowdall, 'Reckoning with Refugeedom,' 77–8.
13 Damousi, 'Child Sponsorship, Development and Aid,' 16.
14 *Manchester Guardian*, 29 March 1893, 3; *Manchester Guardian*, 13 April 1901, 5.
15 Damousi, 'Humanitarianism in the Interwar Years.'
16 Matthews-Jones, '"I Still Remain One of the Old Settlement Boys",' 195–211.
17 Wills, 'Delinquency, Masculinity and Citizenship,' 183.
18 Here, we build on Barbara Rosenwein's influential model of emotional communities: Rosenwein, *Emotional Communities*; Rosenwein, *Generations of Feeling*. For an insightful survey of this rich field, see Plamper, *The History of Emotions*.
19 Barron and Langhamer, 'Feeling through Practice,' 105.
20 Summerfield, *Histories of the Self*, 44–6.
21 Barron and Langhamer, 'Feeling through Practice,' 117. Mass Observation was a social research movement that was established in 1937 by anthropologist Tom Harrisson, film-maker Humphrey Jennings and journalist Charles Madge in order to create 'an anthropology of ourselves,' through the study everyday life in Britain.'
22 Steedman, *The Tidy House*; Greenhalgh, '"Till We Hear the Last All Clear"'; Benninghaus, "Mothers' Toil and Daughters' Leisure.'
23 Letter to Birt, 6 May 1899, MG28-1470.
24 Pavlakis, 'Reputation and the Sexual Abuse of Boys,' 332.
25 See Waller, *Democracy and Sectarianism*.
26 For ambitious Catholic fundraising campaigns, see the attempt to build the second largest cathedral in the world in 1930s Liverpool: Wildman, *Urban Redevelopment and Modernity*, 167–89.
27 *Liverpool Mercury*, 19 December 1894.
28 *Liverpool Daily Post*, 25 September 1902.
29 Pavlakis, 'Reputation and the Sexual Abuse of Boys,' 337–9.
30 See Ayerst, *Guardian*.
31 *Manchester Courier and Lancashire General Advertiser*, 19 April 1890. See also, *Liverpool Echo*, 16 September 1921; *Liverpool Journal of Commerce*, 3 May 1907; *Liverpool Daily Post*, 2 June 1913.
32 *Liverpool Echo*, 25 April 1887; *Manchester Evening News*, 22 April 1887;

Birkenhead and Cheshire Advertiser, 9 August 1884; *Liverpool Echo*,9 May 1884.

33 We used a range of key words to search all the North West based titles held by the British Newspaper Archive in addition to the *Manchester Guardian* archive.

34 Lynch, *UK Child Migration to Australia*, 33.

35 Swartz, 'Children In Between,' 81; Mair, *Religion and Relationship in Ragged Schools*, 174.

36 Roddy, Strange, and Taithe, *The Charity Market*, 97.

37 *Birkenhead News*, 19 November 1884. See also, *Liverpool Mercury*, 4 December 1888.

38 *Manchester Guardian*, 29 March 1893, 3.

39 *Manchester Guardian*, 21 March 1900, 3.

40 *Manchester Guardian*, 13 April 1901, 5.

41 Lynch, *Remembering Child Migration*, 47.

42 *Liverpool Weekly Courier*, 9 April 1881; see also *Liverpool Daily Post*, 8 April 1881.

43 *Liverpool Weekly Courier*, 16 April 1881; see also *Liverpool Mercury*, 13 April 1881.

44 *Liverpool Echo*, 27 May 1881; see also *Liverpool Weekly Courier*, 28 May 1881.

45 *Liverpool Echo*, 3 June 1881; see also *Liverpool Daily Post*, 4 June 1881.

46 *Liverpool Mercury*, 23 March 1883.

47 *Liverpool Mercury*, 16 December 1897.

48 'Boys' and Girls' Refuges,' *Manchester Guardian*, 5 April 1905, 12.

49 See Daunton, *Wealth and Welfare*, 521–73; Thane, 'The Working Class and State "Welfare" in Britain.'

50 *Manchester Guardian*, 4 November 1904, 12.

51 *Manchester Guardian*, 5 November 1904, 6.

52 *Manchester Guardian*, 26 November 1904, 6.

53 Ibid.

54 *Manchester Guardian*, 1 December 1904, 7.

55 *Manchester Guardian*, 3 December 1904, 6.

56 *Manchester Guardian*, 9 May 1905, 5.

57 *Manchester Guardian*, 18 March 1907, 5.

58 Thane, *Foundations of the Welfare State*; Atkins, 'School Milk in Britain, 1900–1934'; Pooley, 'Parenthood, Citizenship and the State.'

59 *Manchester Guardian*, 11 March 1908, 5.

60 *Manchester Guardian*, 9 March 1908, 5.

61 *Manchester Guardian*, 12 March 1908, 9.

62 *Manchester Guardian*, 4 April 1910, 12.
63 *Manchester Guardian*, 21 April 1910, 9.
64 *Manchester Guardian*, 4 February 1911, 6.
65 Soares, *A Home from Home?*, 94.
66 Letter, 28 December 1912, M189/7/2/3.
67 Marchmont Home Report Form, 30 July 1913; 16 July 1912, M189/7/3/20.
68 Mair, *Religion and Relationship in Ragged Schools*, 196.
69 Letter, 4 June 1899. M189/7/2/3.
70 Swartz, 'Children's Experiences,' 29.
71 Letter, 23 September 1900, M189/7/3/17
72 Ayre, *The Socialist*, 24.
73 Letter, 8 May 1903, M692.
74 Letter to Birt, 26 December 1893, MG28-1470.
75 Letter, 2 January 1913, M189/7/2/5.
76 Soares, '"Dear Sir, Remember Me Often If Possible",' 91.
77 Letter, 23 September 1900, M189/7/3/17.
78 Ayre, *The Socialist*, 21.
79 Letter, 14 February 1908, M189/7/3/20.
80 Birt letters, letter to Birt, 31 Oct 1895, MG28-1470.
81 Letter, 9 January 1911, M189/7/3/10.
82 Letter, 2 January 1913. M189/7/2/5.
83 Letter to Birt, 15 November 1897, MG28-1470.
84 Letter, N.D., M189/7/3/10.
85 Ayre, *The Socialist*, 22.
86 Letter, 1 April 1912, M189/7/3/10.
87 Swartz, 'Children's Experiences,' 29.
88 Letter, 23 September 1900, M189/7/3/17.
89 Boyd, *Manliness and the Boys' Story Paper*.
90 Letter, ND. Emigrated 1888, M189/7/3/1.
91 Letter, 28 November 1907, M189/7/3/20.
92 Letter to Wallace, 25 August 1908, M189/7/3/20.
93 Ayre, *The Socialist*, 26.
94 Hamlett, *At Home in the Institution*, 35–7.
95 Letter, 16 July 1906, M692.
96 Letter, 9 January 1911, M189/7/3/10.
97 Roper, *The Secret Battle*, 55; Matthews-Jones, '"I Still Remain One of the Old Settlement Boys"', 201.
98 Letter, 21 January 1901, M189/7/3/17.
99 Letter, 23 September 1900, M189/7/3/17.

100 Davidoff, *Thicker than Water*, 24.
101 Letter, N.D., M189/7/3/22.
102 Letter, 28 November 1907, M189/7/3/20.
103 Letter, 26 July 1911, M189/7/3/20.
104 Marchmont Home Report Form, 28 September 1918, M189/7/3/20.
105 Holtzman, 'The Pursuit of Married Love.'
106 Letter to Birt, 15 November 1897, MG28-1470.
107 Letter, N.D., M189/7/3/10.
108 Ibid.
109 MG28-1470, letter to Birt, 6 October 1898.
110 Soares, *A Home from Home?*, 93.
111 Ayre, *The Socialist*, 22.
112 Letter, 14 February 1907, M189/7/3/19.
113 Letter, 21 December 1909, M189/7/3/19.
114 'Correspondence,' *Manchester Guardian*, 21 April 1910, 9.
115 Ayre, *The Socialist*, 26–7.
116 Ibid., 39.
117 Ibid., 40.
118 Ibid., 43.
119 Letter to Birt, 5 August 1900, MG28-1470.
120 Letter to Birt, 6 May 1900, MG28-1470.
121 Letter to Birt, 5 August 1900, MG28-1470.
122 Letter, 28 November 1907, M189/7/3/20.
123 Letter, 14 February 1908, M189/7/3/20.
124 Marchmont Home Report Form, 10 May 1911, M189/7/3/20
125 Barron and Langhamer, 'Feeling through Practice,' 117.
126 Scheer, 'Are Emotions a Kind of Practice,' 214.
127 Carter, '"Experimental" Secondary Modern Education in Britain'; Tisdall, *A Progressive Education?*.

CHAPTER FOUR

1 Sessional Paper No. 25, Edward VII, A. (1908), 112. Archive of Dave Lorente (henceforth ADL).
2 British Home Children Research and Advocacy Association (BHCRAA), 'Canadian Government Bonus Paid for the Children.'
3 For a useful overview of the etymology and varied scholarly uses of the term 'moral economy' following E.P. Thompson, see Götz, '"Moral Economy".'
4 Hay, *The Origins of the Liberal Welfare Reforms*, 11.

5 Roddy, Strange, and Taithe, *The Charity Market*, 7.
6 Parr, *Labouring Children*, 11.
7 Strange, *Fatherhood and the British Working Class*.
8 *Father Berry's Homes: Tenth Annual Report*, 1902, 7. LHU, NCA 005.
9 Parr, *Labouring Children*, 88.
10 A similar relationship between charitable fundraising and local dignitaries is highlighted in Starkey, '"Temporary Relief"'.
11 Roddy, Strange, and Taithe, *The Charity Market*, 131, 134.
12 Shapely, 'Charity, Status and Leadership.'
13 Letter from Maria Rye to Hon. W. Hardy, 11 February 1880. AO: MS847/22.
14 Kershaw and Sacks, *New Lives for Old*, 21–3; ATA: Sessional Papers (No. 13), 61 Victoria, A1898. W.F. Boardman, 'Appendix: Memorandum of Juvenile Emigration', 1898, 5.
15 Kershaw and Sacks, *New Lives for Old*, 25–6.
16 Ibid., 24.
17 Letter from Maria Rye to Mr D. Spence, Immigration Office, Toronto, 26 December 1877. AO: MS 847/12.
18 Roddy, Strange and Taithe, *The Charity Market*, 2, 10–13.
19 Burley, 'Hardy, Arthur Sturgis.'
20 Letter from Hardy, Toronto, to Maria Rye, Niagara, February 1880. AO: MS 847/22.
21 Sangster, *One Hundred Years of Struggle*, 58–84; King, *Women, Welfare and Local Politics*; Moss, 'Sexual Harassment.'
22 Burton, 'States of Injury.'
23 Diamond, *Emigration and Empire*, 40.
24 *Father Berry's Homes: Tenth Annual Report*, 1902, 18. LHU: NCA 005.
25 *Father Berry's Homes: Eleventh Annual Report*, 1903, 4. LHU: NCA 005.
26 Rev. J. Bennet, 'Emigration of Catholic Boys and Girls,' Liverpool, 1929. LHU: NCA 122.
27 Perren, *Agriculture in Depression*.
28 Boyer and Hatton, 'Did Joseph Arch Raise Agricultural Wages?.'
29 Malchow, 'Trade Unions and Emigration,' 109.
30 *Boys Refuge Certified Industrial School (St. Anne's Street Liverpool) Finance Journal*, 1907–22. LRO: 364 NUG 5/8/1.
31 Letter to Mr Mitchell from Superintendent of Immigration, 21 July 1915. LAC: C7834.
32 Memorandum from G. Bogue Smart to Mr Scott, 13 December 1920, LAC, C7834; LRO: 364 NUG 1/12/10, *St. George's School Freshfield: Cash Book*, 1924–31.

33 'Report on Emigration 1930–31,' (1931); Rooke and Schnell, 'Imperial Philanthropy and Colonial Response,' 58. LHU: NCA 123.
34 'Report on Emigration 1930–31.' LHU: NCA 123.
35 *Boys Refuge Certified Industrial School (St. Anne's Street Liverpool) Finance Journal*, 1907–22. LRO: 364 NUG 5/8/1.
36 *Department of Agriculture: General Correspondence No. 47939*, 1885. LAC: RG17/439. Sir Hugh Allan, the founder of the Allan Line steamship company, had such a large personal wealth that he was able to donate $300,000 to the Canadian Conservative Party's campaign in 1872, precipitating the 'Pacific Scandal' over bribes of Canadian government officials. See "Sir Hugh Allan." *Encyclopedia Britannica*.
37 *Boys Refuge Certified Industrial School (St. Anne's Street Liverpool) Accounts Book*, 1914–21. LRO: 364 NUG 5/6/3.
38 Roddy, Strange, and Taithe, *The Charity Market*, 2.
39 ATA, Sessional Papers, 1924–1925: The Hon L.C.M.S. Amery M. P., Secretary of State for the Colonies and President of the Oversea Settlement Committee 'Oversea Settlement Delegation to Canada, 1924,' 1924, 17.
40 Eichengreen, 'The British Economy between the Wars,' 318–20.
41 Letter to Mr J.A. Donaldson from John McMurray, 27 April 1878. AO: MS847/14.
42 Letter to Mr D. Spence from J. Ealond, 10 May 1886. AO: MS847/22.
43 *Father Berry's Homes: Twelfth Annual Report*, 1904, Appendix 31. LHU: NCA 005.
44 Emigration Diary of Arthur Chilton Thomas, 1904, LRO: 364 NUG. 14/4; 'Father Foley, of Fallowfield'; Letter from Dr M. Feely to Mr Thomas of Canada, 16 July 1905.
45 Ibid., entry dated 13 November 1904.
46 Ibid.
47 Interview conducted by Margaret Humphreys with Florence, referenced in: Humphreys, *Empty Cradles*, 156–7; interview reprinted and transcribed at greater length, including the quote above, in Bean and Melville, *Lost Children of the Empire*, 11–12.
48 In an earlier article on this case in *History Compass*, the authors stated that the discrepancy was first discovered in September 1906 by W.T.R. Preston, but was found to be an error after further research; a correction was submitted to the journal accordingly. Eloise Moss, Charlotte Wildman, and Ruth Lamont, 'Reintegrating Agency.'
49 Letter from the Office of the Auditor General to Mr Beddoe, 20 December 1905, LAC: C7834; Sinclair, *Cordial but Not Cosy*, 34; Creighton, 'McDougall, John Lorn (1838–1909).'

50 1906, LAC: RG 25/198.
51 Roddy, Strange, and Taithe, *The Charity Market*, 89.
52 Ibid., 90–2.
53 Ibid., 92.
54 Ibid., 89; Strange, 'Tramp,' 245–6.
55 Letter from W.D. Scott to High Commissioner for Canada, London, England, 29 March 1906. LAC: C7834.
56 Reford, 'Smith, Donald Alexander, Reford, 1st Baron Strathcona and Mount Royal.'
57 Letter from W.T.W. Preston, Commissioner of Emigration, to the Right Hon Lord Strathcona & Mount Royal, 20 July 1906, LAC: C7834.
58 Letter from Mr Fostier, Acting Superintendent of Immigration, to the High Commissioner for Canada in London, 8 August 1906, LAC: C7834.
59 Letter from W.T.R. Preston, Commissioner of Emigration, 11–18 Charing Cross London, W.C., to The Right Hon. Lord Strathcona & Mount Royal, 1 September 1906, LAC: C7834. Letter also copied in LAC: RG 25/198, 1906.
60 Letter to W.D. Scott from Bruce Walker, Assistant Superintendent of Emigration, 17 November 1906. LAC: C7834
61 See, for example, Letter from Arthur Chilton Thomas to G. Bogue Smart, 31 October 1905, LAC: C7834.
62 Reford, 'Smith, Donald Alexander, 1st Baron Strathcona and Mount Royal.'
63 Kristen Guest, 'The Subject of Money'; On the interrelation of consumption, cultures of gifting, and masculinity earlier in the century, see Finn, 'Men's Things.'
64 The last letter regarding bonus payments addressed to Cecil Arden in the file is dated 30 March 1907, LAC: C7834.
65 Reverend Hudson, 'Catholic Emigration Association: Secretary's Report on the Change of Staff at the St. George's Home,' 18 November 1907, 3, LRO: 364/14/5.
66 Roddy, Strange, and Taithe, *The Charity Market*.
67 Letter from W.D. Scott to Reverend Mother Evangelist O'Keeffe, 15 July 1908, LAC: C7834.
68 See, for example, letters from O'Keeffe to Scott dated 14 July 1910, 5 October 1911, 17 January 1912, 23 September 1912, and 17 October 1916. LAC: C7834.
69 Letter from Reverend Mother Evangelist O'Keeffe to W.D. Scott, 7 July 1908, LAC: C7834.

70 Letter from W.D. Scott to Reverend Mother Evangelist O'Keeffe, 15 July 1908, LAC: C7834.
71 Letter from Reverend Mother Evangelist O'Keeffe to G. Bogue Smart, 6 January 1915, LAC: C7834; Letter from Reverend Mother Evangelist O'Keeffe to G. Bogue Smart, 15 December 1916, LAC: C7834.
72 Letter from W.D. Scott to Reverend Mother Evangelist O'Keeffe, 26 February 1917, LAC: C7834.
73 See chapter 1.
74 Letter from G. Bogue Smart to Reverend Mother Evangelist O'Keeffe, 18 March 1918, LAC: C7834.
75 Letter from Reverend Mother Evangelist O'Keeffe to G. Bogue Smart, 14 January 1919, LAC: C7834.
76 *St. George's Cash Book*, 1924–1931, LRO: 364 NUG 1/12/10.
77 *Boys' Refuge Finance Journal*, 1907–1922, LRO: 364 NUG 5/8/1.

CHAPTER FIVE

1 *Toronto Star*, 27 February 2016, 3.
2 British Home Children in Canada, 'British Home Children Park Lawn Monument.'
3 Truth and Reconciliation Commission of Canada, *They Came for the Children*, 10. See also Milloy, *A National Crime*.
4 Hanson, Gamez, and Manuel, 'The Residential School System.'
5 Wells, '"It Was Devastating."'
6 Truth and Reconciliation Commission of Canada, *They Came for the Children*, 29.
7 See https://bylinetimes.com/2022/12/07/red-tory-to-blue-labour-how-spiked-and-unherd-are-keeping-national-populism-alive/.
8 Rouillard, 'In Kamloops, Not One Body Has Been Found.'
9 Kennedy, 'Biggest Fake News Story in Canada.'
10 Flanagan, 'The Truth about Canada's Indian Graves.' See also: Stannus, 'The Mystery of Canada's Indigenous Mass Graves'; Reilly, 'The Myth of the Kamloops Mass Grave'; Kennedy, 'Biggest Fake News Story in Canada'; Kay, 'A Media-Fueled Social Panic Over Unmarked Graves'; Glavin, 'The Year of the Graves.'
11 Corntassel, Chaw-win-is, and T'lakwadzi, 'Indigenous Storytelling, Truth-telling, and Community', 151.
12 See: https://www.cbc.ca/news/politics/judge-approves-23-billion-first-nations-child-welfare-agreement-1.7006351.

13 Brandon, 'Cecilia Jowett.'
14 Jowett, *No Thought for Tomorrow*, vi.
15 Strange, *Fatherhood and the British Working Class*, 12.
16 de Groot, 'The Genealogy Boom'; Evans, 'Genealogy and Family History.'
17 Oschefski, 'Ups and Downs – British Home Children in Canada.'
18 Letters to the editor: *Toronto Star*, 4 March 2016, 14.
19 British Home Children in Canada, 'Home Page'; British Home Children Advocacy and Research Association. 'About'; Library and Archives Canada, 'Home Children, 1869–1932.
20 British Home Children Advocacy and Research Association, 'Beacons of Light.'
21 National Museums Liverpool, 'On Their Own: Britain's Child Migrants.'
22 Humphreys, *Empty Cradles*.
23 Truth and Reconciliation Commission of Canada, *They Came for the Children*, 31.
24 Tseshaht First Nation's Newsletter, 'Residential School Finally Offers Some Closure,' 1–2, 8. As quoted in Corntassel, Chaw-win-is, and T'lakwadzi, 'Indigenous Storytelling, Truth-telling, and Community,' 143. See also *They Came for the Children*, 39–42.
25 Corntassel, Chaw-win-is, and T'lakwadzi, 'Indigenous Storytelling, Truth-telling, and Community', 143.
26 Wilk, Maltby, and Cooke, 'Residential Schools.'
27 'Don't Call Me Resilient,' *The Conversation* podcast: EP 14, [00:01:00]
28 Daigle, 'The Spectacle of Reconciliation,' 704.
29 Corntassel, Chaw-win-is, and T'lakwadzi, 'Indigenous Storytelling, Truth-telling, and Community', 140. See also Coulthard, 'Subjects of Empire.'
30 Razack, 'Making Canada White,' 177.
31 Brandon, *Promises of Home*, Foreword, np.
32 Ibid., Author's Note, np.
33 Ibid.
34 Neatby and Hodgins, 'Introduction,' 12.
35 Ibid., 9.
36 Truth and Reconciliation Commission of Canada, *Honouring the Truth*.
37 Anderson, 'Museums, Decolonization, and Indigenous Artists,' 174.
38 Razack, 'Making Canada White,' 174.
39 Kwak, 'Still Making Canada White,' 468.
40 Mantel, 'The Day Is for the Living.'
41 Mantel, 'Can These Bones Live?.'
42 Wineapple, in Frank, Wineapple, Michaels et.al., 'Symposium on Historical Fiction', 21.

43 Atwood, 'In Search of Alias Grace,' 1511.
44 Razack, 'Making Canada White,' 174.
45 Loughran, 'Historical Novels,' 259.
46 British Home Children Advocacy and Research Association. 'About.'
47 Graham, *The Forgotten Home Child*, 3.
48 Turansky, *No Ocean Too Wide*, 3.
49 Ayre, *The Socialist*, 21.
50 Jowett, *No Thought for Tomorrow*, 92.
51 Graham, *The Forgotten Home Child*, 66.
52 Ibid., 130.
53 Turansky, *No Ocean Too Wide*, 64.
54 Finley, *The Forsaken Children*, 15, 41.
55 Tisdall, *A Progressive Education?*; Zahra, *The Lost Children*.
56 Jowett, *No Thought for Tomorrow*, vi–vii.
57 Ayre, *The Socialist*, 25.
58 Ibid., 25–6.
59 Jowett, *No Thought for Tomorrow*, 20.
60 Cooper, *Doll in the Woodpile*, 11.
61 Turansky, *No Ocean Too Wide*, 174.
62 Ibid., 249, 251.
63 Graham, *The Forgotten Home Child*, 120.
64 Claudia Soares, '"The Many Lessons Which the Care of Some Gentle, Loveable Animal Would Give",' 262.
65 Jowett, *No Thought for Tomorrow*, 103.
66 Strange, 'When John Met Benny,' 232.
67 Matthews-Jones, 'Translocal Homemaking.'
68 Clark, *The Home Child*.
69 Graham, *The Forgotten Home Child*, 76.
70 British Home Children in Canada, 'Charles Bradbury.'
71 Ayre, *The Socialist*, 42.
72 Finley's, *The Forsaken Children*, 45.
73 Graham, *The Forgotten Home Child*, 90.
74 Finley, *The Forsaken Children*, 159.
75 Ibid., 148.
76 Jowett, *No Thought for Tomorrow*, vii.
77 Phillips, *A Pilgrim Passing Through*, n.p.
78 Graham, *The Forgotten Home Child*, 166.
79 Razack, 'Making Canada White,' 174.
80 Ayre, *The Socialist*, 29.
81 Jowett, *No Thought for Tomorrow*, 20.

82 Brandon, *Promises of Home*, n.p.
83 Ayre, *The Socialist*, 37.
84 Ibid., 43.
85 Graham, *The Forgotten Home Child*, 160.
86 Finley, *The Forsaken Children*, 173.
87 Kroeker, *Heaven and Earth*.
88 Cooper, *Doll in the Woodpile*, 54.
89 *Toronto Star*, 28 February 1987.
90 Cooper, *Doll in the Woodpile*, 90.
91 Finley, *The Forsaken Children*, 135.
92 Graham, *The Forgotten Home Child*, 155–7.
93 Finley, *The Forsaken Children*, 77.
94 Higonnet, 'Suicide,' 109.
95 Young, *Chasing Grandma*, 44–5.
96 Brandon, *Promises of Home*, n.p.
97 Young, *Chasing Grandma*, 12, 13.
98 Cooper, *Doll in the Woodpile*, 195.
99 Finley, *The Forsaken Children*, 173.
100 *Toronto Star*, 28 February 1987.
101 Brandon, *Promises of Home*, n.p.
102 Ibid.
103 Ayre, *The Socialist*, 118.
104 Jowett, *No Thought for Tomorrow*, 89–90.
105 Ibid., 94.
106 Ibid., 2.
107 Ibid., 19.
108 Ayre, *The Socialist*, 48.
109 Ibid., 113.
110 Brandon, *Promises of Home*, n.p.
111 Young, *Chasing Grandma*, 11.
112 Ibid., 14, 119.
113 Johnson, 'Settler Colonial Structures of Domestication,' 3.

CONCLUSION

1 Moss, 'Oral History Interview with Dennis Kelly.'
2 National Museums Liverpool, 'Liverpool Sheltering Homes Trunk,' c. 1925.
3 Ibid.
4 Boucher, *Empire's Children*.

5 Bertsch, *Storytelling*, 23.
6 Swaim, *Pilgrim's Progress*, 40.
7 Uprichard, 'Children as "Beings and Becomings",' 307.
8 Skinner, *Behind Closed Doors*, 226.
9 Lowe, 'English Adoption Law.'
10 Chambers, *A Legal History of Adoption*, 13–14.
11 O'Halloran, *The Politics of Adoption*, 400; Chambers, *A Legal History of Adoption*.
12 These cases involve Grace Potts, emigrated without her father's approval in 1910 (following which her father, Robert Potts, attempted an unsuccessful appeal with the Home Office), and the above-mentioned case of Amelia Mason; see Lamont, Moss, and Wildman, 'Who Cares?.' See also Letter from Thomas Worlock to Rev. John Seddon re Daniel Lynch, 23 July 1881, ATA: AE05/07.
13 Letter from Thomas Worlock to Rev. John Seddon re Daniel Lynch, 23 July 1881.
14 Dutton, (ed.), *Madge Gill by Myrninerest*.
15 Frost, *Victorian Childhoods*.
16 O'Halloran, *The Politics of Adoption*, 27.
17 Thoburn, 'The Adoptive Kinship Network,' 235.
18 See Sloan, 'Post-Adoption Contact Reform.'
19 Ryan, 'Contact between Children in Care.' A similar practice of open adoptions has developed in the Canadian jurisdictions.
20 Lamont, Fenton-Glynn, 'Cross-border Public Care.'
21 First attempted in the Children Act 1948. See, for example, Lord Laming, *The Victoria Climbie Inquiry*; Part IV, Children Act 1989. See, for example, Broadhurst et al., 'Final Report: Vulnerable Birth Mothers and Recurrent Care Proceedings,' which reports on the use of repeat care proceedings to remove children at birth where the mother poses a significant risk, e.g. due to addiction. Individual mothers have had more than five children removed from their care at birth.
22 s.84, Adoption and Children Act 2002.
23 Lamont, 'Child Protection in International Family Law.'
24 UK Parliament Joint Committee on Human Rights (2022–23), *The Violation of Family Life: Adoption of Children of Unmarried Women 1949–1976*, (HC 270; HL 43).
25 Fortin, 'Children's Right to Know Their Origins.'
26 App.No.58757/00 (2006) 47 EHRR 702, para 38. The Court permitted a sixty-seven-year-old applicant to exhume the body of his putative biological father to confirm the relationship through DNA testing under a

right to identity derived from Article 8 ECHR, the right to respect for private and family life.

27 Moss, Wildman, Lamont, and Kelly, 'Rethinking Child Welfare.'

28 Dennis Kelly interview.

29 Ibid.

Bibliography

PRIMARY SOURCES

Manuscript Sources

Archdiocese of Toronto Archives.
Archive of Dave Lorente
Archives of the Manchester and Salford Refuge, the Together Trust and Manchester Central Library Local Archives
Birt letters MG28-1470, Libraries and Archives Canada
Department of Immigration and Employment Fonds, Libraries and Archives Canada
Ministry of Health, Overseas Settlement Office, The National Archives
Nugent Care Archive, Liverpool Hope University
Nugent Care Archives, Liverpool Record Office, Liverpool Central Library
Overseas Settlement Board 1/SOS/14, London School of Economics Archives
Papers relating to Maria Rye's Emigration Home for Destitute Little Girls, University of Liverpool Archives
Records of the Department of Immigration, Archives of Ontario
Sir Wilfred Laurer Fonds, Libraries and Archives Canada

Newspapers

Birkenhead and Cheshire Advertiser
Birkenhead News
Denton and Haughton Examiner
Guardian
Liverpool Daily Post

Liverpool Echo
Liverpool Journal of Commerce
Liverpool Mercury
Liverpool Weekly Courier
Manchester Courier and Lancashire General Advertiser
Manchester Evening News
Manchester Guardian
New York Post
New York Times
The Spectator
Toronto Star

Reports and Legislation

UK Parliament Joint Committee on Human Rights (2022–23), *The Violation of Family Life: Adoption of Children of Unmarried Women 1949–1976*, HC 270; HL 43.

'Child Migration Programmes: Investigation Report,' HC954-II, Independent Inquiry into Child Sexual Abuse, March 2018.

Adoption and Children Act 2002.

Child Welfare Acts, Amended to 28 April 1928.

Adoption Act 1926.

Adoption Act 1921 (Ontario).

Children Act 1908.

Children Act 1948.

Children Act 1989.

Children and Young Persons Act 1933.

Custody of Children Act 1891.

Elementary Education Act 1880.

Hansard.

Industrial Schools Act 1861.

Industrial Schools Act 1866.

Lord Laming, *The Victoria Climbie Inquiry: Report of an Inquiry by Lord Laming* (28 January 2003), [accessed 4 June 2023] https://www.gov.uk/government/publications/the-victoria-climbie-inquiry-report-of-an-inquiry-by-lord-laming.

Poor Law Act 1889.

Poor Law Amendment Act 1834.

Prevention of Cruelty to Children Act 1894; subsequently s.21(6), Children Act 1908.

Reformatory and Industrial Schools Act 1891.

Sections from the Criminal Code, Toronto, 1928.

Truth and Reconciliation Commission of Canada, *Honouring the Truth, Reconciling for the Future Summary of the Final Report of the Truth and Reconciliation Commission of Canada*, Ottawa, ON, 2015.

Truth and Reconciliation Commission of Canada, *They Came for the Children: Canada, Aboriginal Peoples, and the Residential Schools*, Ottawa, ON:, 2012.

Twentieth Report of Superintendent Neglected and Dependent Children of Ontario: Year Ending December 30th, 1912, Toronto: L.K. Cameron, 1913.

University of Ottawa Law Library, Sessional Papers 17:59 Victoria (A.1896), *Third Report of Work under the Children's Protection Act of Ontario for the Year Ending December 31st, 1895*, Toronto, 1896.

OTHER SOURCES

Anderson, Stephanie. 'Museums, Decolonization, and Indigenous Artists as First Cultural Responders at the Canadian Museum for Human Rights.' *Museum & Society*, 17 no. 2 (2019): 173–92.

Archive for the Roman Catholic Diocese of East Anglia, 'Keating, William Frederick Rev.'. (1859–1928), [accessed 1 August 2021]. https://archive.rcdea.org.uk/index.php/keating-william-f.

Atkins, Peter. 'School Milk in Britain, 1900–1934.' *Journal of Policy History*, 19 no. 4 (2007): 395–427.

Atwood, Margaret. 'In Search of Alias Grace: On Writing Canadian Historical Fiction'. *The American Historical Review* 103, no. 5 (1998): 1503–16.

Austin, Ian. 'Canada's Grim Legacy of Cultural Erasure, in Poignant School Photos.' *New York Times*, 5 July 2021, updated 27 October 2021. Accessed 16 June 2022. https://www.nytimes.com/2021/07/05/world/canada/Indigenous-residential-schools-photos.html.

Ayerst, David. *Guardian: Biography of a Newspaper* (London: Collins, 1991).

Ayre, Joe. *The Socialist*. Burnett Archive of Working Class Autobiographies, Brunel University, 1978. 24. Accessed 15 November 2020. http://bura.brunel.ac.uk/handle/2438/9360.

Bagnell, Kenneth. *The Little Immigrants: The Orphans Who Came to Canada*. Toronto: MacMillan of Canada, 1980.

Barron, Hester, and Claire Langhamer. 'Feeling through Practice: Subjectivity and Emotion in Children's Writing.' *Journal of Social History*, 51 no. 1 (2017): 101–23.

Bates, Rebecca. 'From Suppression to Sponsorship: Juvenile Emigration and the Preservation of Pre-Industrial Labour.' In *International Migrations in the Victorian Era*, edited by Marie Ruiz, 507–31. Leiden, NE: Brill, 2018.

Bates, Victoria. *Sexual Forensics in Victorian and Edwardian England*. London: Palgrave MacMillan, 2016.

Baughan, Emily. '"Every Citizen of Empire Implored to Save the Children!": Empire, Internationalism and the Save the Children Fund in Inter-War Britain'. *Historical Research* 86, no. 231 (2013): 116–37.

BBC Radio 4. 'Can These Bones Live? Hilary Mantel on Writing Historical Fiction.' BBC Reith Lectures 2017, part four. 6 July 2017. https://medium.com/@bbcradiofour/can-these-bones-live-b015dc8397c6.

– 'The Day Is for the Living: Hilary Mantel on Writing Historical Fiction.' BBC Reith Lectures 2017, part one. 13 June 2017. https://medium.com/@bbcradiofour/hilary-mantel-bbc-reith-lectures-2017-aeff8935ab33.

Bean, Philip, and Joy Melville. *Lost Children of the Empire*. London: Routledge, 1989.

Behlmer, George K. *Child Abuse and Moral Reform in England, 1870–1908*. Stanford, CA: Stanford University Press, 1982.

Belchem, John. *Merseypride: Essays in Liverpool Exceptionalism*. Liverpool: Liverpool University Press, 2000.

–. *Irish, Catholic and Scouse: The History of the Liverpool-Irish, 1800–1940*. Liverpool: Liverpool University Press, 2007.

Benninghaus, Christina. 'Mothers' Toil and Daughters' Leisure: Working-Class Girls and Time in 1920s' Germany.' *History Workshop Journal* 50, no. 1 (2000): 45–72.

Bertsch, Janet. *Storytelling in the Works of Bunyan, Grimmelshausen, Defoe, and Schnabel*. Woodbridge, GB: Boydell and Brewer, 2004.

Bingham, Adrian, Lucy Delap, Louise Jackson, and Louise Settle, 'Historical Child Sexual Abuse in England and Wales: The Role of Historians.' *History of Education* 45, no. 4 (2016): 411–29.

Boucher, Ellen. *Empire's Children: Child Emigration, Welfare, and the Decline of the British World, 1869–1967*. Cambridge: Cambridge University Press, 2014.

Boyd, Kelly. *Manliness and the Boys' Story Paper in Britain: A Cultural History, 1855–1940*. London: Palgrave Macmillan, 2003.

Boyer, George, and Timothy Hatton, 'Did Joseph Arch Raise Agricultural Wages?: Rural Trade Unions and the Labour Market in Late Nineteenth-Century England'. *Economic History Review* 47, no. 2 (1994): 310–34.

Briggs, Laura. 'Mother, Child, Race, Nation: The Visual Iconography of Rescue and the Politics of Transnational and Transracial Adoption.' *Gender and History* 15, no. 2 (2003): 179–200.

British Isles Family History Society of Greater Ottawa, site hosted by Facebook, posts dated 21 May 2015 and 12 December 2019. Accessed 23 August 2022. https://www.facebook.com/page/1497883484371 26/search /?q=Sayers.

British Home Children Advocacy and Research Association. 'About.' Accessed 23 August 2022. https://www.britishhomechildren.com /president-ms-lori-oschefski.

– 'Beacons of Light.' Accessed 22 June 2022. https://www.britishhome children.com/beacons-of-light-2019.

British Home Children in Canada. 'British Home Children Park Lawn Monument'. Accessed 22 June 2022. https://canadianbritishhome children.weebly.com/the-park-lawn-cemetery-monument.html.

– 'Canadian Government Bonus Paid for the Children.' Accessed 20 August 2021. https://canadianbritishhomechildren.weebly.com/bonuss-paid-for-children.html.

– 'Charles Bradbury.' Accessed 8 December 2022. https://canadianbritishhomechildren.weebly.com/charles-bradbury.html.

– 'Home Page.' Accessed 22 June 2022. https://canadianbritishhomechildren.weebly.com/.

Broadhurst, Karen, Claire Mason, Stuart Bedston, et al., 'Vulnerable Birth Mothers and Recurrent Care Proceedings,' Report for the Nuffield Foundation, 2–17.' Accessed 4 June 2023. https://www.nuffieldfoundation .org/wp-content/uploads/2019/11/a7pppykncjiwcpiovgbi6a2prk glcc7v.pdf.

Burley, David G. 'Hardy, Arthur Sturgis,' *Dictionary of Canadian Biography*. Toronto: University of Toronto/Université Laval, 2003, 13. Accessed 23 August 2021. http://www.biographi.ca/en/bio/hardy_arthur_sturgis _13E.html.

Burton, Antoinette. 'States of Injury: Josephine Butler on Slavery, Citizenship and the Boer War.' In *Women's Suffrage in the British Empire: Citizenship, Nation and Race*, edited by Ian Christopher Fletcher, Philippa Levine, and Laura E. Nym Mayhall, 18–32. London: Routledge, 2000.

Canadiana Héritage, *British Children Emigrated to Canada by Authority of Boards of Guardians 1880–1916*, RG76 C4a, microfilm T-537. Accessed 17 August 2022. https://heritage.canadiana.ca/view/oocihm.lac_reel_t537.

Carpenter, Mary. *Our Convicts, Vol. II*. London: Longman, Green, Roberts & Green, 1864.

Carter, Laura. '"Experimental" Secondary Modern Education in Britain, 1948–1958.' *Cultural and Social History* 13, no. 1 (2016): 23–41.

Chambers, Lori, *A Legal History of Adoption in Ontario, 1921–2015*. Toronto: University of Toronto Press, 2016.

Child Migrants Trust, 'Retrieving Archives and Obtaining Birth Certificates.' Accessed 18 August 2022. https://www.childmigrantstrust.com/services/retrieving-files-from-government-departments.

Clapton, Gary, Vivienne E. Cree, and Mark Smith, 'Moral Panics and Social Work: Towards a Sceptical View of UK Child Protection.' *Critical Social Policy* 33, no. 2 (2012): 197–217.

Clark, Anna. *Women's Silence, Men's Violence: Sexual Assault in England, 1770–1845*. London: Routledge, 1987.

Clark, Lynn L. *The Home Child: A Supernatural Novel*. Oxford Station, ON: The Plaid Raccoon Press, 2014.

Cockburn, Tom. *Rethinking Children's Citizenship*. Palgrave Macmillan: London, 2018.

Constantine, Stephen. '"Dear Grace … Love Maidie": Interpreting a Migrant's Letters from Australia, 1926–67.' In *Empire, Migration and Identity in the British World*, Edited by Kent Fedorowich and Andrew S. Thompson, 192–213. Manchester: Manchester University Press, 2013.

–. 'The British Government, Child Welfare, and Child Migration to Australia after 1945.' *Journal of Imperial and Commonwealth History* 30, no. 1 (2002): 99–132.

Cooper, Tanya. *Doll in the Woodpile: A Home Child's Journey from England to Canada in 1908*. CreateSpace Independent Publishing Platform: Kindle edition, 2017.

Corntassel, Jeff, Chaw-win-is, and T'lakwadzi. 'Indigenous Storytelling, Truth-telling, and Community: Approaches to Reconciliation.' *ESC: English Studies in Canada* 35, no. 1 (2009): 137–59.

Coulthard, Glen S. 'Subjects of Empire: Indigenous Peoples and the "Politics of Recognition" in Canada.' *Contemporary Political Theory* 6, no. 4 (2007): 437–60.

Creighton, Philip. 'John Lorn, McDougall (1838–1909).' *Dictionary of Canadian Biography*, vol. 13, Toronto: University of Toronto/Université Laval, 2003. Accessed 25 August 2021. http://www.biographi.ca/en/bio/mcdougall_john_lorn_1838_1909_13E.html.

Cresswell, Tim. *The Tramp in America*. London: Reaktion Books, 2001.

Cretney, Stephen. *Family Law in the Twentieth Century: A History*. Oxford: Oxford University Press 2003.

Daunton, Martin J. *Wealth and Welfare: An Economic and Social History of Britain, 1851–1951*. Cambridge: Cambridge University Press, 2007.

Daigle, Michelle. 'The Spectacle of Reconciliation: On (the) Unsettling

Responsibilities to Indigenous Peoples in the Academy.' *Environment and Planning D: Society and Space* 37, no. 4 (2019): 703–21.

Damousi, Joy. 'Child Sponsorship, Development and Aid: PLAN and UNICEF in Australia, 1945–1975.' *History Australia* 17, no. 4 (2020): 711–27.

– . 'Humanitarianism in the Interwar Years: How Australians Responded to the Child Refugees of the Armenian Genocide and the Greek-Turkish Exchange'. *History Australia* 12, no. 1 (2015): 95–115.

Davidoff, Leonore. *Thicker than Water: Siblings and their Relations, 1780–1920*. Oxford: Oxford University Press, 2011.

– . 'Gender and the "Great Divide": Public and Private in British Gender History'. *Journal of Women's History* 15, no. 1 (2003): 11–27.

Davie, Neil. 'Criminal Man Revisited? Continuity and Change in British Criminology, c. 1865–1918.' *Journal of Victorian Culture* 8, no. 1 (2003): 1–32.

Davin, Anna. 'When Is a Child Not a Child?' In *Politics of Everyday Life: Continuity and Change in Work and the Family*, edited by Helen Corr and Lynn Jamieson, 37–62. Basingstoke, GB: MacMillan, 1990.

D'Cruze, Shani. 'Sex, Violence, and Local Courts: Working-Class Respectability in a Mid-Nineteenth Century Lancashire Town.' *British Journal of Criminology* 39, no. 1 (1999): 39–55.

de Groot, Jerome. 'The Genealogy Boom: Inheritance, Family History and the Popular Historical Imagination.' In *The Impact of History? Histories at the Beginning of the 21st Century*, edited by Pedro Ramos Pinto and Bertrand Taithe, 21–34. Routledge: London, 2015.

Delap, Lucy. '"Thus Does Man Prove His Fitness to Be the Master of Things": Shipwrecks, Chivalry, and Masculinities in Nineteenth- and Twentieth-Century Britain.' *Cultural and Social History* 3, no. 1 (2006): 45–74.

Diamond, Marion. *Emigration and Empire: The Life of Maria S. Rye*. London: Garland Publishing, 1999.

Durbach, Nadja. B*odily Matters: The Anti-Vaccination Movement in England, 1853–1907*. Durham, NC/London: Duke University Press, 2004.

Dutton, Sophie (ed.). *Madge Gill by Myrninerest*. London: Rough Trade Books, 2019.

Eekelaar, John. 'The Chief Glory: The Export of Children from the United Kingdom'. *Journal of Law and Society* 21, no. 4 (1994): 487–504.

– . 'Victims or Threats? Children in Care Proceedings.' *The Journal of Social Welfare and Family Law* 4, no 2 (1982): 68–82.

Eichengreen, Barry. 'The British Economy between the Wars.' In *The Cam-*

bridge Economic History of Modern Britain Volume 2: Economic Maturity 1860–1939, edited by Roderick Floud and Paul Johnson, 314–43. Cambridge: Cambridge University Press, 2004.

Encyclopedia Britannica, 'Sir Hugh Allan.' Accessed 19 December 2022. https://www.britannica.com/biography/Hugh-Allan.

Evans, Tanya. 'Genealogy and Family History.' In *A Companion to Public History*, edited by David Dean, 175–85. Chichester, GB: John Wiley & Son, 2018.

Fehrenbach, Heide. 'Children and Other Civilians: Photography and the Politics of Humanitarian Image-Making.' In *Humanitarian Photography: A History*, edited by Heide Fehrenbach and Davide Rodogno, 165–99. Cambridge: Cambridge University Press, 2015.

Finley, Naomi. *The Forsaken Children (The British Home Children Book 1)*. N.P.: Huntson Press, 2021.

Fink, Janet. 'Children of Empire: The Alignments of Church, State and Family in the Creation of Mobile Children.' *Cultural Studies* 21, no. 6 (2007): 847–65.

Finn, Margot. 'Men's Things: Masculine Possession in the Consumer Revolution'. *Social History* 25, no. 2 (2000): 133–155.

Flanagan, Tom. 'The Truth about Canada's Indian Graves.' *Unherd.Com*, 29 June 2022. Accessed 12 May 2023. https://unherd.com/2022/06/the-truth-about-canadas-indian-graves/.

Folkes, Louise. 'Moving beyond Shopping List Positionality: Using Kitchen Table Reflectivity and In/visible Tools to Develop Reflexive Qualitative Research'. *Qualitative Research* (2022) doi: 10.1177/14687941221098922.

Fortin, Jane. 'Children's Right to Know Their Origins – Too far, too fast?' *Child and Family Law Quarterly* 31, no.3 (2009): 336–55.

Frank, Edwin, Brenda Wineapple, Katharine Michaels, et. al. 'Symposium on Historical Fiction'. *The Threepenny Review*, 149 (2017): 20–3.

Frost, Ginger. *Victorian Childhoods*. Santa Barbara, CA: Praeger, 2008.

Gatrell, Peter, Anindita Ghoshal, Katarzyna Nowak, and Alex Dowdall. 'Reckoning with Refugeedom: Refugee Voices in Modern History.' *Social History* 46, no. 1 (2021): 70–95.

Gerber, David. 'The Immigrant Letter between Positivism and Populism: American Historians' Uses of Personal Correspondence.' In *Epistolary Selves: Letters and Letter-writers, 1600–1945*, Edited by Rebecca Earle, 37–55. Aldershot, GB: Routledge, 1998.

Glavin, Terry. 'The Year of the Graves: How the World's Media Got It Wrong on Residential School Graves.' *National Post*, 26 May 2022. Accessed 12 May 2023. https://nationalpost.com/opinion/the-year-of-the-graves-how-the-worlds-media-got-it-wrong-on-residential-school-graves ?ref=quillette.com.

Godfrey, Barry, Pamela Cox, Heather Shore, and Zoe Alker, *Young Criminal Lives: Life Courses and Life Chances from 1850*. Oxford: Oxford University Press, 2017.

Götz, Norbert. '"Moral Economy": Its Conceptual History and Analytical Prospects'. *Journal of Global Ethics* 11, no. 2 (2015): 147–62.

Graham, Genevieve. *The Forgotten Home Child*. New York: Simon & Schuster, 2020.

Greenhalgh, James. '"Till We Hear the Last All Clear": Gender and the Presentation of Self in Young Girls' Writing about the Bombing of Hull during the Second World War'. *Gender and History* 26, no. 1 (2014): 167–83.

Griffin, Emma. *Bread Winner: An Intimate History of the Victorian Economy*. London: Yale University Press, 2020.

Guest, Kristen. 'The Subject of Money: Late Victorian Melodrama's Crisis of Masculinity'. *Victorian Studies* 49, no. 4 (2007): 636–7.

Hadley, Elaine. 'Natives in a Strange Land: The Philanthropic Discourse of Juvenile Emigration in Mid-Nineteenth Century England.' *Victorian Studies* 33, no. 3 (1990): 413–14.

Hamlett, Jane. *At Home in the Institution: Material Life in Asylums, Lodging Houses and Schools in Victorian and Edwardian England*. Basingstoke, GB: Palgrave Macmillan, 2014.

Hanson, Erin, Daniel P. Gamez, and Alexa Manuel. 'The Residential School System'. Accessed 5 May 2023. https://indigenousfoundations.arts.ubc.ca/the_residential_school_system/#what-were-residential-schools.

Harrison, Phyllis, ed. *The Home Children*. Winnipeg, MB: Watson and Dwyer, 1979.

Higonnet, Margaret. 'Suicide: Representations of the Feminine in the Nineteenth Century.' *Poetics Today* 6, no. 1/2, The Female Body in Western Culture: Semiotic Perspectives (1985): 103–18.

Hilton, Matthew. 'Ken Loach and the Save the Children Film: Humanitarianism, Imperialism, and the Changing Role of Charity in Postwar Britain'. *Journal of Modern History* 87, no. 2 (2015): 357–94.

Holtzman, Ellen. 'The Pursuit of Married Love: Women's Attitudes toward Sexuality and Marriage in Great Britain, 1918—1939.' *Journal of Social History* 16, no. 2 (1982): 39–51.

Home Children Canada. 'Our Story.' Accessed 23 August 2022. https://www.britishhomechildren.com/.

Horn, Pamela. *Young Offenders: Juvenile Delinquency 1700–2000*. Stroud, GB: Amberley Publishing, 2010.

Humphreys, Margaret. *Empty Cradles*. London: Doubleday, 1994.

Johnson, Morgan Brie. 'Settler Colonial Structures of Domestication: British Home Children in Canada.' *Genealogy* 5, no. 3 (2021): 1–10.

Kay, Jonathan. 'A Media-Fueled Social Panic over Unmarked Graves.' *Quillette*, 22 July 2022.

Kay, Joseph. *The Social Condition and Education of the People in England*. New York: Harper & Brothers, 1863. First published 1850.

Kershaw, Roger and Janet Sacks. *New Lives for Old: The Story of Britain's Child Migrants*. Kew, GB: National Archives, 2008.

Kidd, Alan. 'Civil Society or the State?: Recent Approaches to the History of Voluntary Welfare'. *Journal of Historical Sociology* 15, no. 3 (2002): 328–42.

King, Steven. *Women, Welfare and Local Politics 1880–1920*. Brighton, GB: Sussex Academic Press, 2006.

Kohli, Marjorie. *The Golden Bridge: Young Immigrants to Canada, 1833–1939*. Toronto: Natural Heritage Books, 2003.

Koven, Seth. *Slumming: Sexual and Social Politics in Victorian London*. Princeton, NJ: Princeton University Press, 2004.

Kroeker, Allan, dir. *Heaven and Earth*. Canada and the UK: Opix Films. Aired on BBC and CBC Television 1 March 1987. 100 minutes.

Kwak, Laura J. 'Still Making Canada White: Racial Governmentality and the Good Immigrant in Canadian Parliamentary Immigration Debates.' *Canadian Journal of Women and the Law* 30. no. 3 (2018): 447–70.

Lamb, Gillian. '"Their Mother Is a Violent Drunken Woman Who Has Been Several Times in Prison": "Saving" Children from Their Families, 1850–1900.' In *Children's Experiences of Welfare in Modern Britain*, edited by Siân Pooley and Jonathan Taylor, 49–72. London: University of London Press, Institute of Historical Research, 2021.

Lamont, Ruth. 'Child Protection in International Family Law and the Determination of Where a Child "Belongs" for the Purpose of Jurisdiction'. *Child and Family Law Quarterly* 34, no.4 (2022): 401–18.

Lamont, Ruth, and Claire Fenton-Glynn. 'Cross-border Public Care and Adoption Proceedings in the European Union.' *Journal of Social Welfare and Family Law* 38, no.1 (2016): 94–102.

Lamont, Ruth, Eloise Moss, and Charlotte Wildman. 'Who Cares? Welfare and Consent to Child Emigration from England to Canada, 1870–1918.' *Liverpool Law Review* 41, no. 1, (2020): 45–65.

Library and Archives Canada. 'Guide to Sending Organisations and Receiving Homes'. Accessed 17 August 2022. https://www.bac-lac.gc.ca/eng/discover/immigration/immigration-records/home-children-1869-1930/home-children-guide/Pages/guide-organizations-receiving-homes.aspx.

– 'Home Children Records (164656).' Accessed 1 August 2021. https://www.bac-lac.gc.ca/eng/discover/immigration/immigration-records/home-children-1869-1930/immigration-records/Pages/item.aspx?IdNumber=164656.

– 'Home Children, 1869–1932.' Accessed 23 August 2022. https://www.bac-lac.gc.ca/eng/discover/immigration/immigration-records/home-children-1869-1930/Pages/home-children.aspx.

Liverpool Hope University Library. 'Nugent – 135 Years of Care.' Accessed 23 August 2022. https://liverpoolhopelibraryblog.wordpress.com/2016/12/09/nugent-135-years-of-care/.

Livesey, Ruth. 'Reading for Character: Women Social Reformers and Narratives of the Urban Poor in Late Victorian and Edwardian London.' *Journal of Victorian Culture* 43, no. 9 (2004): 43–67.

Loach, Jim. dir. *Oranges and Sunshine*. Australia and the UK: See-Saw and Sixteen Films. Released on 1 April 2011 in UK and 9 June 2011 in Australia. 135 minutes.

Logan, Anne. '"A Suitable Person for Suitable Cases": The Gendering of Juvenile Courts in England, c. 1910–39.' *Twentieth Century British History* 16, no. 2 (2005): 129–45.

Loughran, Tracey. 'Historical Novels.' In *A Practical Guide to Studying History: Skills and Approaches*, edited by Tracey Loughran, 249–62. London: Bloomsbury, 2017.

Lowe, Nigel. 'English Adoption Law: Past, Present and Future.' In *Cross Currents: Family Law and Policy in the US and England*, Edited by Sanford Katz, John Eekelaar, and Mavis Maclean, 307–40. Oxford: Oxford University Press, 2000.

Lynch, Gordon. *Remembering Child Migration: Faith, Nation-Building and the Wounds of Charity*. London: Bloomsbury, 2016.

– *UK Child Migration to Australia, 1945–1970: A Study in Policy Failure*. London: Palgrave: 2021.

Mair, Laura. *Religion and Relationship in Ragged Schools: An Intimate History of Educating the Poor, 1844–1870*. London: Routledge, 2019.

Malchow, Howard L. 'Trade Unions and Emigration in Late Victorian England: A National Lobby for State Aid.' *Journal of British Studies* 15, no. 2 (1976): 92–116.

Matthews-Jones, Lucinda. '"I Still Remain One of the Old Settlement Boys": Cross-Class Friendship in the First World War Letters of Cardiff University Settlement Lads' Club.' *Cultural and Social History* 13, no. 2 (2016): 195–211.

– 'Translocal Homemaking and Home Unmaking in the Letter Memoir of

Alice Lucy Hodson.' *Women's History Review* Special Issue: Challenging Domesticity in Britain, 32, no. 4 (2023): 474–95.

Maxwell-Stuart, Hamish, and Deborah Oxley. 'Convicts and the Colonisation of Australia, 1788–1868.' *Digital Panopticon* (2017). Accessed 1 August 2021. https://www.digitalpanopticon.org/Convicts_and_the_Colonisation_of_Australia,_1788-1868.

McCarthy, Angela. 'Personal Letters, Oral Testimony and Scottish Migration to New Zealand in the 1950s: the Case of Lorna Carter.' *Immigrants and Minorities* 23, no. 1 (2005): 59–79.

McCormick Brandon, Rose. *Promises of Home – Stories of Canada's British Home Children*. Magnolia Press: Kindle version, 2015.

–. 'Cecilia Jowett: A Little Girl with a Big Dream.' Accessed 16 June 2022. https://littleimmigrants.wordpress.com/2013/01/30/cecilia-jowett-a-little-girl-with-a-big-dream/.

Milloy, John S. *A National Crime: The Canadian Government and the Residential School System, 1879–1986*. Winnipeg: University of Manitoba Press, 1999.

Moss, Eloise. 'Oral History Interview with Dennis Kelly,' Ottawa Public Library, 20 August 2018. Reproduced here by kind permission of Dennis Kelly.

– . 'Sexual Harassment, Victimhood and Affective Self-Fashioning in Victorian England: The Bolton Workhouse Scandal, 1889–1890.' *Gender & History* 32, no. 2 (2020): 46581.

Moss, Eloise, Charlotte Wildman, and Ruth Lamont. 'Reintegrating Agency, Regulation and the Economy into Histories of Child Emigration from North West England to Canada, 1860–1930.' *History Compass* 19, no. 1 (2021): 1–11.

Moss, Eloise, Charlotte Wildman, Ruth Lamont, and Luke Kelly. 'Rethinking Child Welfare and Emigration Institutions, 1870–1914.' *Cultural and Social History* 14, no. 5 (2017): 647–68.

Mukherjee, Sumita. 'Indian Child Migration in the British Empire.' *History Compass* 19, no. 8 (August 2021), e12687.

Murdoch, Lydia. *Imagined Orphans: Poor Families, Child Welfare, and Contested Citizenship in London*. New Brunswick, NJ: Rutgers University Press, 2006.

Myers, Kevin. 'The Ambiguities of Aid and Agency: Representing Refugee Children in England, 1937–38.' *Cultural and Social History* 6, no. 1 (2009): 29–46.

National Museums Liverpool. 'Liverpool Sheltering Homes Trunk,' c. 1925, donated by Dennis Kelly. Accessed 20 December 2022.

https://www.liverpoolmuseums.org.uk/william-kelly-child-migrant-liverpool-1909-1980.

– 'On Their Own: Britain's Child Migrants.' Accessed 22 June 2022. https://www.liverpoolmuseums.org.uk/whatson/merseyside-maritime-museum/exhibition/their-own-britains-child-migrants.

Neatby, Nicole, and Peter Hodgins. 'Introduction.' In *Settling and Unsettling Memories: Essays in Canadian Public History*, edited by Nicole Neatby and Peter Hodgins, 2–23. Toronto: University of Toronto Press: 2012.

Nugent Care, 'Central Library Exhibition Marks 135 Years of Nugent.' Accessed 23 August 2022. https://wearenugent.org/news/central-library-exhibition/.

Nunn, Heather. 'Emotional Death: The Charity Advert and Photographs of Childhood Trauma'. *Journal for Cultural Research* 8, no. 3 (2004): 271–92.

O'Halloran, Kerry. *The Politics of Adoption: International Perspectives on Law, Policy and Practice*. Cham, CH: Springer, 2021.

Oschefski, Lori. 'Ups and Downs – British Home Children in Canada.' Accessed 8 December 2022. https://upsanddownsofhomechildren.wordpress.com/lori-oschefski/.

Parker, Roy. *Uprooted: The Shipment of Poor Children to Canada 1867–1917*. Bristol, GB: Policy Press, 2008.

Parr, Joy. *Labouring Children: British Immigrant Apprentices to Canada, 1969–1924*. Montreal: McGill-Queen's University Press, 1980.

Pavlakis, Dean. 'Reputation and the Sexual Abuse of Boys: Changing Norms in Late Nineteenth-century Britain.' *Men and Masculinities* 17, no. 3 (2014): 325–46.

Perren, Richard. *Agriculture in Depression, 1870–1940*. Cambridge: Cambridge University Press, 1995.

Peters, Laura. *Victorian Orphans, Culture and Empire*. Manchester, GB: Manchester University Press, 2000.

Phillips, Gloria V. *A Pilgrim Passing Through*. Collingwood, ON: Rogdah Publishing, 2011.

Pimm-Smith, Rachel. 'A New-born of Respectable Class Would Have Weighed More: Class, Gender and Neglect in Late-nineteenth-century England'. *Child and Family Law Quarterly* 34, no.2 (2022): 189–210.

Plamper, Jan. *The History of Emotions. An Introduction*. Oxford: Oxford University Press, 2015.

Pooley, Siân. 'Child Philanthropy, Family Care and Young Bodies in Britain, 1876—1914.' In *Children's Experiences of Welfare in Modern Britain*, edited by Siân Pooley and Jonathan Taylor, 99–122. London: University of London Press, 2021.

– 'Parenthood, Citizenship and the State in England, c.1870–1914.' In *Parenting and the State in Britain and Europe, c. 1870-1950: Raising the Nation*, edited by Hester Barron and Claudia Siebrecht, 25–47. London: Palgrave Macmillan Cham 2017.

Pooley, Siân, and Jonathan Taylor. 'Introduction.' In *Children's Experiences of Welfare in Modern Britain*, edited by Siân Pooley and Jonathan Taylor, 1–26. London: University of London Press, 2021.

Razack, Sherene H. 'Making Canada White: Law and the Policing of Bodies of Colour in the 1990s.' *Canadian Journal of Law and Society* 14, no. 1 (1999): 159–84.

Reford, Alexander. 'Smith, Donald Alexander, 1st Baron Strathcona and Mount Royal,' *Dictionary of Canadian Biography*, vol. 14, University of Toronto/Université Laval, 2003. Accessed August 25, 2021. http://www.biographi.ca/en/bio/smith_donald_alexander_14E.html.

Reilly, Wilfred. 'The Myth of the Kamloops Mass Grave.' *Spiked-Online*, 9 August 2022. Accessed 12 May 2023. https://www.spiked-online.com/2022/08/09/the-myth-of-the-kamloops-mass-grave/.

Roddy, Sarah, Julie-Marie Strange, and Bertrand Taithe. *The Charity Market and Humanitarianism in Britain, 1870–1912*. London: Bloomsbury, 2019.

Rooke, Patricia T., and R.L. Schnell. 'Imperial Philanthropy and Colonial Response: British Juvenile Emigration to Canada, 1896–1930.' *The Historian* (1983): 56–77.

Roper, Michael. *The Secret Battle: Emotional Survival in the Great War*. Manchester, GB: Manchester University Press, 2009.

Rose, Clare. 'Raggedness and Respectability in Barnardo's Archive.' *Childhood in the Past* 1, no. 1 (2009): 136–50.

Rose, June. *For the Sake of the Children: Inside Barnardo's 120 Years of Caring for Children*. London: Hodder & Stoughton, 1987.

Rosenwein, Barbara H. *Emotional Communities in the Early Middle Ages.* London: Cornell University Press, 2007.

– *Generations of Feeling: A History of Emotions, 600–1700*. Cambridge: Cambridge University Press, 2016.

Sangster, Joan. *One Hundred Years of Struggle: The History of Women and the Vote in Canada*. Vancouver, CA: UBC Press, 2018.

Scheer, Monique. 'Are Emotions a Kind of Practice (and Is That What Makes Them Have a History)? A Bourdieuian Approach to Understanding Emotion'. *History and Theory* 51, no. 2 (2012): 193–220.

Shapely, Peter. 'Charity, Status and Leadership: Charitable Image and the Manchester Man'. *Journal of Social History* 32, no. 1 (1998): 157–77.

Shore, Heather. *Artful Dodgers: Youth and Crime in Early 19th-Century London*. Woodbridge, GB: The Boydell Press, 1999.

Sinclair, Sonja. *Cordial but Not Cosy: A History of the Office of the Auditor General*. Toronto: McClelland and Stewart, 1979.

Skinner, Annie. *Behind Closed Doors: Hidden Histories of Children Committed to Care in the Late Nineteenth Century, 1882–1889*. Oxford: Peter Lang, 2021.

Smith, Karen. *The Government of Childhood: Discourse, Power and Subjectivity*. Basingstoke, GB: Palgrave Macmillan, 2014.

Snell, Keith. 'The Sunday-School Movement in England and Wales: Child Labour, Denominational Control and Working-Class Culture.' *Past and Present* 164, no. 1 (1999): 122–68.

Soares, Claudia. '"Dear Sir, Remember Me Often If Possible": Family, Belonging and Identity for Children in Care in Britain, c.1870–1920.' In *Children's Experiences of Welfare in Modern Britain*, edited by Siân Pooley and Jonathan Taylor, 73–98. London: University of London Press, 2021.

– *A Home from Home?: Children and Social Care in Victorian and Edwardian Britain, 1870–1920*. Oxford: Oxford University Press, 2023.

– '"The Many Lessons Which the Care of Some Gentle, Loveable Animal Would Give": Animals, Pets, and Emotions in Children's Welfare Institutions, 1870–1920.' *The History of the Family* 26, no. 2 (2021): 236–65.

– 'Neither Waif nor Stray: Home, Family and Belonging in the Victorian Children's Institution, 1881–1914.' PhD diss., University of Manchester, 2014.

Starkey, Pat. '"Temporary Relief for Specially Recommended or Selected Deserving Persons': The Mission of the House of Charity, Soho, 1846–1914.' *Urban History* 35, no. 1 (2008): 96–115.

Steedman, Carolyn. *The Tidy House*. London: Virago, 1982.

Strange, Julie-Marie. *Fatherhood and the British Working Class, 1865–1914*. Cambridge: Cambridge University Press, 2015.

– 'Tramp: Sentiment and the Homeless Man in the Late-Victorian and Edwardian City'. *Journal of Victorian Culture* 16 no. 2 (2011): 242–58.

– 'When John Met Benny: Class, Pets and Family Life in Late Victorian and Edwardian Britain.' *The History of the Family*, 26 no. 2, (2021): 214–35.

Summerfield, Penny. *Histories of the Self: Personal Narratives and Historical Practice*. London: Routledge, 2018.

Swaim, Kathleen M. *Pilgrim's Progress, Puritan Progress: Discourses and Contexts*. Chicago: University of Illinois Press, 1993.

Swain, Shurlee. 'Sweet Childhood Lost: Idealized Images of Childhood in the British Child Rescue Literature.' *Journal of the History of Childhood and Youth* 2, no. 2 (2009): 198–214.

Swartz, Rebecca. 'Children In Between: Child Migrants from England to the Cape in the 1830s.' *History Workshop Journal* 91, no. 1 (2021): 71–90.

– 'Children's Experiences of the Children's Friend Society Emigration Scheme to the Colonial Cape, 1833–41: Snapshots from Compliance to Rebellion.' In *Children's Experiences of Welfare in Modern Britain*, edited by Siân Pooley and Jonathan Taylor, 27–48. London: University of London Press, 2021.

Thane, Pat. *Foundations of the Welfare State*. Abingdon, GB: Longman, 2013.

– 'The Working Class and State "Welfare" in Britain, 1880–1914.' *Historical Journal* 27, no. 4 (1984): 877–900.

The Conversation. 'Unmarked Graves of 215 Indigenous Children Were Found in Kamloops a Year Ago: What's Happened Since?' *Don't Call Me Resilient, The Conversation Podcast*, released in the UK on 18 May 2022. 40 minutes.

Thoburn, June. 'The Adoptive Kinship Network: Issues around Birth Family Contact in Adoption.' In *Adoption from Care: International Perspectives on Children's Rights, Family Preservation and State Intervention*, edited by Tarja Pöjö, Marit Skivenes, and June Thoburn, 233–48. Bristol, GB: Bristol University Press, 2021.

Tisdall, Laura. *A Progressive Education?: How Childhood Changed in Mid-twentieth-century English and Welsh Schools*. Manchester, GB: Manchester University Press, 2020.

Together Trust, 'Our History.' Accessed 16 December 2022. https://www.togethertrust.org.uk/our-history

Tosh, John. *Manliness and Masculinities in Nineteenth-Century Britain: Essays on Gender, Family, and Empire*. London: Routledge, 2005.

Turansky, Carrie. *No Ocean Too Wide*. Colorado Springs, CO: Multnomah, 2019.

Union of Catholic Christian Rationalists, 'Canadian Historian: No Natives Killed in Catholic Schools.' Accessed 12 May 2023. https://www.uccronline.it/eng/2022/04/05/canadian-historian-no-indigenous-killed-in-catholic-schools/.

Uprichard, Emma. 'Children as 'Being and Becomings': Children, Childhood and Temporality'. *Children and Society* 22, no.4 (2008): 303–13.

Voce, Antonio, Leyland Cecco, and Chris Michael. '"Cultural Genocide": The Shameful History of Canada's Residential Schools – Mapped.' *Guardian*, 6 September 2021. Accessed 16 June 2022. https://www.theguardian.com/world/ng-interactive/2021/sep/06/canada-residential-schools-indigenous-children-cultural-genocide-map.

Wagner, Gillian. 'Barnardo, Thomas John (1845–1905)', Oxford Dictionary of National Biography (23 September 2004), online at: https://doi.org/10.1093/ref:odnb/30600 [accessed 27 October 2023].

– *Children of the Empire* London: Weidenfeld and Nicolson, 1982.

Waller, Phillip J. *Democracy and Sectarianism: Political and Social History of Liverpool, 1868–1939*. Liverpool, GB: Liverpool University Press, 1981.

Ward, Rebecca. 'An Alternative Approach to Child Rescue: Child Emigration Societies in Birmingham and Manchester, 1870–1914'. Master's thesis, Durham University, 2010.

Watkins, Emma. *Life Courses of Young Convicts Transported to Van Diemen's Land*. London: Bloomsbury, 2020.

Wells, Nick. '"It Was Devastating," Chief Recalls after Remains of 215 Children Found in B.C.'. Accessed 5 May 2023. https://www.thestar.com/news/canada/2021/05/28/bc-premier-horrified-at-discovery-of-remains-at-kamloops-residential-school-site.html.

Wiener, Martin. *Reconstructing the Criminal: Culture, Law, and Policy in England, 1830–1914*. Cambridge: Cambridge University Press, 1990.

Wildman, Charlotte. *Urban Redevelopment and Modernity in Liverpool and Manchester, 1918–1939*. London: Bloomsbury, 2016.

Wills, Abigail. 'Delinquency, Masculinity and Citizenship in England 1950–1970'. *Past and Present*, 187 no. 1, (2005): 157–85.

Zahra, Tara. *The Lost Children: Reconstructing Europe's Families after World War II*. Cambridge, MA: Harvard University Press, 2011.

Index

Pages with (f) refer to illustrations; pages with (t) refer to tables.